TOP 15 THINGS YOU NEED TO KNOW ABOUT LITERATURE

This feature provides a checklist of the 15 reading strategies and literary elements that are most likely to appear in questions and answer choices on the SAT Literature Test.

The list provides you with a hint about how to answer a question about each element or strategy. Two sample questions are provided, showing you how questions relating to each element or strategy are likely to be worded.

See "Test-Taking Strategies for the Literature Test" for specific types of questions and how to approach them.

1. CHARACTER/MOTIVATION

Understand why a character does or says something and what a character may be thinking or feeling based on clues in the passage. Be able to locate specific words or phrases in a passage that support your interpretation.

Examples

Which best characterizes the speaker?
Which is NOT a reasonable conclusion to draw about the captain?

2. SETTING

Know how to identify a time or place based on clues in a passage or poem, how setting relates to mood or tone, and how setting affects characters. Look for hints in the selection.

Examples

The setting of this passage is best described as
How does the setting affect the mood of the poem?

3. THEME

Know how to identify the theme of a passage or poem. Remember that the theme of a literary work is its implied message—a universal statement about life. Because themes are usually implied, not stated directly, you may have to spend a little extra time on a theme question. Use specific details in the passage to help identify the theme.

Examples

Which major theme does the passage address?
Which best sums up the speaker's message to the beloved?

4. TONE

Be able to describe the tone of a passage or poem, or how a specific extract from the poem or passage affects the tone. Remember that the tone of a work is the author's attitude toward the subject; do not confuse tone with mood, which is the impact of the work on the reader.

Which best describes the tone of the passage?
The poet uses the words "dark," "night," "shade," and "shadow" in order to achieve a tone of

5. SYMBOLISM

Know how to identify the larger symbolic importance of a character, object, or action from the passage or poem. Because authors usually imply what something symbolizes rather than stating this information directly, questions about symbolism can take a little more time to answer. Use specific details in the passage to understand the symbolism of a passage.

Examples

When the author says that Raggles sees a city as "an individual conglomeration of life," he suggests that the city symbolizes which of the following?
What does the black-and-red color scheme of the suite's seventh room symbolize?

6. ALLUSIONS

Recognize allusions—references to historical events, great works of literature, and art. By definition, allusions are unexplained; the author takes for granted that the reader will recognize an allusion. The strategy of eliminating obvious wrong answers can come in handy when you are not sure of the right answer to an allusion question.

Examples

The line "I do not find / The Hanged Man" is an allusion to which of the following?
When the author says that Jim was "tilting at windmills," he is alluding to

7. USING CONTEXT CLUES TO DEFINE VOCABULARY

Use context clues and knowledge of roots and affixes to define an unfamiliar vocabulary word. Make sure to identify the word's part of speech; this can also help you eliminate wrong choices. You can also use context clues when the word in the question is familiar but has more than one definition.

Examples

The word "concatenation" is best defined as
In what sense does the speaker use the word "forward"?

8. AUTHOR'S PURPOSE

Be able to identify the author's main purpose in writing a speech or passage. In order to determine why an author included a particular detail, think about the effect that detail had on you and then find the answer choice that best matches your reaction.

Examples

The author includes the information in the last paragraph in order to
Why does the author include the final sentence, when its ideas were already expressed in the previous sentence?

9. SONNET

Be sure you know that a sonnet is a 14-line poem in iambic pentameter, and that when you see a sonnet that deviates from the standard sonnet form, you can identify what makes it different. This book contains a few sonnets in the practice tests and other sample poems that you can examine as examples.

Example

The poem meets all of the usual standards for a sonnet EXCEPT

10. METER AND RHYTHM

In poetry, meter refers to the number of metric feet per line, and rhythm refers to the pattern of stressed and unstressed syllables. Be sure not to confuse these terms with one another. Practice scanning verse so that you will be confident in your ability to identify rhythm and meter.

Examples

Which best describes the relationship between the poem's main theme and its rhythm?
Which best describes the effect of the poem's meter?

11. INTERPRETING FIGURATIVE LANGUAGE

Be able to interpret similes, metaphors, and examples of personification. The test is more likely to ask you to interpret a simile or a metaphor than to simply identify one. When interpreting figurative language, look for the answer choice that is best supported by the overall meaning of the passage or poem.

Examples

Which best describes the effect of the speaker's comparison of the "half-deserted streets" "that follow like a tedious argument / Of insidious intent"?
The metaphor "white sails" refers to

12. UNDERSTANDING ARCHAIC LANGUAGE

Make sure that you understand archaic and old-fashioned language, such as occurs in the poems and plays of Shakespeare. (Roughly 60 percent of the test questions will be on literary selections written before 1900.)

Examples

Which of the following best paraphrases the lines "More will I do; / Though all that I can do is nothing worth, / Since that my penitence comes after all, / Imploring pardon"?

When the speaker says "Then if for my love thou my love receivest, / I cannot blame thee for my love thou usest," he means

13. MAKING INFERENCES

Know how to make an inference about why a character does something, what a character may be thinking, why an author included a particular detail, and so forth. Be able to weigh the clues in the passage and use surrounding details to find the best answer.

Examples

When the speaker says "I have measured out my life with coffee-spoons," he means
The information in the second paragraph allows you to conclude which of the following?

14. FINDING THE MAIN IDEA

Be able to identify the main idea of a passage. To do this, it is best to ask yourself the question "What was this passage about?" Look among the answer choices for the one that best matches your answer to this question. It may be more difficult to identify an implied main idea than one that is stated directly. (HINT: Many authors state the main idea at the beginning or end of a paragraph.)

Examples

Which sentence from the passage best states its main idea?
Which statement best summarizes the speaker's message?

15. RHETORICAL DEVICES

Know how to describe the effect of rhetorical devices, such as parallelism and repetition. To answer these questions, first consider the effect the rhetorical element had on you as a reader, then look for the choice that best matches your answer.

Examples

What is the effect of the repetition of the phrase "my God, my kingdom, and my people"?
The author starts almost every sentence of the essay with the phrase "I want a wife who . . . " because

McGRAW-HILL'S

SAT

SUBJECT TEST

LITERATURE

Stephanie Muntone

New York | Chicago | San Francisco | Lisbon | London | Madrid | Mexico City
Milan | New Delhi | San Juan | Seoul | Singapore | Sydney | Toronto

The McGraw·Hill Companies

Library of Congress Cataloging-in-Publication Data

Muntone, Stephanie.
  McGraw-Hill's SAT subject test : literature / Stephanie Muntone.
       p.   cm.
  ISBN-13: 978-0-07-160928-9
  ISBN-10: 0-07-160928-8
  1. Literature—Examinations, questions, etc.   2. SAT (Educational
test)—Study guides.   3. College entrance achievement tests—Study
guides.   I. Title.   II. Title: SAT subject test : literature.
  PN62.M86   2009
  807.6—dc22

                                                          2008041735

1 2 3 4 5 6 7 8 9   QPD/QPD   0 4 3 2 1 0 9

ISBN 978-0-07-160928-9
MHID 0-07-160928-8

McGraw-Hill books are available at special quantity discounts for use
as premiums and sales promotions, or for use in corporate training
programs. For more information, please write to the Director of Special Sales, McGraw-Hill Professional, Two Penn Plaza, New York, NY,
10121-2298. Or contact your local bookstore.

This publication is designed to provide accurate and authoritative
information in regard to the subject matter covered. It is sold with the
understanding that neither the author nor the publisher is engaged
in rendering legal, accounting, or other professional services. If legal
advice or other expert assistance is required, the services of a compe-
tent professional person should be sought.

> *—From a Declaration of Principles jointly adopted*
> *by a Committee of the American Bar*
> *Association and a Committee of Publishers*

SAT is a registered trademark of the College Entrance Examination
Board, which was not involved in the production of, and does not
endorse, this product.

This book is printed on acid-free paper.

|CONTENTS

PART I

INTRODUCTION TO THE SAT LITERATURE TEST

ALL ABOUT THE SAT LITERATURE TEST

ABOUT THE LITERATURE TEST

The SAT Literature Test is one of the Subject Tests offered by the College Board. The test is a one-hour exam consisting of approximately 60 multiple-choice questions. It is designed to measure how well you have learned to read and interpret literature.

The SAT Subject Tests (formerly known as the SAT II tests or Achievement Tests) are the lesser-known counterpart to the SAT, offered by the same organization—the College Board. Whereas the SAT covers general verbal, writing, and mathematical reasoning skills, the SAT Subject Tests cover specific knowledge in a variety of subjects, including English, mathematics, history, science, and foreign languages. SAT Subject Tests are only one hour long and thus are significantly shorter than the SAT. Furthermore, you can choose which SAT Subject Tests to take and how many (up to three) to take on one test day, but you cannot register for both the SAT and the SAT Subject Tests on the same test day.

The SAT Literature Test usually includes four to twelve literary texts. Each text is followed by a set of six to eight questions based on that text. The test covers the topics shown in the table:

Genre	Percentage
Prose passages (primarily excerpts from fiction and essays)	50%
Poetry (primarily entire poems, though some selections are excerpts from larger works)	50%
Drama (included in Prose passages) (many tests, but not all, contain one dramatic selection)	20%
Period	
Before 1700	30%
Between 1701 and 1900	30%
After 1900	40%
National Tradition	
Authors from the United States	50%
Authors from Great Britain	50%
Authors from other English-speaking traditions (India, Ireland, Canada, and the Caribbean)	As much as 20%

The SAT Literature Test measures not only how well you understand the subject matter of each text, but also how well you understand specific literary concepts, such as theme, genre, tone, and characterization. You may be asked about the structure and organization of a text, or you may be asked about the author's use of narrative voice. You may also be asked about syntax, diction, vocabulary, and the author's use of figurative language, including imagery. You should be familiar with these concepts from your English and language arts classes.

When determining which SAT Subject Tests to take and when to take them, consult your high school guidance counselor and pick up a copy of the "Taking the SAT Subject Tests" bulletin published by the College Board. Research the admissions policies of colleges to which you are considering applying to determine their SAT Subject Test requirements and the average scores students receive. Also, visit the College Board's Web site at www.college-board.com to learn more about which tests are offered.

Use this book to become familiar with the content, organization, and level of difficulty of the SAT Literature Test. Knowing what to expect on the day of the test will allow you to do your best.

WHEN TO TAKE THE TEST

For the SAT Literature Test, the College Board simply recommends that you have as much experience as possible in reading and carefully analyzing a variety of American and British literary works from different historical periods and in different genres. The more texts you have read and closely studied, the better prepared you will be. Note, however, that there is no particular reading list for the test, so you cannot know beforehand which literary works you will encounter on the exam you take.

Many students take the SAT Literature Test at the end of their junior year or at the beginning of their senior year. If you are unsure when you should take this exam, consult your teacher or school counselor.

Colleges look at SAT Subject Test scores to see a student's academic achievement, because the test results are less subjective than are other parts of a college application, such as grade point average, teacher recommendations, student background information, and the interview. Many colleges require at least one SAT Subject Test score for admission, but even schools that do not require SAT Subject Tests may review your scores to get an overall picture of your qualifications. Colleges may also use SAT Subject Test scores to enroll students in appropriate courses. If English is your strongest subject, then a high SAT Literature score, combined with good grades on your transcript, can convey that strength to a college or university.

To register for SAT Subject Tests, pick up a copy of the *Registration Bulletin*, "Registering for the SAT: SAT Reasoning Test, SAT Subject Tests" from your guidance counselor. You can also register at www.collegeboard.com or contact the College Board directly at:

College Board SAT Program
901 South 42nd Street
Mount Vernon, IL 62864
(866) 756-7346

General inquiries can be directed via e-mail through the College Board's Web site e-mail inquiry form or by telephone at the number listed above.

The SAT Literature Test is administered six Saturdays (or Sunday if you qualify because of religious beliefs) a year in October, November, December, January, May, and June. Students may take up to three SAT Subject Tests per test day.

SCORING

The scoring of the Literature test is based on a 200–800-point scale, similar to that of the math and verbal sections of the SAT. You receive one point for each correct answer and lose one quarter of a point for each incorrect answer. You do not lose any points for omitting a question. In addition to your scaled score, your score report shows a percentile ranking indicating the percentage of students scoring below your score.

Score reports are mailed, at no charge, approximately 5 weeks after the test day. Score reports are available approximately 3 weeks after the test day at www.collegeboard.com. Just as with the SAT, you can choose up to four college/scholarship program codes to which to send your scores, and the College Board will send a cumulative report of all of your SAT and SAT Subject Test scores to these programs. Additional score reports can be requested, for a fee, online or by telephone.

TEST-TAKING STRATEGIES FOR THE LITERATURE TEST

TEST-TAKING STRATEGIES FOR THE LITERATURE TEST

The SAT Literature Test will present you with several poems and prose passages, all originally written in the English language. In many cases, the poems and passages will be excerpted from longer works; in some cases, they will be complete. Each passage will have the date of its original publication at the end. (Knowing when the passage or poem was written will often help you as you approach the questions.) You will not be expected to identify the authors or to have read these works before.

This section contains a number of strategies that you can use to help yourself earn a high score on the SAT Literature Test. The first strategy will help you prepare for the test before you take it. The other strategies address the types of questions on the test and describe some methods that will help prevent you from making careless or unnecessary errors in choosing your answer. Each strategy is accompanied by a sample question. Try using the strategy to answer the question, and then go over the answer explanation provided.

On the actual SAT Literature Test—as well as on the practice tests in Part III of this book—each poem or passage will be followed by a set of approximately 6 to 12 questions. Read the passage or poem, then answer the questions. Try these strategies on the practice tests to help prepare yourself for the actual test day.

STRATEGY: Read fiction, nonfiction, poetry, and drama actively and often.

The best way to get a high score on the SAT Literature Test is to be an avid and active reader. You won't be required to have read any specific literary works or to memorize authors' names or lists of the books and poems they wrote. Prior familiarity with the passages that appear on the test probably won't affect your score. However, it will help to be generally familiar with literature of different periods, because writing styles and vocabulary changed a great deal between the Renaissance and modern times.

It is also best to get into the habit of thinking about what you read, because that is what the test will ask you to do. You will have to analyze passages, to identify specific details, and to draw conclusions. You can practice this skill the same way as any other. Every time you read a book or a story, ask yourself questions about it as you go. Use homework assignments from English class to help yourself prepare for the test. The more accustomed you are to thinking about what you read, and to picking up clues and implications in a text, the stronger position you will be in to do well on the Literature Test.

STRATEGY: Skip difficult poems or passages and return to them later.

The literary works and excerpts that appear on the SAT Literature Test were chosen with college-bound high school students in mind. In other words, these works should be appropriate to your current reading level. However, everyone brings different knowledge and experience to literature, and everyone has different areas of difficulty.

The best way to earn a high score on the test is to choose as many correct answers as possible and as few wrong answers. Therefore, it is a smart strategy to read through, or at least glance at, all the passages before you look at any of the questions. Begin with the easiest selection, then go back and work on the more challenging ones. Because you are free to answer the questions in any order you choose, it's best to concentrate on the easy poems and passages first. This will give you confidence and help you accumulate a stock of correct answers to build on.

With some questions, you may be able to eliminate two or even three wrong answer choices. If you can narrow your choices down to two or three from the original five, it's probably a good idea to answer these questions. However, you should only go back to them after you have answered all the questions of which you are sure of the answers.

STRATEGY: Weigh three given options to decide if one, two, or all three are correct.

The SAT Literature Test uses a question format you may not have encountered before. Some of the questions will ask you which of three options is correct. It then will give you five lettered choices that show different combinations of those three options. Any one, any two, or all three of the options may be correct.

First, read the three options and eliminate any that do not answer the question correctly. Cross out the Roman numerals of those options in your test booklet. Any remaining options should constitute the correct answer. Look among the five answer choices to see if there is one that agrees with your answer. If there isn't, go back and check the numbered options against the original passage.

Read the following passage, then try the sample question that follows.

The grill-room clock struck eleven with the respectful unobtrusiveness of one whose mission in life is to be ignored. When the flight of time should really have rendered abstinence and migration imperative the lighting apparatus would signal the fact in the usual way.

5 Clovis approached the supper-table, in the blessed expectancy of one who has dined sketchily and long ago.

"I'm starving," he announced, making an effort to sit down gracefully and read the menu at the same time.

"So I gathered," said his host, "from the fact that you were nearly punc-
10 tual. I ought to have told you that I'm a Food Reformer. I've ordered two bowls of bread-and-milk and some health biscuits. I hope you don't mind."

Clovis pretended afterwards that he didn't go white above the collar-line for the fraction of a second.

"All the same," he said, "you ought not to joke about such things. There
15 really are such people. I've known people who've met them. To think of all the adorable things there are to eat in the world and then to go through life munching sawdust and being proud of it."

"They're like the Flagellants of the Middle Ages, who went about morti-fying themselves."

20 "They had some excuse," said Clovis. "They did it to save their immortal souls, didn't they? You needn't tell me that a man who doesn't love oys-ters and asparagus and good wines has got a soul, or a stomach either. He's simply got the instinct for being unhappy highly developed."

(1911)

Example

1. The author most likely wrote this work from which this passage is taken in order to

    I. persuade readers not to eat health food
    II. entertain readers with an amusing story
    III. inform readers what it is like to be a Food Reformer

(A) I only
(B) I and II only
(C) II only
(D) II and III only
(E) III only

Read the question, then read Options I–III. Cross out any options that do not answer the question correctly. Then look at the lettered choices to see if your answer is among them. That will be the correct answer.

Remember that any one, any two, or all three of the numbered options may be correct. Do not hesitate to choose any of the lettered answers simply because they contain one, two, or all of the three options.

The writer does not mention any benefits that would accrue to the reader from eating health food, so you can cross out Option I. The story is entertaining and amusing, so Option II is correct. The writer does not dwell on what it's like to be a Food Reformer. He mentions the idea of health food simply in order to create an amusing moment between the host and Clovis. Therefore, you can cross out Option III.

Only Option II is left which means only Choice C can be the correct answer.

STRATEGY: Learn how to answer questions about vocabulary.

The SAT Literature Test will ask you to choose the correct definition of a word from a passage or poem. The best way to answer such a question is to go back to the passage to find the word, then mentally replace it with each of the five answer choices. The correct answer will be the one that best fits the sense of the sentence in the original.

The question may ask about a word you have never seen before. Don't panic. Often, the context in which a word is used will make the meaning clear, or at least will enable you to eliminate two or three obviously wrong answers. You will then have good odds of guessing the correct answer.

Use your knowledge of prefixes, suffixes, and roots when asked about unfamiliar vocabulary words. For example, you know that the prefix *uni-* means "one." This would help you define the word *unicycle* if you had never seen it before.

Never answer a vocabulary question without looking back at the word in the original passage. Many English words have more than one meaning. *Cleave,* for instance, can mean "to cling together" or "to split apart." If you don't look back at the passage, you won't know which definition of a multiple-meaning word is correct.

The sample question refers to the passage above.

Example

2. The word "unobtrusiveness" in the first sentence (line 1) means

   (A) anger
   (B) inconspicuousness
   (C) heartiness
   (D) sullenness
   (E) invisibility

If you know the meaning of *unobtrusiveness,* good; you can answer the question without taking any further time. If not, go back to the passage and circle the word. Try each of the five answer choices in its place. Which one makes the most sense?

The context clues are "respectful" and "mission in life is to be ignored." Therefore you are looking for a word that conveys a meaning of quietness, modesty, and keeping a low profile. *Anger* and *heartiness* clearly do not fit with the notion of being ignored. *Invisibility* is too extreme and does not fit the idea of a clock striking, which is a sound rather than a sight. *Sullenness* goes with the idea of being ignored, but not with being respectful. Choice B, *inconspicuousness,* is a perfect synonym for *unobtrusiveness. Inconspicuous* means "not obvious, apparent, or noticeable." It makes perfect sense in the context and is the correct answer.

STRATEGY: If you don't know the answer, make an educated guess.

Most questions on the SAT Literature Test will refer you back to the passage, asking you to draw a conclusion or correctly identify a detail. However, some questions will ask about literary terms. If you don't know the definitions of those terms, you may have trouble with the question. It is a good idea to study the meaning of literary terms such as *allusion, sonnet,* and *metaphor* before you take the test. See Chapter 1 of this book for a glossary of common literary terms.

If you come across unfamiliar literary terms on the test, you should still be able to make an educated guess. You will probably recognize one or two of the terms in the answer choices. You may be able to figure out the meaning of others just by looking at them. For instance, the word *simile* looks enough like the word *similar* that you might be able to approximate its meaning for the purposes of answering a multiple-choice question.

Read the poem, then try the sample question that follows.

The Man He Killed

"Had he and I but met
By some old ancient inn,
We should have sat us down to wet
Right many a nipperkin!

5   "But ranged as infantry,
And staring face to face,
I shot at him as he at me,
And killed him in his place.

"I shot him dead because—
10   Because he was my foe,
Just so: my foe of course he was;
That's clear enough; although

"He thought he'd 'list, perhaps,
Off-hand like—just as I—
15   Was out of work—had sold his traps—
No other reason why.

"Yes; quaint and curious war is!
You shoot a fellow down
You'd treat, if met where any bar is,
20   Or help to half-a-crown."

(1917)

Example

3. This poem represents or includes all of the following EXCEPT

(A) enjambment
(B) dialect
(C) dramatic monologue
(D) exact rhyme
(E) ballad

If you know the meaning of the five literary terms in the answer choices, then you can answer this question right away without wasting any time. If you only know one or two of them, you are in a good position to make an educated guess.

Go through the terms one by one. You may not recognize *enjambment*; if not, move on to the next choice. You probably will remember that *dialect* refers to colloquial or regional speech, which you can see in the poem in such expressions as "wet / Right many a nipperkin." You can use your knowledge of word parts to break down the word *monologue* and define it as "a speech made by one character." This poem, which is spoken aloud by one person, fits that meaning. You should conclude that the term *exact rhyme* is self-explanatory; It refers to words that rhyme exactly. Such pairs as *perhaps/traps* and *down/crown* show that this poem includes exact rhymes. You may or may not know exactly what kind of poem a *ballad* is.

You have eliminated three of the five choices. Now you have a 50% chance of guessing the correct answer, and you probably should take a chance on it. It is probably best to go through the rest of the questions first, answering all the ones you are quite sure of, then return and answer questions like this one where you have a good chance of getting it right.

(In fact, *enjambment* refers to lines of poetry that do not end in punctuation marks, but instead continue a sentence or complete thought to the next line or lines without pause. A *ballad* is a narrative poem that features four-line stanzas with alternate lengths of six and eight syllables. This poem does feature enjambment; several of the lines carry a thought on to the next one without a pause. It is clearly influenced by the ballad form, but does not quite fit the definition, as each stanza has a different pattern of syllables. Therefore, *ballad* is the one term that is not included or represented in the poem, and E is the correct answer.)

STRATEGY: Learn how to answer quotation questions.

The SAT Literature Test will feature a number of questions that quote a specific sentence, line, or phrase in the passage or poem. The best strategy in this case is to read the question, go back to the passage, read the phrase or line in its context, and then look at the answer choices to see which one is best.

Read the poem, then try the sample question that follows.

> That time of year thou may'st in me behold
> When yellow leaves, or none, or few, do hang
> Upon those boughs which shake against the cold,
> Bare ruined choirs, where late the sweet birds sang.
> 5 In me thou see'st the twilight of such day
> As after sunset fadeth in the west;
> Which by and by black night doth take away,
> Death's second self, that seals up all in rest.
> In me thou see'st the glowing of such fire,
> 10 That on the ashes of his youth doth lie,
> As the deathbed whereon it must expire,
> Consumed with that which it was nourished by.
> This thou perceiv'st, which makes thy love more strong.
> To love that well which thou must leave ere long.

(1609)

Example

4. "Death's second self" (line 8) refers to

    (A) sleep
    (B) twilight
    (C) night
    (D) old age
    (E) sunset

You notice that the question tells you the line number where you can find this phrase in the original poem. The SAT Literature Test will always provide you with the line number of a quotation so you won't have to reread the entire passage to find it.

Look back at line 8 of the poem to find the reference to "Death's second self." Read back a few lines to find the beginning of the sentence. Remember that in poems, lines are not the same thing as sentences. In this case, the sentence begins at line 5, "In me thou see'st." In line 7 you find the phrase "black night," which is what the speaker describes as "Death's second self." The correct answer is choice C.

STRATEGY: Understand archaic word order and usage.

The SAT Literature Test will feature selections from the premodern era. For example, the sonnet you read for question 4 comes from the English Renaissance of the late sixteenth and early seventeenth centuries. At that time, English usage differed from the modern usage to which you are accustomed. For example, this poem uses a verb tense that we no longer use: the familiar second-person pronoun *thou* and the verbs that go with it, ending in *–st*. When questions ask you about the meanings of words and phrases, you need to consider carefully how those words and phrases are being used in a selection that dates back to a time before 1800. This is especially true of poetry.

The sample question refers to the sonnet above.

Example

5. Which of the following best paraphrases the final two lines of the sonnet (lines 13–14)?

   (A) Your love for me is stronger than my love for you.
   (B) Since you can see how old I am, there is no sense in you loving me so much.
   (C) Your love is strong because I am too old for you.
   (D) You are brave to love me when you know that you are bound to lose me to death before long.
   (E) I love you, so I regret that I will die long before you will.

This question asks you to rephrase two lines of a poem in modern language. The best way to do that is to go over those two lines to be sure you understand exactly what they say. You may want to rewrite the lines yourself, then see which answer comes closest to your version. Remember that a paraphrase must include all the same ideas as the original.

"This thou perceiv'st, which makes thy love more strong.
To love that well which thou must leave ere long"
You need to know that *ere* means *before* and that *thou perceiv'st* means *you perceive*. You also need to know that *thy* is the possessive form of *thou*.

Your version might say:

Your ability to see my old age makes your love more admirable.

It takes great strength to love someone who will soon leave you because he will soon die of old age.

This paraphrase includes all the ideas expressed in the original. Note that you have to read back a little further than line 13 to figure out exactly what the speaker means.

You can see right away that the speaker does not refer at all to his own feelings toward the person he is addressing; therefore you can eliminate choices A and E. You can eliminate choice B because the speaker says nothing about the love being unwise. Choice D encompasses the important ideas expressed in the two lines and is the correct answer.

STRATEGY: Pay attention to capitalized words in the questions, such as NOT and EXCEPT.

Make sure you do not carelessly misread a question. Some questions on the SAT Literature Test contain the capitalized word NOT or EXCEPT. If you miss this word, you will misinterpret the question and choose the wrong answer. The best strategy is to circle this word when you see it in a question. That will help you concentrate on what the question is really asking you to find.

Read the passage and then try the sample question that follows.

When Jane and Elizabeth were alone, the former, who had been cautious in her praise of Mr. Bingley before, expressed to her sister how very much she admired him.

"He is just what a young man ought to be," said she, "sensible, good-
5 humored, lively; and I never saw such happy manners!—so much ease, with such perfect good-breeding!"

"He is also handsome," replied Elizabeth; "which a young man ought likewise to be, if he possibly can. His character is thereby complete."

"I was very much flattered by his asking me to dance a second time. I
10 did not expect such a compliment."

"Did not you? *I* did for you. But that is one great difference between us. Compliments always take *you* by surprise, and *me* never. What could be more natural than his asking you again? He could not help seeing that you were about five times as pretty as every other woman in the
15 room. No thanks to his gallantry for that. Well, he certainly is very agreeable, and I give you leave to like him. You have liked many a stupider person."

"Dear Lizzy!"

"Oh! you are a great deal too apt, you know, to like people in general.
20 You never see a fault in anybody. All the world are good and agreeable in your eyes. I never heard you speak ill of a human being in my life."

"I would not wish to be hasty in censuring anyone; but I always speak what I think."

25 "I know you do; and it is *that* which makes the wonder. With *your* good sense, to be so honestly blind to the follies and nonsense of others! Affectation of candour is common enough—one meets it everywhere. But to be candid without ostentation or design—to take the good of everybody's character and make it still better, and say nothing of the
30 bad—belongs to you alone."

(1813)

Example

6. Which of the following does NOT characterize Jane?

   (A) friendliness
   (B) perceptiveness
   (C) pleasantness
   (D) popularity
   (E) modesty

Circle the word NOT in the question. This word tells you that four of the choices should describe Jane accurately, while the other one does not. The one that does not describe her accurately is the correct answer.

Look over the four choices. Anyone who sees the good in others and never comments on the bad is bound to be friendly, popular, and pleasant. In addition, because *friendly* and *pleasant* mean more or less the same thing, they must both be either wrong or right. Because there is only one right answer to every test question, both must be wrong. Therefore you can eliminate choices A, C, and D. Elizabeth's statements "Compliments always take you by surprise" and "you were about five times as pretty as any other woman in the room" make it clear that Jane is modest; a pretty woman should not be surprised at a compliment, unless she is unusually modest about her own good looks. This leaves choice B, *perceptiveness*. You know from Elizabeth's comment "so honestly blind to the follies and nonsense of others" that Jane sees the good but not the bad in people. This makes her kind, but not truly perceptive. Choice B is the correct answer.

DIAGNOSTIC TEST
LITERATURE

The following diagnostic test is designed to be just like the real SAT Subject Test in Literature. It matches the actual test in content coverage and degree of difficulty.

Once you finish the diagnostic test, determine your score. Carefully read the answer explanations of the questions you answered incorrectly. Identify any weaknesses in your literature skills by determining the areas in which you made the most errors. Review those sections of this book first. Then, as time permits, go back and review your strengths.

Allow one hour to take the test. Time yourself and work uninterrupted. If you run out of time, take note of where you stopped when time ran out. Remember that you lose a quarter point for each incorrect answer, but you do not lose points for questions you leave blank. Therefore, unless you can eliminate one or more of the five choices, it is best to leave a question unanswered.

Use the following formula to calculate your score:

(number of correct answers) – ¼ (number of incorrect answers)

If you treat this diagnostic test just like the actual exam, it will accurately reflect how you are likely to perform on test day. Here are some hints on how to create test-taking conditions similar to those of the actual exam:

- Complete the test in one sitting. On test day, you will not be allowed to take a break.
- Tear out the answer sheet and fill in the ovals just as you will on the actual test day.
- Have a good eraser and more than one sharp pencil handy. On test day, you will not be able to go get a new pencil if yours breaks.
- Do not allow yourself any extra time; put down your pencil after exactly one hour, no matter how many questions are left to answer.
- Become familiar with the directions on the test. If you go in knowing what the directions say, you will not have to waste time reading and thinking about them on the actual test day.

DIAGNOSTIC TEST
LITERATURE

ANSWER SHEET

Tear out this answer sheet and use it to mark your answers.

1. Ⓐ Ⓑ Ⓒ Ⓓ Ⓔ	16. Ⓐ Ⓑ Ⓒ Ⓓ Ⓔ	31. Ⓐ Ⓑ Ⓒ Ⓓ Ⓔ	46. Ⓐ Ⓑ Ⓒ Ⓓ Ⓔ
2. Ⓐ Ⓑ Ⓒ Ⓓ Ⓔ	17. Ⓐ Ⓑ Ⓒ Ⓓ Ⓔ	32. Ⓐ Ⓑ Ⓒ Ⓓ Ⓔ	47. Ⓐ Ⓑ Ⓒ Ⓓ Ⓔ
3. Ⓐ Ⓑ Ⓒ Ⓓ Ⓔ	18. Ⓐ Ⓑ Ⓒ Ⓓ Ⓔ	33. Ⓐ Ⓑ Ⓒ Ⓓ Ⓔ	48. Ⓐ Ⓑ Ⓒ Ⓓ Ⓔ
4. Ⓐ Ⓑ Ⓒ Ⓓ Ⓔ	19. Ⓐ Ⓑ Ⓒ Ⓓ Ⓔ	34. Ⓐ Ⓑ Ⓒ Ⓓ Ⓔ	49. Ⓐ Ⓑ Ⓒ Ⓓ Ⓔ
5. Ⓐ Ⓑ Ⓒ Ⓓ Ⓔ	20. Ⓐ Ⓑ Ⓒ Ⓓ Ⓔ	35. Ⓐ Ⓑ Ⓒ Ⓓ Ⓔ	50. Ⓐ Ⓑ Ⓒ Ⓓ Ⓔ
6. Ⓐ Ⓑ Ⓒ Ⓓ Ⓔ	21. Ⓐ Ⓑ Ⓒ Ⓓ Ⓔ	36. Ⓐ Ⓑ Ⓒ Ⓓ Ⓔ	51. Ⓐ Ⓑ Ⓒ Ⓓ Ⓔ
7. Ⓐ Ⓑ Ⓒ Ⓓ Ⓔ	22. Ⓐ Ⓑ Ⓒ Ⓓ Ⓔ	37. Ⓐ Ⓑ Ⓒ Ⓓ Ⓔ	52. Ⓐ Ⓑ Ⓒ Ⓓ Ⓔ
8. Ⓐ Ⓑ Ⓒ Ⓓ Ⓔ	23. Ⓐ Ⓑ Ⓒ Ⓓ Ⓔ	38. Ⓐ Ⓑ Ⓒ Ⓓ Ⓔ	53. Ⓐ Ⓑ Ⓒ Ⓓ Ⓔ
9. Ⓐ Ⓑ Ⓒ Ⓓ Ⓔ	24. Ⓐ Ⓑ Ⓒ Ⓓ Ⓔ	39. Ⓐ Ⓑ Ⓒ Ⓓ Ⓔ	54. Ⓐ Ⓑ Ⓒ Ⓓ Ⓔ
10. Ⓐ Ⓑ Ⓒ Ⓓ Ⓔ	25. Ⓐ Ⓑ Ⓒ Ⓓ Ⓔ	40. Ⓐ Ⓑ Ⓒ Ⓓ Ⓔ	55. Ⓐ Ⓑ Ⓒ Ⓓ Ⓔ
11. Ⓐ Ⓑ Ⓒ Ⓓ Ⓔ	26. Ⓐ Ⓑ Ⓒ Ⓓ Ⓔ	41. Ⓐ Ⓑ Ⓒ Ⓓ Ⓔ	56. Ⓐ Ⓑ Ⓒ Ⓓ Ⓔ
12. Ⓐ Ⓑ Ⓒ Ⓓ Ⓔ	27. Ⓐ Ⓑ Ⓒ Ⓓ Ⓔ	42. Ⓐ Ⓑ Ⓒ Ⓓ Ⓔ	57. Ⓐ Ⓑ Ⓒ Ⓓ Ⓔ
13. Ⓐ Ⓑ Ⓒ Ⓓ Ⓔ	28. Ⓐ Ⓑ Ⓒ Ⓓ Ⓔ	43. Ⓐ Ⓑ Ⓒ Ⓓ Ⓔ	58. Ⓐ Ⓑ Ⓒ Ⓓ Ⓔ
14. Ⓐ Ⓑ Ⓒ Ⓓ Ⓔ	29. Ⓐ Ⓑ Ⓒ Ⓓ Ⓔ	44. Ⓐ Ⓑ Ⓒ Ⓓ Ⓔ	59. Ⓐ Ⓑ Ⓒ Ⓓ Ⓔ
15. Ⓐ Ⓑ Ⓒ Ⓓ Ⓔ	30. Ⓐ Ⓑ Ⓒ Ⓓ Ⓔ	45. Ⓐ Ⓑ Ⓒ Ⓓ Ⓔ	60. Ⓐ Ⓑ Ⓒ Ⓓ Ⓔ

DIAGNOSTIC TEST

Directions: This test consists of selections from literary works and questions on their content, form, and style. After reading each passage or poem, choose the best answer to each question, and then fill in the corresponding oval on the answer sheet.

Note: Pay particular attention to the requirements of questions that contain the words NOT or EXCEPT.

Questions 1–9. Read the following poem carefully before you choose your answers.

Loving in truth, and fain in verse my love to show,
That she (dear She) might take some pleasure of my pain:
Pleasure might cause her read, reading might make her know,
Knowledge might pity win, and pity grace obtain;
5 I sought fit words to paint the blackest face of woe,
Studying inventions fine, her wits to entertain:
Oft turning others' leaves, to see if thence would flow
Some fresh and fruitful showers upon my sun-burn'd brain.
But words came halting forth, wanting Invention's stay,
10 Invention, Nature's child, fled step-dame Study's blows,
And others' feet still seem'd but strangers in my way.
Thus, great with child to speak, and helpless in my throes,
Biting my truant pen, beating myself for spite—
"Fool," said my Muse to me, "look in thy heart and write."

(circa 1581)

1. "Turning others' leaves . . . fruitful showers" in lines 7–8 refers to

   (A) looking to the beauties of nature for inspiration
   (B) sitting in the shade because the sunlight was too strong
   (C) calling to his muse to help him write about his love
   (D) searching for ideas in the work of other poets
   (E) praying for help when he is unable to think of anything to write

2. Which of the following best describes the speaker's reasoning in lines 1–4?

   (A) If she reads what I write, she may fall in love with me.
   (B) If she feels sorry for me, she will turn away from me in disgust.
   (C) If she reads my poems, she will admire me as a writer.
   (D) As long as I love her, I will be unable to write anything good.
   (E) As long as she loves me, I cannot concentrate on my work.

3. Which of the following does the Muse's response in line 14 imply?

   I. that the speaker is trying too hard
   II. that if the speaker writes what he feels, he will achieve his goal
   III. that appealing to a Muse will not help a writer out of difficulties

   (A) I only
   (B) I and II only
   (C) I, II, and III
   (D) II only
   (E) II and III only

4. Which of the following best describes the speaker's mood throughout the poem?

   (A) optimistic and energetic
   (B) frustrated and anxious
   (C) discouraged and melancholy
   (D) bitter and jealous
   (E) introspective and pensive

5. The sonnet makes extensive use of which of the following types of figurative language?

   (A) poetry
   (B) metaphor
   (C) simile
   (D) hyperbole
   (E) contrast

6. Which of the following does the speaker imply that "She" feels toward him?

   (A) indifference
   (B) love
   (C) anger
   (D) friendship
   (E) warmth

GO ON TO THE NEXT PAGE

DIAGNOSTIC TEST—*Continued*

7. Which of the following best describes the relationship between the speaker and the poem's author?

    I. The speaker and the author are the same person.
    II. The speaker and the author are both poets.
    III. The speaker and the author may or may not be the same person.

    (A) I and II only
    (B) I and III only
    (C) II and III only
    (D) II only
    (E) III only

8. The speaker describes his pen as "truant" (line 13) in order to

    (A) suggest that his muse has abandoned him
    (B) explain that his pen is missing
    (C) blame his faulty tools for his bad writing
    (D) point out that his pen is not nourishing food
    (E) emphasize his inability to write

9. Which of the following elements of this poem does NOT conform to the normal standards for a sonnet?

    (A) the number of lines
    (B) the rhyme scheme
    (C) the subject matter
    (D) the first-person point of view
    (E) the meter

Questions 10–17. Read the following passage carefully before you choose your answers.

The afternoon sun was pouring in at the back windows of Mrs. Farmer's long, uneven parlour, making the dusky room look like a cavern with a fire at one end of it. The furniture was
5 all in its cool, figured summer cretonnes. The glass flower vases that stood about on little tables caught the sunlight and twinkled like tiny lamps. Claude had been sitting there for a long while, and he knew he ought to go.
10 Through the window at his elbow he could see rows of double hollyhocks, the flat leaves of the sprawling catalpa, and the spires of the tangled mint bed, all transparent in the gold-powdered light. They had talked about everything but the
15 thing he had come to say. As he looked out into the garden he felt that he would never get it out. There was something in the way the mint bed burned and floated that made

one a fatalist,—afraid to meddle. But after he
20 was far away, he would regret; uncertainty would tease him like a splinter in his thumb.

He rose suddenly and said without apology: "Gladys, I wish I could feel sure you'd never marry my brother."

25 She did not reply, but sat in her easy chair, looking up at him with a strange kind of calmness.

"I know all the advantages," he went on hastily, "but they wouldn't make it up to you.
30 That sort of a—compromise would make you awfully unhappy. I know."

"I don't think I shall ever marry Bayliss," Gladys spoke in her usual low, round voice, but her quick breathing showed he had
35 touched something that hurt. "I suppose I have used him. It gives a school-teacher a certain prestige if people think she can marry the rich bachelor of the town whenever she wants to. But I am afraid I won't marry him,—because
40 you are the member of the family I have always admired."

Claude turned away to the window. "A fine lot I've been to admire," he muttered.

"Well, it's true, anyway. It was like that when
45 we went to High School, and it's kept up. Everything you do always seems exciting to me."

Claude felt a cold perspiration on his forehead. He wished now that he had never come. "But that's it, Gladys. What *have* I ever done,
50 except make one blunder after another?"

She came over to the window and stood beside him. "I don't know; perhaps it's by their blunders that one gets to know people,—by what they can't do. If you'd been like all the
55 rest, you could have got on in their way. That was the one thing I couldn't have stood."

Claude was frowning out into the flaming garden. He had not heard a word of her reply. "Why didn't you keep me from making
60 a fool of myself?" he asked in a low voice.

GO ON TO THE NEXT PAGE

DIAGNOSTIC TEST—*Continued*

"I think I tried—once. Anyhow, it's all turning out better than I thought. You didn't get stuck here. You've found your place. You're sailing away. You've just begun."

65 "And what about you?"

She laughed softly. "Oh, I shall teach in the High School!"

Claude took her hands and they stood looking searchingly at each other in the swim-
70 ming golden light that made everything transparent. He never knew exactly how he found his hat and made his way out of the house. He was only sure that Gladys did not accompany him to the door. He glanced back
75 once, and saw her head against the bright window.

(1922)

10. Which of the following best explains why Gladys is hurt by Claude's reference to Bayliss?

  (A) She feels guilty for having made use of Bayliss.
  (B) She has already agreed to marry Bayliss.
  (C) She has always wanted to marry Claude.
  (D) She knows that Bayliss doesn't want to marry her.
  (E) She doesn't want to lose face in the town by rejecting Bayliss.

11. Which of the following best describes the tone of the passage?

  (A) rueful
  (B) nostalgic
  (C) matter-of-fact
  (D) gentle
  (E) unhappy

12. Which of the following best describes the relationship between Gladys and Claude?

  (A) They are lovers.
  (B) They are husband and wife.
  (C) They are old friends.
  (D) They are acquaintances.
  (E) They are cousins.

13. Which of the following best explains why Claude turns away from Gladys and wishes "that he had never come" (line 48)?

  (A) Claude regrets having spoken to Gladys about his brother.
  (B) Claude is confused because Gladys has paid him a compliment.
  (C) Claude is embarrassed at Gladys's implication that she would like to marry him.
  (D) Claude is upset because he has made Gladys angry.
  (E) Claude realizes that he loves Gladys, but he does not have the courage to say so.

14. The society in which Claude and Gladys live is best characterized as

  (A) conventional
  (B) wealthy
  (C) dishonest
  (D) artistic
  (E) decadent

15. Which of the following best describes Claude's reason for visiting Gladys?

  (A) to say goodbye before he leaves town
  (B) to urge her not to marry his brother
  (C) to tell her that he loves her
  (D) to ask why she has always admired him
  (E) to ask what she will do after he leaves

16. Claude's hesitation to say "the thing he had come to say" (lines 14–15) adds to the portrayal of his character by

  (A) revealing that he does not concern himself with other people
  (B) proving that he has always been blunt and outspoken
  (C) suggesting that speaking out is against his better judgment
  (D) implying that he is not on comfortable terms with Gladys
  (E) showing that he is sensitive to other people's feelings

GO ON TO THE NEXT PAGE

DIAGNOSTIC TEST—*Continued*

17. Which of the following does Gladys imply by saying "If you'd been like all the rest, you could have got on in their way. That was the one thing I couldn't have stood" (lines 54–56)?

> I. Claude has blundered because he was trying to achieve something extraordinary.
> II. Gladys has always been in love with Claude.
> III. Gladys admires Claude because he is different from their friends and neighbors.

(A) I only
(B) I and II only
(C) I and III only
(D) II and III only
(E) III only

Questions 18–23. Read the following excerpt carefully before you choose your answers.

(It is the night before the Battle of Agincourt, which will be fought between the British, led by King Henry V, and the French, led by the Dauphin (crown prince) of France. The British are outnumbered five to one.)

(*Enter Erpingham*)

Erpingham

1 My lord, your nobles, jealous of your absence,
Seek through your camp to find you.

King Henry V

                     Good old knight,
Collect them all together at my tent:
I'll be before thee.

Erpingham

                I shall do't, my lord. (*Exit*)

King Henry V

5 O God of battles! steel my soldiers' hearts;
Possess them not with fear; take from them now
The sense of reckoning, if the opposed numbers
Pluck their hearts from them. Not to-day, O Lord,
O, not to-day, think not upon the fault
10 My father made in compassing the crown!
I Richard's body have interred anew;
And on it have bestow'd more contrite tears
Than from it issued forced drops of blood:
Five hundred poor I have in yearly pay,
15 Who twice a-day their wither'd hands hold up
Toward heaven, to pardon blood; and I have built
Two chantries, where the sad and solemn priests

Sing still for Richard's soul. More will I do;
Though all that I can do is nothing worth,
20 Since that my penitence comes after all,
Imploring pardon.

(*Enter Gloucester*)

Gloucester

My liege!

King Henry V

My brother Gloucester's voice? Ay;
I know thy errand, I will go with thee:
25 The day, my friends and all things stay for me.

                          (1599)

18. Which of the following best paraphrases King Henry's prayer "Take from them now . . . their hearts from them" (lines 6–8)?

(A) Help my soldiers to be brave even though we are outnumbered.
(B) Remind my soldiers that there is safety in numbers.
(C) Reassure my soldiers that you, God of battles, are on our side.
(D) If my soldiers fear being outnumbered, make them forget how to count.
(E) Don't let my soldiers desert just because we are outnumbered.

19. All of the following support the implication that King Henry's father "compassed" the crown unjustly or illegally (line 10) EXCEPT

(A) "think not upon the fault" (line 9)
(B) "my penitence comes after all" (line 20)
(C) "forced drops of blood" (line 13)
(D) "I know thy errand" (line 24)
(E) "I have built / Two chantries" (lines 16–17)

GO ON TO THE NEXT PAGE

DIAGNOSTIC TEST—*Continued*

20. Which of the following explains why the King believes that his prayer for his soldiers will not be answered?

    (A) He has a premonition that he will be killed in the battle.
    (B) He has no real hope that his soldiers can win the battle the next day.
    (C) He thinks God will not forgive him for the crimes his father committed.
    (D) He does not believe God has the power to affect the battle's outcome.
    (E) He knows that his attempts to atone for his father's crime are not sincere.

21. In line 5, the verb "steel" means

    (A) take without payment
    (B) fill with courage
    (C) harden against compassion
    (D) remove surgically
    (E) melt in a furnace

22. King Henry speaks at length of his attempts to atone for his father's actions in order to

    (A) explain that his father was not guilty of any crime
    (B) express the distaste and disgust he feels at his father's deeds
    (C) assert his divine right to the crown of England
    (D) insist that Richard was a greater criminal than Henry's own father
    (E) persuade the Lord to help his army win the battle

23. Which of the following best conveys the meaning of the phrase "jealous of your absence" (line 1)?

    (A) worried about your state of mind
    (B) urgently in need of your presence
    (C) angry that you are not present
    (D) bitter over your neglect of them
    (E) wondering where you are

Questions 24–31. Read the following speech carefully before you choose your answers.

Fourscore and seven years ago our fathers brought forth on this continent a new nation, conceived in Liberty, and dedicated to the proposition that all men are created equal.

5 Now we are engaged in a great civil war, testing whether that nation, or any nation so conceived and so dedicated, can long endure.

We are met on a great battlefield of that war. We have come to dedicate a portion of that
10 field as a final resting-place for those who here gave their lives that that nation might live. It is altogether fitting and proper that we should do this.

But, in a larger sense, we cannot dedicate—
15 we cannot consecrate—we cannot hallow—this ground. The brave men, living and dead, who struggled here, have consecrated it, far above our poor power to add or detract. The world will little note, nor long remember,
20 what we say here, but it can never forget what they did here.

It is for us the living, rather, to be dedicated here to the unfinished work which they who fought here have thus far so nobly advanced.
25 It is rather for us here to be dedicated to the great task remaining before us—that from these honored dead we take increased devotion to that cause for which they gave the last full measure of devotion—that we here
30 highly resolve that these dead shall not have died in vain—that this nation, under God, shall have a new birth of freedom—and that government of the people, by the people, for the people, shall not perish from the earth.

(1863)

24. Which of the following contains the main idea of the speech?

    (A) "all men are created equal" (line 4)
    (B) "we are engaged in a great civil war" (line 5)
    (C) "it can never forget what they did here" (lines 20–21)
    (D) "we cannot hallow this ground" (line 15)
    (E) "these dead shall not have died in vain" (lines 30–31)

25. In the first sentence, the speaker compares the founding of the United States to

    (A) independence
    (B) equality
    (C) war
    (D) childbirth
    (E) slavery

GO ON TO THE NEXT PAGE

DIAGNOSTIC TEST—*Continued*

26. The final sentence of the speech is characterized mainly by

    (A) parallel structure
    (B) metaphor
    (C) personification
    (D) realism
    (E) allusion

27. Which of the following best describes the tone of the speech?

    (A) triumphant
    (B) solemn
    (C) angry
    (D) vengeful
    (E) victorious

28. In the opening sentence of the third paragraph, the speaker uses the words "consecrate" and "hallow" (lines 14–16) to convey which of the following?

    I.   the sense that the battlefield is a cemetery for the dead soldiers
    II. the belief that the soldiers' sacrifice of their lives was a holy thing
    III. the belief that he cannot give a speech honoring the dead as they deserve

    (A) I only
    (B) I and II only
    (C) I and III only
    (D) II and III only
    (E) III only

29. The contents of the speech suggest that the speaker chooses to speak so briefly because

    (A) he knows that the soldiers are too busy fighting the war to listen for long
    (B) he knows that he is unpopular with his audience
    (C) he believes that speeches are unimportant compared to soldiers' lives
    (D) he is awkward with words and does not know what to say
    (E) he thinks the occasion is not important enough for a longer speech

30. Which of the following best paraphrases the sentence "The world will little note . . . what they did here" (lines 18–21)?

    (A) The soldiers' sacrifice of their lives is far more meaningful than a speech in their honor.
    (B) No one will ever forget what the soldiers did on this battleground.

    (C) The world will not pay any attention to the speeches we make today.
    (D) Speeches made during a war are rarely remembered; people remember battles and those who fought.
    (E) Our speeches are forgettable, but their actions are unforgettable.

31. The speaker repeats the word "cannot" (lines 14–15) in order to

    (A) emphasize the failure of the armies to end the war
    (B) emphasize that a speech is an empty gesture compared to the sacrifice of a life
    (C) ensure that his audience will always remember his words
    (D) give himself time to remember what he was going to say next
    (E) remind the audience that the battle is over, but the war continues to be fought

Questions 32–40. Read the following passage carefully before you choose your answers.

Reaching the ground floor they naively avoided the hotel candy counter, descended the wide front staircase, and walking through several corridors found a drugstore in the
5 Grand Central Station. After an intense examination of the perfume counter she made her purchase. Then on some mutual unmentioned impulse they strolled, arm in arm, not in the direction from which they had come,
10 but out into Forty-third Street.

The night was alive with thaw; it was so nearly warm that a breeze drifting low along the sidewalk brought to Anthony a vision of an unhoped-for hyacinthine spring. Above in the
15 blue oblong of sky, around them in the caress of the drifting air, the illusion of a new season carried relief from the stiff and breathed-over atmosphere they had left, and for a hushed moment the traffic sounds and the murmur of
20 water flowing in the gutters seemed an illusive and rarefied prolongation of that music to which they had lately danced. When Anthony spoke it was with surety that his words came from something breathless and desirous that
25 the night had conceived in their two hearts.

GO ON TO THE NEXT PAGE →

DIAGNOSTIC TEST—*Continued*

"Let's take a taxi and ride around a bit!" he suggested, without looking at her.

Oh, Gloria, Gloria!

A cab yawned at the curb. As it moved off like
30 a boat on a labyrinthine ocean and lost itself among the inchoate night masses of the great buildings, among the now stilled, now strident, cries and clangings, Anthony put his arm around the girl, drew her over to him
35 and kissed her damp, childish mouth.

She was silent. She turned her face up to him, pale under the wisps and patches of light that trailed in like moonshine through a foliage. Her eyes were gleaming ripples in
40 the white lake of her face; the shadows of her hair bordered the brow with a persuasive unintimate dusk. No love was there, surely; nor the imprint of any love. Her beauty was cool as this damp breeze, as the moist soft-
45 ness of her own lips.

(1920)

32. Which of the following best describes the setting of this passage?

(A) a slum neighborhood
(B) a large city
(C) a drugstore in a train station
(D) a small town
(E) a hotel bedroom

33. The tone of the second paragraph is best described as

(A) hopeful
(B) suspenseful
(C) passionate
(D) somber
(E) humorous

34. Anthony and Gloria's stroll in the night most likely takes place in

(A) April
(B) May
(C) July
(D) October
(E) December

35. This passage represents the perspective of which of the following characters?

(A) Anthony
(B) Gloria
(C) the cab driver
(D) the author
(E) an omniscient narrator

36. Which of the following best describes Gloria's attitude toward Anthony?

(A) She loves him.
(B) She does not understand him.
(C) She is indifferent to him.
(D) She is fond of him.
(E) She is afraid of him.

37. Which of the following best describes the theme of the passage?

(A) the cruelty of indifference toward a lover
(B) the romance of being alone with one's beloved
(C) the anonymity of public places in a large city
(D) the miracle of the change in seasons
(E) the foolishness of young men in love

38. The author uses the word "labyrinthine" (line 30) to describe

(A) the size of the ocean
(B) the maze of city streets
(C) the darkness of the night
(D) the romance of the situation
(E) the beauty and youth of Gloria

39. The writer compares the taxi to "a boat on a labyrinthine ocean" (line 30) in order to

I. emphasize the isolation and privacy of being in the taxi together
II. heighten the sense of romance and adventure Anthony feels at being alone with Gloria
III. convey to the reader a sense of the vastness of the city

(A) I only
(B) I and II only
(C) III only
(D) II and III only
(E) I, II, and III

GO ON TO THE NEXT PAGE

DIAGNOSTIC TEST—*Continued*

40. Anthony probably looks away from Gloria when he suggests a taxi ride (line 27) in order to

    (A) conceal from her how much he wants to be alone with her
    (B) look up and down the street for an empty taxi
    (C) irritate her with his lack of good manners
    (D) persuade her to return with him to the train station
    (E) manipulate her into suggesting some other way to pass the time

Questions 41–49. Read the following poems carefully before you choose your answers.

Ode on a Grecian Urn

Thou still unravish'd bride of quietness,
   Thou foster-child of Silence and slow Time,
Sylvan historian, who canst thus express
   A flowery tale more sweetly than our rhyme.
5 What leaf-fringed legend haunts about thy shape
   Of deities or mortals, or of both,
      In Tempe or the dales of Arcady?
   What men or gods are these? What maidens loth?
What mad pursuit? What struggle to escape?
10   What pipes and timbrels? What wild ecstasy?

Heard melodies are sweet, but those unheard
   Are sweeter; therefore, ye soft pipes, play on;
Not to the sensual ear, but, more endear'd,
   Pipe to the spirit ditties of no tone:
15 Fair youth, beneath the trees, thou canst not leave
   Thy song, nor ever can those trees be bare;
      Bold Lover, never, never canst thou kiss,
Though winning near the goal—yet, do not grieve;
      She cannot fade, though thou hast not thy bliss,
20   For ever wilt thou love, and she be fair!

Ah, happy, happy boughs! that cannot shed
   Your leaves, nor ever bid the Spring adieu;
And, happy melodist, unwearièd,
   For ever piping songs for ever new;
25 More happy love! more happy, happy love!
   For ever warm and still to be enjoy'd,
      For ever panting, and for ever young;
All breathing human passion far above,
   That leaves a heart high-sorrowful and cloy'd,
30   A burning forehead, and a parching tongue.

Who are these coming to the sacrifice?
   To what green altar, O mysterious priest,
Lead'st thou that heifer lowing at the skies,
   And all her silken flanks with garlands drest?

35 What little town by river or sea-shore
   Or mountain-built with peaceful citadel,
      Is emptied of its folk, this pious morn?
And, little town, thy streets for evermore
   Will silent be; and not a soul, to tell
40   Why thou art desolate, can e'er return.

O Attic shape! fair attitude! with brede
   Of marble men and maidens overwrought,
With forest branches and the trodden weed
   Thou, silent form! dost tease us out of thought
45 As doth eternity: Cold Pastoral!
   When old age shall this generation waste,
      Thou shalt remain, in midst of other woe
   Than ours, a friend to man, to whom thou say'st,
'Beauty is truth, truth beauty,—that is all
50   Ye know on earth, and all ye need to know.'

                       (1819)

41. The word "timbrels" (line 10) most probably means

    (A) carts
    (B) drums
    (C) shepherds
    (D) poems
    (E) trees

42. Which of the following explains why the Grecian urn is "a friend to man" (line 48)?

    (A) The decorations on the urn present valuable information about the past.
    (B) The characters pictured on the urn tell a universal story of love.
    (C) The urn is a useful article to people in all periods of history.
    (D) The urn's beauty thrills the beholder and reminds him of what is truly important in life.
    (E) The urn will continue to inspire poets as long as it remains whole and unbroken.

GO ON TO THE NEXT PAGE

DIAGNOSTIC TEST—*Continued*

43. Which of the following can be used to support the statement "Heard melodies are sweet, but those unheard / Are sweeter" (lines 11–12)?

    (A) "Thou still unravish'd bride of quietness" (line 1)
    (B) "She cannot fade, though thou hast not thy bliss" (line 19)
    (C) "Thy streets forevermore / Will silent be" (lines 38–39)
    (D) "When old age shall this generation waste, / Thou shalt remain" (lines 46–47)
    (E) "Beauty is truth, truth beauty" (line 49)

44. Which of the following is the best paraphrase of lines 3–4?

    (A) A poet can tell a love story better than anyone else.
    (B) The decorations on the urn tell a love story better than a poet can tell it.
    (C) The urn depicts a love story that takes place in the woods.
    (D) A writer of history can tell as wonderful love stories as a poet.
    (E) The urn depicts a story that the poet finds flowery and sweet.

45. "With brede / Of marble men and maidens over-wrought" (lines 41–42) means that the urn is

    (A) used by the children of the men and women pictured on it
    (B) upsetting to the men and women who see it
    (C) crafted by angry men and unhappy women
    (D) made of marble by men and women working together
    (E) decorated with raised figures of men and women

46. Why does the speaker believe that the lover is better off not catching and kissing the maiden?

    (A) She is not a real person, only an image of one.
    (B) She will not always be young and beautiful, as she is now.
    (C) She does not want to be caught.
    (D) She is running toward another lover.
    (E) She will never love him as much as he loves her.

47. Lines 11–14 and 31–34 share which of the following literary elements?

    I. slant rhyme
    II. meter
    III. personification

    (A) I only
    (B) I and II only
    (C) II only
    (D) II and III only
    (E) I, II and III

48. The mood of the poem is best described as

    (A) passionate
    (B) matter-of-fact
    (C) poignant
    (D) rueful
    (E) eerie

49. Which of the following is a major theme of the poem?

    I. Death is a merciful ending to a disappointing life.
    II. Dying for truth or beauty is worthwhile and noble.
    III. Truth and beauty are stronger than death.

    (A) I only
    (B) II only
    (C) III only
    (D) I and II only
    (E) I and III only

Questions 50–60. Read the following passage carefully before you choose your answers.

He was an inch, perhaps two, under six feet, powerfully built, and he advanced straight at you with a slight stoop of the shoulders, head forward, and a fixed from-under stare which
5 made you think of a charging bull. His voice was deep, loud, and his manner displayed a kind of dogged self-assertion which had nothing aggressive in it. It seemed a necessity, and it was directed apparently as much
10 at himself as at anybody else. He was spotlessly neat, apparelled in immaculate white from shoes to hat, and in the various Eastern ports where he got his living as shipchandler's water-clerk he was very popular.

GO ON TO THE NEXT PAGE

DIAGNOSTIC TEST—*Continued*

15 A water-clerk need not pass an examination
in anything under the sun, but he must have
Ability in the abstract and demonstrate it
practically. His work consists in racing under
sail, steam, or oars against other water-clerks
20 for any ship about to anchor, greeting her
captain cheerily, forcing upon him a card—
the business card of the ship-chandler—and
on his first visit on shore piloting him firmly
but without ostentation to a vast, cavern-like
25 shop which is full of things that are eaten and
drunk on board ship; where you can get
everything to make her seaworthy and beautiful, from a set of chain-hooks for her cable
to a book of gold-leaf for the carvings of her
30 stern; and where her commander is received
like a brother by a ship-chandler he has
never seen before. There is a cool parlour,
easy-chairs, bottles, cigars, writing imple-
ments, a copy of harbour regulations, and a
35 warmth of welcome that melts the salt of a
three months' passage out of a seaman's
heart. The connection thus begun is kept up,
as long as the ship remains in harbour, by the
daily visits of the water-clerk. To the captain
40 he is faithful like a friend and attentive like a
son, with the patience of Job, the unselfish
devotion of a woman, and the jollity of a
boon companion. Later on the bill is sent in.
It is a beautiful and humane occupation.
45 Therefore good water-clerks are scarce.
When a water-clerk who possesses Ability in
the abstract has also the advantage of having
been brought up to the sea, he is worth to his
employer a lot of money and some humouring.
50 Jim had always good wages and as much
humouring as would have bought the fidelity
of a fiend. Nevertheless, with black ingrati-
tude he would throw up the job suddenly and
depart. To his employers the reasons he gave
55 were obviously inadequate. They said 'Confounded fool!' as soon as his back was
turned. This was their criticism on his exquisite sensibility.

To the white men in the waterside business
60 and to the captains of ships he was just Jim—
nothing more. He had, of course, another
name, but he was anxious that it should not
be pronounced. His incognito, which has as
many holes as a sieve, was not meant to hide
65 a personality but a fact. When the fact
broke through the incognito he would leave

suddenly the seaport where he happened to
be at the time and go to another—generally
farther east. He kept to seaports because he
70 was a seaman in exile from the sea, and had
Ability in the abstract, which is good for no
other work but that of a water-clerk. He
retreated in good order toward the rising
sun, and the fact followed him casually but
75 inevitably.

(1900)

50. The narrator's attitude toward Jim is best described
as

(A) respectful and admiring
(B) wary and distrustful
(C) intrigued and curious
(D) objective but friendly
(E) disapproving but compassionate

51. What does the narrator mean by the phrase "Ability
in the abstract" (used for the first time in line 17)?

(A) the ability to understand abstract concepts
(B) the ability to perform manual labor
(C) the appearance of one who can carry out most
tasks
(D) a sharp intelligence that cannot easily be fooled
(E) secret abilities that other people cannot see

52. In this context, "exquisite sensibility" (lines 57–58)
means

(A) cowardice
(B) foolishness
(C) stubbornness
(D) common sense
(E) oversensitivity

53. You can infer that Jim left the sea because

(A) he is no longer physically able to work as a
sailor
(B) there is a disgraceful secret in his past
(C) ship's crews do not like working with him
(D) he is lazy and not good at his work on board
ship
(E) he argues too much with his superiors

GO ON TO THE NEXT PAGE

DIAGNOSTIC TEST—*Continued*

54. Which is the best description of Jim's character?

    (A) reserved and secretive
    (B) temperamental and emotional
    (C) bitter and cynical
    (D) friendly and outgoing
    (E) reckless and brave

55. His employers call Jim a "confounded fool" (lines 55–56) because

    (A) they know he is lying about his reasons for quitting his job
    (B) his lack of ability causes him to make stupid mistakes
    (C) he refuses to tell anyone his real name
    (D) he is giving up a good job for no particular reason
    (E) they believe he thinks he is better than them

56. When the narrator says that Jim's incognito "had as many holes as a sieve" (lines 63–64), he means that

    (A) people only pretend not to know Jim's true history
    (B) it would be easy to discover Jim's real name
    (C) Jim is ashamed to talk about his experiences
    (D) Jim no longer remembers his real name
    (E) no one believes what Jim says about himself

57. Why might Jim's self-assertion be "directed . . . at himself" (lines 9–10)?

    (A) to prove to others that he is capable and worthy of respect
    (B) to discourage anyone he meets from asking him questions
    (C) to impress his employers and persuade them to pay him well
    (D) to reassure himself that he is a strong and able person
    (E) to convince the narrator to tell his story in a favorable way

58. Jim's constant retreat from the "fact" implies which of the following about his character?

    (A) He is disloyal.
    (B) He is careless.
    (C) He is unfriendly.
    (D) He is impatient.
    (E) He is cowardly.

59. The fact that Jim is such a good water-clerk suggests which of the following about him?

    I. He can play a role convincingly.
    II. He is highly skilled at many tasks.
    III. He has great leadership ability.

    (A) I only
    (B) II only
    (C) I and II only
    (D) II and III only
    (E) III only

60. The statement "the fact followed him casually but inevitably" (lines 74–75) suggests that

    (A) Jim will eventually be forced to come to terms with his past
    (B) the narrator knows Jim's secret and will reveal it
    (C) people will only learn Jim's secret after his death
    (D) a specific enemy is chasing Jim and will expose him in the end
    (E) Jim can escape his past for good if he travels far enough

STOP

IF YOU FINISH BEFORE TIME IS CALLED, YOU MAY CHECK YOUR WORK ON THIS TEST ONLY.

DO NOT TURN TO ANY OTHER TEST IN THIS BOOK.

ANSWER KEY

1. D	21. B	41. B
2. A	22. E	42. D
3. B	23. B	43. B
4. B	24. E	44. B
5. B	25. D	45. E
6. A	26. A	46. B
7. C	27. B	47. B
8. E	28. C	48. C
9. E	29. C	49. C
10. A	30. E	50. D
11. D	31. B	51. C
12. C	32. B	52. E
13. C	33. C	53. B
14. A	34. E	54. A
15. B	35. A	55. D
16. E	36. C	56. E
17. C	37. B	57. D
18. D	38. B	58. E
19. D	39. E	59. A
20. C	40. A	60. A

ANSWERS AND EXPLANATIONS

1. **Correct Choice: D**
   The "leaves" in the phrase are pages of books, not leaves on trees. The speaker has been "turning others' leaves," or looking in books of verse by other poets, for inspiration.

2. **Correct Choice: A**
   In effect, the speaker reasons that "She" may read his verses, understand that he loves her, take pity on his suffering, and be kind to him.

3. **Correct Choice: B**
   The speaker has spent the entire sonnet describing how hard he has been trying to write his poem, so Option I must be correct. Option II must also be correct because it paraphrases what the Muse actually says in line 14. Option III cannot be among the answers because the Muse gives the speaker very good advice.

4. **Correct Choice: B**
   The speaker is frustrated by his inability to get his feelings down on paper. He does not mention being jealous of any other man, and his tone cannot be described as bitter, because he keeps trying throughout and because the poem ends on a note of hope.

5. **Correct Choice: B**
   A metaphor is a direct comparison between two unlike things, stating in effect that A is B. The poet uses many metaphors in this sonnet.

6. **Correct Choice: A**
   "She" evidently knows him but does not know of his love for her. This suggests that they are not friends. They are certainly not lovers. He does not suggest that she is angry at him. It is her indifference that has determined him to try to win her love.

7. **Correct Choice: C**
   Option I cannot be correct because, with rare exceptions such as Walt Whitman's *Song of Myself*, there is never any proof that a speaker and the poet who created that speaker are one and the same. A speaker in a poem is like a first-person narrator in a novel; he or she is a character like any other character. Option II is obviously correct. Option III is obviously correct.

8. **Correct Choice: E**
   By "truant pen," the speaker implies that his pen has metaphorically left him; in other words, that he cannot write. The other four choices either misconstrue his meaning altogether or take it too literally.

9. **Correct Choice: E**
   This sonnet is written in iambic hexameter, which has six metric feet per line instead of the usual five. The other four elements meet the usual standards for a sonnet.

10. **Correct Choice: A**
    Gladys says, "I suppose I have used him." The impression of her character as shown in this passage suggests that she has a conscience and thus would feel badly about having used him.

11. **Correct Choice: D**
    The author shows a quiet, gentle regard for her two characters and their situation.

12. **Correct Choice: C**
    They went to high school together, Claude feels free to bring up the very personal topic of Gladys's marriage, and Gladys also speaks very personally to Claude. This makes it clear that they are old friends, not mere acquaintances. Nothing in the passage suggests that they are cousins. Because they talk about Gladys's marriage to someone else, they are neither lovers nor married to each other.

13. **Correct Choice: C**
    In effect, Gladys has said she will not marry Claude's brother because she likes Claude better. This is a strong hint that she would like to marry Claude. Given the date of 1922 and the obviously conventional environment, this is naturally embarrassing for a sensitive person like Claude. (If you recognize the passage, you know that in fact Claude is already—very unhappily—married, which is further reason for his embarrassment. It is the reason he says a bad marriage "would make you awfully unhappy. I know" and that he once "made a fool of himself.")

14. **Correct Choice: A**
    Claude's hesitation to speak out on a personal matter shows that he respects convention. The phrase "without apology" shows that normally a person would apologize for saying something personal. Gladys's comments about acquiring prestige by being able to "marry the rich bachelor of the town" and "if you'd been like the rest, you could have got on in their way" show that they are surrounded by people who stick to certain social conventions.

15. **Correct Choice: B**
    Claude hesitates to say "the thing he had come to say." This makes it clear that although he does also want to say goodbye before leaving, the real, crucial motive for the visit is to reassure himself that Gladys will not throw her life away by marrying the wrong man.

16. **Correct Choice: E**
    Claude's hesitation indicates that he is a sensitive person. He wants to speak about an intimate, personal concern that is not really his business, but because he cares deeply for Gladys, he nerves himself to be "insensitive" and to speak out.

17. **Correct Choice: C**
    "If you'd been like all the rest" makes it clear Claude is different from them, and Gladys clearly likes this quality about him. Claude himself says that he has always made mistakes; Gladys suggests that a lack of mistakes means a person has not reached after anything difficult to achieve, and therefore has nothing particular to be proud of.

18. **Correct Choice: D**
    "Take from them now their sense of reckoning" means "take away their ability to count." If they can't count, they won't know that they are outnumbered, and they won't be afraid.

19. **Correct Choice: D**
    It is the only choice that does not refer to the past crimes or to repentance for them.

20. **Correct Choice: C**
    Henry says "my penitence comes after all," meaning that it is too late to be sorry for the sins of his father. He is afraid his sincere repentance will count for nothing with God, and that therefore God will not help the English army in the battle.

21. **Correct Choice: B**
    "Steel my soldier's hearts" means "fill my soldier's hearts with courage." The following line "possess them not with fear" suggests that the presence of courage, not the absence of compassion, is most important to Henry.

22. **Correct Choice: E**
    Henry prays to God to help his side win the battle. To make his case more persuasive, he points out in his prayer that he has tried his best to atone for his father's sins; therefore those sins should not be counted against him when he and his army are badly outnumbered and need divine assistance.

23. **Correct Choice: B**
    The following line, "seek through the camp to find you" makes it clear that they are not "jealous" in the modern, everyday sense of the word. They simply need him to join them as soon as possible.

24. **Correct Choice: E**
    The most important point of the speech is that those who hear it should do everything they can to ensure that the soldiers did not die in vain. They should take up the soldiers' cause and help end the war and reunite the nation.

25. **Correct Choice: D**
    The speaker uses the language of childbirth in the phrase "our fathers brought forth a new nation, conceived in liberty."

26. **Correct Choice: A**
    Parallel structure means using the same grammatical pattern in each clause of a sentence. In this case, parallel elements include: "that we take; that we resolve; that this nation shall have, that government shall not perish" and "of the people, by the people, for the people."

27. **Correct Choice: B**
    The event where this speech takes place is the dedication of a battlefield as a cemetery for fallen soldiers. Clearly, a solemn tone is most appropriate for such an occasion.

28. **Correct Choice: C**
    This sentence does not talk about the soldiers having already consecrated the battlefield. That idea appears in the next sentence. Therefore Option II is incorrect. The ideas described in Options I and III are present in this sentence.

29. **Correct Choice: C**
    The speaker points out that "the world will little note, nor long remember, what we say here" and also states that speeches have only "poor power" to commemorate the dead. He is brief because he feels that brevity is appropriate.

30. **Correct Choice: E**
    This paraphrase includes all the information in the sentence itself and echoes its grammatical structure. The other choices convey only parts of the sentence's ideas and information or change its meaning by their choice of words.

31. **Correct Choice: B**
    The repetition of "we cannot dedicate—we cannot consecrate—we cannot hallow" hammers home the idea that speeches in honor of the dead, although appropriate, are meaningless in comparison to the soldiers' sacrifice of their lives for a cause in which they believed.

32. **Correct Choice: B**
    Even if the reader did not identify New York City from the references to Grand Central Station and Forty-third Street, any city with that many numbered streets must be large. Choice C is wrong because the characters do not remain inside the drugstore. Choice A is wrong because it would not be easy to find a taxi or a major train station in a slum.

33. **Correct Choice: C**
    Words and phrases like "the night was alive," "caress," "hushed moment," and "something breathless and desirous" all suggest passion.

34. **Correct Choice: E**
    Because the night's improbably moderate temperature makes Anthony look forward to spring, it must be winter now.

35. **Correct Choice: A**
"Perspective" refers to the point of view represented in the passage. In this passage, the reader experiences the night and the taxi ride through Anthony's eyes and Anthony's emotions.

36. **Correct Choice: C**
The sentence "No love was there, surely; nor the imprint of any love" makes it clear that Gloria is indifferent to Anthony.

37. **Correct Choice: B**
The passage is all about the romance of being alone with Gloria in the night. Anthony is not foolish in his own eyes; the themes of anonymity and the change of season are only alluded to briefly; and Anthony does not seem to feel that Gloria is cruel to him.

38. **Correct Choice: B**
The common noun *labyrinth* comes from the Labyrinth of Greek mythology—a maze no one could find the way out of. A metaphorical ocean of city streets is "labyrinthine" because, like the paths of a maze, the streets crisscross one another and offer a wide choice of possible paths.

39. **Correct Choice: E**
A boat on an ocean conveys a tremendous sense of privacy, isolation, and adventure. The comparison suggests that the city, like the ocean, is huge.

40. **Correct Choice: A**
The passage emphasizes that while Anthony passionately desires Gloria, Gloria is indifferent to Anthony. Anthony does not want to alienate Gloria, so he tries to "play it cool" by not looking at her, making the suggestion in an offhand manner, as if he doesn't really care whether they take a taxi ride or not.

41. **Correct Choice: B**
The context of "pipes and timbrels" and "melodies" makes it clear that timbrels, like pipes, are musical instruments. In fact, a timbrel is a type of drum.

42. **Correct Choice: D**
The speaker's main point about the urn throughout the poem is that it is a thing of beauty that far surpasses any beauty in real life and that it is more beautiful than his own poems. Because of its beauty, it inspires everyone who looks at it. Its beauty, shared with the world, makes the world a better place. To the speaker, this is the real importance of being alive—being able to appreciate beauty and recognize its great importance.

43. **Correct Choice: B**
The speaker believes that the pleasure of the imagination is greater than the pleasure of actual possession, because living things deteriorate while works of art endure. Therefore it is

sweeter to imagine a song than to hear one, and sweeter to dream about a lover than to kiss her. A real maiden would "fade"—grow old—but the one pictured on the urn will always be beautiful and young.

44. **Correct Choice: B**
The "sylvan historian" is the urn itself. The speaker is not asking it a question, but making a statement about it—that it can "express a flowery tale more sweetly than our rhyme."

45. **Correct Choice: E**
Brede is an archaic word that refers to ornament or decoration, and *overwrought* in this context means "elaborated, ornamented" (as wrought iron is worked into decorative shapes).

46. **Correct Choice: B**
The speaker directly tells the lover not to grieve because the woman will be fair forever and will not fade.

47. **Correct Choice: B**
Slant rhyme (or off rhyme) occurs when poets use approximate rather than exact rhymes. *Unheard/endeared, on/tone, (sacri)fice/skies,* and *priest/drest* are slant rhymes. The poem never changes meter; it has five metric feet per line throughout. The pipes are personified in lines 11–14, addressed as if they have the power to play on their own; but there is no personification in lines 31–34.

48. **Correct Choice: C**
Poignant means "moving, affecting, touching." This describes the poet's attitude toward the urn's images of a love that will never be consummated.

49. **Correct Choice: C**
The speaker stresses that beauty and truth endure beyond death. He suggests more than once that although people will age and wither, beautiful works of art and imagination like the urn will endure. He does not suggest that death is noble nor that it will redeem a disappointing life.

50. **Correct Choice: D**
The narrator describes Jim's appearance and manner without apparent emotion or bias, but notes that Jim is popular and that he seems to like Jim well enough.

51. **Correct Choice: C**
"Ability in the abstract" suggests its opposite; a lack of ability in the concrete. The implication is that one who has ability in the abstract *seems* very capable, but in reality lacks skills. This is supported by the description of the water-clerk's job, which consists of being pleasant and charming, rather than doing any real work. It is the appearance of competence and skill, not the reality.

52. **Correct Choice: E**
    Today, a *sensible* person is one who shows common sense; this meaning does not fit the context of the sentence. In an earlier time, *sensibility* referred to a too-great susceptibility to emotion. Jim's employers feel that he is touchy or unreasonably sensitive.

53. **Correct Choice: B**
    The word *exile* suggests that Jim did not stop sailing due to his own choice but because he was forced to do so. It seems likely that the mysterious "fact" that he tries to hide must be the reason for his exile. The passage suggests that he works hard, gets along well with others, and is not prone to argue, which makes the other choices incorrect.

54. **Correct Choice: A**
    The passage clearly shows that Jim keeps his own counsel and does not show much emotion.

55. **Correct Choice: D**
    The narrator states that the employers find Jim's reasons for quitting "inadequate"; they think anyone who would give up a well-paid job for such reasons is a fool.

56. **Correct Choice: E**
    An incognito is a disguise or a false account of oneself. If your story about who you are is full of holes, that means it is not very believable. Other information in the passage suggests that choice C is a true statement, but it is not the answer to why Jim's incognito is "full of holes."

57. **Correct Choice: D**
    Jim would not need to assert himself to himself unless he needed reassurance; he evidently suffers from self-doubt and must constantly remind himself that there is no need to feel insecure. The other choices are wrong because they address why Jim might assert himself toward others, not toward himself.

58. **Correct Choice: E**
    To run away from one's name and one's past suggests that one does not have the courage to confront them.

59. **Correct Choice: A**
    A good water-clerk must act out a part; he pretends to be the best friend of every ship's captain who comes to port. Option II is incorrect because a water-clerk is a salesman, not someone who performs skilled labor. Option III is incorrect because a water-clerk is not a leader, but one who works for a boss.

60. **Correct Choice: A**
    The word *inevitably* suggests that Jim cannot avoid the secret in his past, no matter how far or how fast he runs from it. This statement foreshadows a confrontation between Jim and his secret. Choices B and E are eliminated by the word *casually;* no specific enemy is trying to ruin Jim.

HOW TO CALCULATE YOUR SCORE

Count the number of correct answers and enter the total below.
Count the number of wrong answers. Do NOT include any questions you did not answer.
Multiply the number of wrong answers by 0.25 and enter the total below.
Do the subtraction. The answer is your raw score. Use the scoring scale to find your scaled score.

$$\underset{\substack{\text{[short WOL]} \\ \text{(number of correct answers)}}}{} - \underset{\substack{\text{[short WOL]} \\ \text{(number of wrong answers} \times 0.25)}}{} = \underset{\substack{\text{[short WOL]} \\ \text{(raw score)}}}{}$$

Raw Score	Scaled Score	Raw Score	Scaled Score	Raw Score	Scaled Score	Raw Score	Scaled Score	Raw Score	Scaled Score
60	800	44	710	28	560	12	420	−4	260
59	800	43	700	27	550	11	410	−5	250
58	800	42	690	26	540	10	400	−6	240
57	800	41	690	25	530	9	390	−7	230
56	800	40	680	24	520	8	380	−8	220
55	800	39	670	23	510	7	370	−9	210
54	790	38	660	22	500	6	360	−10	200
53	790	37	650	21	500	5	350	−11	200
52	780	36	640	20	490	4	340	−12	200
51	770	35	630	19	490	3	330	−13	200
50	760	34	620	18	480	2	320	−14	200
49	750	33	610	17	470	1	310	−15	200
48	740	32	600	16	460	0	300		
47	740	31	590	15	450	−1	290		
46	730	30	580	14	440	−2	280		
45	720	29	570	13	430	−3	270		

Note: This is only a sample scoring scale. Scoring scales differ from exam to exam.

PART II
TOPIC REVIEW FOR THE LITERATURE TEST

CHAPTER 1
LITERARY TERMS

LITERARY TERMS

Literary terms are the words and phrases students and scholars use to discuss and interpret works of literature. This chapter contains an alphabetical glossary of literary terms likely to appear in questions and answer choices on the SAT Literature Test. You can use this chapter to review the meaning of these literary terms. The examples are all taken from literary works like those you will find on the SAT Literature Test.

Chapter 1 concludes with a sample passage and questions, which you can use to test your knowledge of the literary terms.

Alliteration

Alliteration occurs when two or more words in a line of verse or a sentence of prose begin with the same sound. There are two types of alliteration: when the repeated sound is a vowel, it is sometimes called *assonance*. When the repeated sound is a consonant, it is sometimes called *consonance*.

Example

> To sit in solemn silence in a dull dark dock,
> In a pestilential prison with a lifelong lock,
> Awaiting the sensation of a short sharp shock
> From a cheap and chippy chopper on a big black block!

Allusion

An **allusion** is a reference to a person, place, thing, or event in history, literature, or the arts. Authors do not explain allusions because usually, in their time, they expected their audience to understand these references automatically.

Example

> One of the ones that Midas touched,
> Who failed to touch us all,
> Was that confiding prodigal,
> The blissful oriole.

(The poet mentions Midas, who was a king in Greek mythology. Even if you do not know who Midas is, the capitalized name provides a clue that this is an allusion.)

Argument

An **argument** can also be called a thesis. It is a strong statement of opinion that an author sets out to prove. The term *argument* is usually used in discussion of nonfiction; it can also be applied to certain kinds of poetry.

Example

The history of the present king of Great Britain is a history of repeated injuries and usurpations, all having in direct object the establishment of an absolute tyranny over these states. To prove this, let facts be submitted to a candid world.

Blank Verse

Blank verse refers to unrhymed lines of **iambic pentameter** (see below). Elizabethan plays were largely written in blank verse. Authority figures, royalty, and members of the nobility usually speak in blank verse, while clowns, servants, and commoners usually speak in prose. Elizabethan playwrights used blank verse because the regular rhythm made the dialogue easier for actors to memorize and the rhythm of iambic pentameter closely approximates the natural rhythm of English speech. In addition, blank verse has a certain stately and majestic quality appropriate to the royal, heroic, and/or noble characters who speak it.

Example

GLOUCESTER.	Now tell me, brother Clarence, what think you Of this new marriage with the Lady Grey? Hath not our brother made a worthy choice?
CLARENCE.	Alas, you know, 'tis far from hence to France; How could he stay till Warwick make return?
SOMERSET.	My lords, forbear this talk. Here comes the King.

Character

The term **character** has two meanings:

1. a person or animal who plays a role in a literary work
2. the personality traits and type of the person or animal

The process of creating and describing a literary character is called **characterization.** In **direct characterization,** an author tells the reader what a character is like. In **indirect characterization,** the author leaves the reader to infer this from the character's words and actions.

Example of direct characterization

Oh! but he was a tight-fisted hand at the grindstone, Scrooge! a squeezing, wrenching, grasping, scraping, clutching, covetous old sinner! Hard and sharp as flint, from which no steel had ever struck out generous fire; secret, and self-contained, and solitary as an oyster.

Dialect

Dialect is colloquial, idiomatic speech used in everyday conversation among uneducated characters. Dialect also refers to speech patterns used in a specific geographic region. The grammatical and spelling patterns of dialects differ from those of Standard English.

Examples

British dialect (London, East End)	American dialect (Missouri regional)
"Let me lay here quiet, and not be chivied no more," falters Jo, "and be so kind any person as is a-passin' nigh where I used fur to sweep, as jist to say to Mr. Sangsby that Jo, wot he known once, is a-moving on right forards with his duty, and I'll be wery thankful."	Pap was standing over me looking sour— and sick too. He says: "What you doin' with this gun?" I judged he didn't know nothing about what he had been doing, so I says: "Somebody tried to get in, so I was laying for him." "Why didn't you roust me out?" "Well, I tried to, but I couldn't; I couldn't budge you." "Well, all right. Don't stand there palavering all day . . ."

Dialogue

Dialogue refers to the words spoken by characters in fiction, poetry, or drama and by the real people who are quoted in works of nonfiction. In a play, the character's name appears at the start of each speech he or she makes. In prose and narrative poetry, dialogue is enclosed in quotation marks.

Examples

Dialogue in drama	Dialogue in prose
PHYLLIS. There's really nothing to choose between you. If one of you would forgo his title, and distribute his estates among his Irish tenantry, why, I should then see a reason for accepting the other. LORD M. Tolloller, are you prepared to make this sacrifice? LORD T. No! LORD M. Not even to oblige a lady? LORD T. No! not even to oblige a lady.	"What did you say his name was?" he asked. "Scratchy Wilson," they answered in chorus. "And will he kill anybody? What are you going to do? Does this happen often? . . . Can he break in that door?" "No, he can't break down that door," replied the barkeeper. "He's tried it three times. But when he comes, you better lay down on the floor, stranger."

End Stopping / Enjambment

An **end-stopped** line of verse ends in a punctuation mark that indicates a pause or a full stop. **Enjambment** occurs when lines do not end in punctuation marks, but rather express thoughts or ideas that continue without pause to the following line(s).

Example

That's my last Duchess painted on the wall,
Looking as if she were alive. I call
That piece a wonder, now; Fra Pandolf's hands
Worked busily a day; and there she stands.

*(Lines 1 and 4 are **end-stopped**; lines 2–4 are an example of **enjambment**, because the complete thought begun on line 2 continues to the end of line 4.)*

Figurative Language

Any figure of speech that has a meaning beyond the literal definition of the words is called **figurative language.** Types of figurative language include **hyperbole, metaphor, simile,** and **personification** (see definitions and examples below).

Free Verse

Free verse is "free" because it does not employ a regular rhythm, meter, or rhyme scheme. However, not all unrhymed poems are free-verse poems. A poem with rhythm and meter is not a free-verse poem, even if it is unrhymed.

Examples

Free verse	Unrhymed poetry; *not* free verse

I sang to you and the moon
But only the moon remembers.
   I sang
O reckless free-hearted
          free-throated rhythms,
Even the moon remembers them
   And is kind to me.
	Gipsy queen of the night, wraith of the fire-lit dark,
	Glittering eyes of ice, sharp as glacier green,
	Lisping falling kisses, syllabled flakes of snow,
	Down on the stubbled fields, over my eyes and hair;
	If on my mouth one falls, it is tasteless and
	   light and cold.

(The regular rhythm and meter of the excerpt on the right prevent it from being free verse.)

Hyperbole

Hyperbole refers to gross exaggeration that no one could mistake for a literal statement of fact. It is usually used for humorous effect.

Example

"How long can you hold him?" asks Bill.

"I'm not as strong as I used to be . . . but I think I can promise you ten minutes."

"Enough," says Bill. "In ten minutes I shall cross the Central, Southern, and Middle Western States, and be legging it trippingly for the Canadian border."

Iambic Pentameter

This term denotes a specific **rhythm** and **meter** (see below) used in verse and verse drama. **Pentameter** refers to a line of verse that has five metric feet (*penta-* is Latin for "five"). **Iambic** means that each metric foot has a weak syllable followed by a strong one. Elizabethan playwrights wrote in iambic pentameter (see **blank verse,** above). **Sonnets** (see below) are also written in iambic pentameter, which is generally a very popular meter for

English poetry. Couplets with a meter of iambic pentameter are called **heroic couplets**.

Example

KING   The mercy that was quick in us of late
                 By your own counsel is suppress'd and kill'd.
                 You must not dare, for shame, to talk of mercy,
                 For your own reasons turn into your bosoms,
                 As dogs upon their masters, worrying you.
                 See you, my princes and my noble peers,
                 These English monsters!

Imagery

Imagery is any descriptive language that appeals to one or more of the five senses. It occurs in all types of writing.

Example

Ah, what can ever be more stately and admirable to me than mast-hemm'd Manhattan?
Rivers and sunset and scallop-edg'd waves of floodtide?
The sea-gulls oscillating their bodies, the hay-boat in the twilight, and the belated lighter?
What gods can exceed these that clasp me by the hand, and with voices I love call me
    promptly and loudly by my nighest name as I approach?

(Details in this excerpt appeal to the senses of sight, touch, and hearing.)

Inference

To make an **inference,** a reader must study the details of a literary text and decide what they mean. Authors do not tell readers everything directly; they often leave readers to figure out meaning for themselves. The reader must **infer** from what the author **implies.**

Example

True! nervous, very, very dreadfully nervous I have been and am; but *why* will you say that I am mad? . . . Hearken! and observe how healthily, how calmly, I can tell you the whole story.

It is impossible to say how first the idea entered my brain . . . I loved the old man. He had never wronged me. He had never given me insult. For his gold I had no desire. I think it was his eye! Yes, it was this! One of his eyes resembled that of a vulture—a pale blue eye with a film over it. Whenever it fell upon me my blood ran cold, and so by degrees, very gradually, I made up my mind to take the life of the old man, and thus rid myself of the eye for ever.

(The reader might reasonably infer that the narrator is in custody for the old man's murder and that he is insane, because his motive for murder is irrational.)

Main Idea

The **main idea** of a literary work is the most important concept the author is writing about—the one he or she most wants the reader to think about. The main idea of a nonfiction work is similar to the **theme** (see below) of a work of fiction, poetry, or drama.

Example, with main idea in boldface

> **Shakespeare is,** above all writers, at least above all modern writers, the poet of nature; **the poet that holds up to his readers a faithful mirror of manners and of life.** His characters are not modified by the customs of particular places, unpracticed by the rest of the world; by the peculiarity of studies or professions, which can operate but upon small numbers; or by the accidents of transient fashions or temporary opinions; they are the genuine progeny of common humanity, such as the world will always supply, and observation will always find.

Metaphor

A **metaphor** is a direct comparison of two apparently unlike things, stating that A is B. In an **implied metaphor,** the author does not say "A is B," but describes A as if it were B. An **extended metaphor** is one that the author continues to develop through several lines of prose or verse.

Examples

Metaphor (stated)	Extended metaphor (implied)

But soft! what light through
    yonder window breaks?
It is the East, and Juliet
    is the sun.
	The yellow fog that rubs its back upon the window-panes,
	The yellow smoke that rubs its muzzle on the window-panes
	Licked its tongue into the corners of the evening,
	Lingered upon the pools that stand in drains,
	Let fall upon its back the soot that falls from chimneys,
	Slipped by the terrace, made a sudden leap,
	And seeing that it was a soft October night,
	Curled once about the house, and fell asleep.

(In the example on the right, instead of saying "The fog is a cat," the poet describes the fog as if it were a cat.)

Meter

In poetry, **meter** refers to the number of times a rhythmic pattern occurs in a line of verse. Meter is measured in **metric feet.** Each repetition of a rhythmic pattern represents one metric foot. The most common meters in English-language poetry are **tetrameter** (four metric feet per line), **pentameter** (five), and **hexameter** (six).

Example

In placid hours well-pleased we dream
Of many a brave unbodied scheme;
But form to lend, pulsed life create,
What unlike things must meet and mate.

(This excerpt is written in tetrameter, with each metric foot containing a weak beat followed by a strong one.)

Mood

In a literary sense, the word **mood** is used to refer to the overall emotional impact of a work on the reader. The mood of a work might be suspenseful, ironic, funny—there are many possibilities. The term *mood* can also be used in its everyday sense to describe how a character feels about something.

Example

"Is matchmaking at all in your line?"

Hugo Peterby asked the question with a certain amount of personal interest.

"I don't specialize in it," said Clovis; "it's all right while you're doing it, but the after-effects are sometimes so disconcerting—the mute reproachful looks of the people you've aided and abetted in matrimonial experiments. It's as bad as selling a man a horse with half a dozen latent vices and watching him discover them piecemeal in the course of the hunting season."

(The author uses the witty dialogue to establish a mood of frivolous humor.)

Narrator

The **narrator** is the character from whose point of view a work of prose fiction is told. The narrator refers to him- or herself as *I* and *me* and may play either a major or a minor role in the plot. The word *narrator* is NOT used in discussing nonfiction; the "narrator" of a nonfiction work is the author. (See also **perspective/point of view,** below.)

Example

Call me Ishmael. Some years ago—never mind how long precisely—having little or no money in my purse, and nothing particular to interest me on shore, I thought I would sail about a little and see the watery part of the world.

Paraphrase

To **paraphrase** a text means to restate it in different words. A paraphrase should restate all the ideas in the original.

Personification

To **personify** an inanimate object means to endow it with the abilities, qualities, or emotions of living creatures. Animals can also be personified, such as in folk or fantasy literature, where they converse, dress up, walk on two legs, and live in houses like human beings.

Example

Besides, the Kettle was aggravating and obstinate. It wouldn't allow itself to be adjusted on the top bar; it wouldn't hear of accommodating itself kindly to the knobs of coal; it would lean forward with a drunken air, and dribble, a very Idiot of a Kettle, on the hearth. It was quarrelsome; and hissed and spluttered morosely at the fire.

Plot

The **plot** is the series of events that make up a prose narrative or a narrative poem. A plot contains five stages:

- **Exposition,** in which the characters and conflicts are introduced
- **Rising action,** in which the conflicts begin to play out
- **Climax,** the point of highest interest, excitement, and suspense
- **Falling action,** in which the characters begin to resolve their conflicts
- **Resolution,** at which point the narrative ends

Point of View/Perspective

An author tells a story from a specific **point of view,** or **perspective.** The narrative point of view determines how the reader will experience and understand the story.

A **limited** point of view means the reader can only see into the thoughts and feelings of one character. Both first-person and third-person narrators can tell a story from a limited point of view.

An **omniscient** point of view means that the reader can see into the thoughts and feelings of all the characters in turn. This is typical of a story narrated in the third person.

Example of omniscient point of view/perspective

Ray . . . was thinking of that afternoon and how it had affected his whole life when a spirit of protest awoke in him. He had forgotten about Hal and muttered words. "Tricked by Gad, that's what I was, tricked by life and made a fool of," he said in a low voice.

As though understanding his thoughts, Hal Winters spoke up. "Well, has it been worth while? What about it, eh? What about marriage and all that?" he asked and then laughed. Hal tried to keep on laughing but he too was in an earnest mood.

Rhyme—Exact Rhyme and Slant Rhyme

To form **exact rhymes,** words must have the same vowel sound on the stressed syllable and the same final consonant. **Slant rhyme** (also called near rhyme or off rhyme) is achieved when the words share beginning and/or final consonants but have different vowel sounds.

Example

1   Now all the truth is out,
     Be secret and take defeat
     From any brazen throat,
     For how can you compete,
5   Being honor bred, with one
     Who, were it proved he lies,
     Were neither shamed in his own
     Nor in his neighbor's eyes?

(The odd-numbered lines form slant rhymes: out/throat *and* one/own. *The even-numbered lines are exact rhymes:* defeat/compete *and* lies/eyes.*)*

Rhythm

Rhythm refers to the pattern of stressed and unstressed syllables in verse. Common rhythmic patterns include the following:

- **Spondaic** STRONG / STRONG / STRONG
- **Anapestic** weak weak STRONG / weak weak STRONG
- **Trochaic** STRONG weak / STRONG weak / STRONG weak
- **Iambic** weak STRONG / weak STRONG / weak STRONG

Setting

The **setting** of a literary work is the time and place in which the events occur. An author's description of a setting can contribute to mood, tone, and character. The setting can also affect the events of the plot.

Example

He lived in an old somber house and from his windows he could look into the disused distillery or upwards along the shallow river on which Dublin is built. The lofty walls of his uncarpeted room were free from pictures. He himself had bought every article of furniture in the room: a black iron bedstead, an iron washstand, four cane chairs, a clothes-rack, a coal-scuttle, a fender and irons and a square table on which lay a double desk.

Simile

A **simile** is a comparison between two apparently unlike things, stating that A is like/as B.

Examples

She raised her head from her arms and dried her eyes with the back of her hand like a child.

Like distant music these words that he had written years before were borne towards him from the past.

Sonnet

A **sonnet** is a fourteen-line poem in **iambic pentameter** (see above). There are two standard rhyme schemes for sonnets:

- An **Italian** or **Petrarchan sonnet** describes a problem or conflict in its first eight lines (the octave). With the final six lines (the sestet), the speaker's thoughts usually take a turn toward some kind of resolution of the conflict. The sestet is set off from the octave by a change in rhyme scheme.
- A **Shakespearean sonnet** asks a question or describes a problem in three quatrains of four lines each, rhymed either ABBA or ABAB, then sums up and resolves the situation in a final rhymed couplet.

Many sonnets deviate from these two patterns. A sonnet can be entirely or partly unrhymed, or it can have a rhyme scheme all its own. As long as it consists of fourteen lines of iambic pentameter, it is still a sonnet.

Example of an Italian sonnet:

Oh soft embalmer of the still midnight!
  Shutting with careful fingers and benign
Our gloom-pleased eyes, embower'd from the light
  Enshaded in forgetfulness divine;
O soothest Sleep! If so it please thee, close
  In midst of this thine hymn, my willing eyes,
Or wait the amen, ere my poppy throws
  Around my bed its lulling charities;
Then save me, or the passèd day will shine
  Upon my pillow, breeding many woes;
Save me from curious conscience, that still lords
  In strength for darkness, burrowing like a mole;
Turn the key deftly in the oiled wards
  And seal the hushèd casket of my soul.

Speaker

The **speaker** is the first-person narrator of a poem, who refers to him- or herself as *I* and *me*. In a **lyric poem,** the speaker may or may not represent the author's views, experiences, and emotions. In a **narrative poem,** the speaker is NOT to be identified with the author, but is simply a character in the poem's story.

Example: Speaker of a narrative poem

Once upon a midnight dreary, while I pondered, weak and weary,
Over many a quaint and curious volume of forgotten lore,
While I nodded, nearly napping, suddenly there came a tapping
As of someone gently rapping, rapping at my chamber door.
"'Tis some visitor," I muttered, "tapping at my chamber door—
                    Only this, and nothing more."

Summary

Unlike a **paraphrase** (see above), a **summary** does not rephrase the original text. A summary briefly recapitulates the major themes or main ideas and the most important supporting details of a literary work.

Symbolism

When an author gives a character, place, or thing in a story or poem a meaning beyond its face value, this is referred to as **symbolism.** In the following example, the city of Christminster has both literal and symbolic meaning. Literally, it is a city of buildings, streets, and people. Symbolically, it represents the main character's fondest dream—his desire to acquire learning and wisdom.

Example

> The air increased in transparency with the lapse of minutes, till the topaz points showed themselves to be the vanes, windows, wet roof slates, and other shining spots upon the spires, domes, freestone-work, and varied outlines that faintly revealed it. It was Christminster, unquestionably; either directly seen, or miraged in the peculiar atmosphere . . . And the city acquired a tangibility, a permanence, a hold on his life, mainly from the one nucleus of fact that the man for whose knowledge and purposes he had so much reverence was actually living there.

Theme

The **theme** is the overall meaning of a literary work. The theme encompasses the most important concept or idea that the author wants the reader to take away and think about. A theme must usually be **inferred** (see above) from details in the text. A theme is usually spoken of as being **universal**—common to human experience in all times, places, and cultures.

Example

> If I should die, think only this of me:
>   That there's some corner of a foreign field,
> That is forever England. There shall be
>   In that rich earth a richer dust concealed;
> A dust whom England bore, shaped, made aware,
>   Gave, once, her flowers to love, her ways to roam,
> A body of England's breathing English air,
>   Washed by the rivers, blest by suns of home.

(The theme of this excerpt is patriotism, or love for one's country.)

Tone

In a literary sense, **tone** refers to the author's attitude toward the subject. An author might write with a nostalgic, humorous, or sarcastic tone, to name only a few possibilities.

Example

"What do we talk of marks and brands, whether on the bodice of her gown, or the flesh of her forehead?" cried another female, the ugliest as well as the most pitiless of these self-constituted judges. "This woman has brought shame upon us all, and ought to die. Is there not law for it? Truly, there is, both in the Scripture and the statute-book. Then let the magistrates, who have made it of no effect, thank themselves if their own wives and daughters go astray!"

(The author's tone is condemnatory; he shows his sympathy for the criminal by painting a harsh and unflattering portrait of her "self-constituted judge.")

REVIEW QUESTIONS

Questions 1–4. Read the following passage carefully before you choose your answers.

"I want to know what I should do—Today, Edgar Linton has asked me to marry him, and I've given him an answer . . . I accepted him, Nelly. Be quick, and say whether I was wrong!"

"You accepted him? then, what good is it discussing the matter? You have pledged your word, and cannot retract."

"But, say whether I should have done so—do!" she exclaimed in an irritated tone, chafing her hands together, and frowning.

"There are many things to be considered, before that question can be answered properly," I said sententiously. "First and foremost, do you love Mr. Edgar?"

"Who can help it? Of course I do," she answered.

Then I put her through the following catechism—for a girl of twenty-two, it was not injudicious.

"Why do you love him, Miss Cathy?"

"Nonsense, I do—that's sufficient."

"By no means; you must say why."

"Well, because he is handsome, and pleasant to be with."

"Bad," was my commentary.

"And because he is young and cheerful."

"Bad, still."

"And because he loves me."

"Indifferent, coming there."

"And he will be rich, and I shall like to be the greatest woman of the neighborhood, and I shall be proud of having such a husband."

"Worst of all! And now, you say how you love him?"

"As everybody loves—You're silly, Nelly."

"Not at all—Answer."

"I love the ground under his feet, and the air over his head, and everything he touches, and every word he says—I love all his looks, and all his actions, and him entirely, and altogether. There now!"

". . . And now, let us hear what you are unhappy about. Your brother will be pleased . . . the old lady and gentleman will not object, I think—you will escape from a disorderly, comfortless home into a wealthy, respectable one; and you love Edgar, and Edgar loves you. All seems smooth and easy—where is the obstacle?"

"*Here*! and *here*!" replied Catherine, striking one hand on her forehead, and the other on her breast: "In whichever place the soul lives—in my soul, and in my heart, I'm convinced I'm wrong! . . . I've no more business to marry Edgar Linton than I have to be in heaven; and if the wicked man in there[1] had not brought Heathcliff so low, I shouldn't have thought of it. It would degrade me to marry Heathcliff, now; so he shall never know how I love him: and that, not because he's handsome, Nelly, but because he's more myself than I am. Whatever our souls are made of, his and mine are the same, and Linton's is as different as a moonbeam from lightning, or frost from fire . . . I want to cheat my uncomfortable conscience, and be convinced that Heathcliff has no notion of these things—he has not, has he? He does not know what being in love is?"

"I see no reason that he should not know, as well as you," I returned; "and if *you* are his choice, he'll be the most unfortunate creature that ever was born! As soon as you become Mrs Linton, he loses friend, and love, and all! Have you considered how you'll bear the separation, and how he'll bear to be quite deserted in the world? Because, Miss Catherine—"

"He quite deserted! we separated!" she exclaimed, with an accent of indignation. "Who is to separate us, pray? They'll meet the fate of Milo! Not as long as I live, Ellen—for no mortal creature. Every Linton on the face of the earth might melt into nothing, before I could consent to forsake Heathcliff! . . . I cannot express it; but surely you and everybody have a notion that there is, or should be, an existence of yours beyond you. What were the use of my creation if I were entirely contained here? My great miseries in this world have been Heathcliff's miseries, and I watched and felt each from the beginning; my great thought in living is himself. If all else perished, and *he* remained, I should still continue to be; and if all else remained, and he were annihilated, the universe would turn to a mighty stranger. I should not seem a part of it. My love for Linton is like the foliage in the woods. Time will change it, I'm well aware, as winter changes the trees. My love for Heathcliff resembles the eternal rocks beneath—a source of little visible delight, but necessary. Nelly, I *am* Heathcliff—he's always, always in my mind—not as a pleasure, any more than I am always a pleasure to myself—but as my own being."

[1]Catherine refers to her older brother Hindley, who abuses Heathcliff and treats him like a servant.

1. From the way they speak to one another, you can infer that Nelly is Catherine's

    (A) friend
    (B) mother
    (C) servant
    (D) sister
    (E) employer

2. Which of the following does NOT represent a use of figurative language, but is meant literally only?

   (A) "I love the ground under his feet, and the air over his head, and everything he touches, and every word he says."
   (B) "Whatever our souls are made of, his and mine are the same, and Linton's is as different as a moonbeam from lightning, or frost from fire."
   (C) "Every Linton on the face of the earth might melt into nothing, before I could consent to forsake Heathcliff!"
   (D) "My great miseries in this world have been Heathcliff's miseries, and I watched and felt each from the beginning; my great thought in living is himself."
   (E) "My love for Linton is like the foliage in the woods. Time will change it, I'm well aware, as winter changes the trees."

3. Catherine's statement "Nelly, I *am* Heathcliff" might be paraphrased as which of the following?

   (A) Heathcliff and I are, in fact, the same person.
   (B) Heathcliff is my twin brother.
   (C) Heathcliff is my best friend.
   (D) Heathcliff and I love each other very much.
   (E) Heathcliff and I are kindred spirits.

4. Catherine's character is best described as

   (A) impulsive and rash
   (B) cautious and prudent
   (C) sensible and reasonable
   (D) good natured and kind
   (E) charming and lively

ANSWERS AND EXPLANATIONS

1. **Correct Choice: C**
   Although they speak to one another frankly and bluntly, as if they were equals, Nelly addressed Catherine as "Miss Cathy" and "Miss Catherine," while Catherine calls Nelly by her first name. This supports choice C—that Nelly is Catherine's servant.

2. **Correct Choice: D**
   Choices A and C are hyperbole—an exaggeration of the love Catherine feels for Linton. (In this case, the hyperbole is made for dramatic rather than comic effect.) Choices B and E contain similes, or imaginative comparisons. This leaves choice D, which Catherine means literally—she has watched Heathcliff suffer; she has herself suffered because she loves and sympathizes with him; and he is the central person in her life.

3. **Correct Choice: E**
   Catherine's earlier statement that "his (soul) and mine are the same" helps explain her meaning. She believes that she and Healthcliff are spiritually akin; that they think and feel the same way about everything; and that they understand one another perfectly and completely. Choice E, "kindred spirits," matches this analysis. Catherine and Heathcliff are obviously two separate individuals, not one. Because Catherine has evidently considered marrying Heathcliff, he cannot be her twin. Details in the passage show that choices C and D are true statements; but Catherine speaks of a bond stronger than friendship or even love when she says, "I *am* Heathcliff."

4. **Correct Choice: A**
   It is fair to use choice A, "impulsive and rash," to describe Catherine. She acts first on the spur of the moment, and only afterward does she think about the consequences of her hasty decision. A cautious or sensible person would have thought things through before acting; a good-natured, kind person would never say something like, "It would degrade me to marry Heathcliff"; and in this passage, Catherine is too serious and earnest to be described as charming or lively.

CHAPTER 2
FICTION

PROSE FICTION

The key word in the definition of **prose fiction** is *imagination*. Fiction consists of imagined stories. Although authors often base works of fiction on their own experiences or on historical events, these stories are considered fiction because they recount actual experiences in an imaginative way.

This chapter contains a brief overview of prose fiction: its forms, structure, and history. Use the sample passages and questions to test your ability to read and understand works of prose fiction.

FORMS OF PROSE FICTION

Prose fiction comes in three forms: the **novel,** the **novella,** and the **short story.**

The Novel and the Novella

A **novel** is a full-length work of prose fiction; a **novella** is a short novel. Roughly speaking, a narrative of about 80 to 150 pages is called a novella; any narrative longer than that is called a novel. The typical novel runs 200 to 350 pages, but there is no outside limit to its length. The longest novels, such as *War and Peace* (Leo Tolstoy, 1865–1869), *In Search of Lost Time* (Marcel Proust, 1913–1927), and *Les Miserables* (Victor Hugo, 1862) run well over 1,000 pages.

Some authors imagine stories of such scope that they must be told over the course of an entire series of novels. In a series of novels, each novel can be read as one long chapter of the extended story. Examples include the Palliser and Barchester novels by Anthony Trollope (6 novels in each series), *The Raj Quartet* by Paul Scott (4 novels), the Rougon-Macquart novels of Emile Zola (20 novels), *A Dance to the Music of Time* by Anthony Powell (12 novels), *Strangers and Brothers* by C. P. Snow (11 novels), and the Aubrey-Maturin novels of Patrick O'Brian (20 novels, plus one left half-finished at the author's death).

Structure of the Novel

A novel employs a full range of literary techniques to tell a story in an imaginative way. In a novel, the author can take all the time he or she wants to describe and develop characters and conflicts.

A novel is rooted in four major elements: **plot, character, setting,** and **theme.** (See Chapter 1 for definitions and examples of these terms). The author imagines people, sets them in a specific time and place, and gives them actions to carry out. The overall story is written to illustrate a meaning beyond itself; something that can be phrased as a statement that readers will recognize as a universal human truth. The only distinction between a novel and a novella is one of length; the author of a novella must deal with these four elements somewhat more concisely.

Because of its length, a novel can cover these four elements in great detail. For example, a novel may have more than one plot. It may have two major plot lines linked in some important way, or one main plot line and one or more **subplots**—chains of events that usually involve minor characters and relate to the central plot line.

In its hundreds of pages, a novel can portray dozens of characters. Some make only brief appearances, while others play major roles in the plot. Novels generally present a variety of settings, as the characters enact the events of the plot in different places. Many novels cover the activities of months or years in the characters' lives; others concentrate on a much shorter period of time. *Ulysses* (James Joyce, 1922) takes nearly 800 pages to recount only one day in the life of its protagonist, Leopold Bloom. A long novel can address a variety of major and minor themes.

Although novels are by definition prose works, authors often play with this convention, borrowing from other forms. For example, *Moby-Dick* (Herman Melville, 1851), *Ulysses,* and *This Side of Paradise* (F. Scott Fitzgerald, 1920) contain sections that are composed entirely of dialogue and stage directions, like play scripts. **Epistolary novels**, such as *Clarissa* (Samuel Richardson, 1748) and *The Ides of March* (Thornton Wilder, 1948) are made up of letters exchanged among the characters. *Dracula* (Bram Stoker, 1897), and *The Moonstone* (Wilkie Collins, 1868) tell their stories in whole or in part by means of journal entries. *Eugene Onegin* (Alexander Pushkin, 1833) is an eight-part story described by its author not as a modern epic poem but as "a novel in verse."

History of the Novel's Development

Literary historians generally agree that the world's first important novel was written in 1022 C.E. by Murasaki Shikibu of Japan. *The Tale of Genji* is a romance set in the Japanese royal palace.

The technological breakthrough that allowed and encouraged the development of long works of fiction was the invention of the printing press that used movable type. This technology was invented in Korea; in the West, it was perfected in Germany around 1450. For the first time, the mass production of books and other printed material was possible. The demand for literature rose along with the supply, as more and more western Europeans learned to read and write.

The first European novels began to appear in the 1500s: *Gargantua and Pantagruel* (François Rabelais, France, 1532), and *Don Quixote* (Miguel de Cervantes, Spain, 1605). *Don Quixote* owes a great deal to the form of the linked short-story collection (see **short story,** below). The novel has been an extraordinarily popular form of entertainment ever since.

The Eighteenth Century

Daniel Defoe, Samuel Richardson, Henry Fielding, and Laurence Sterne are the fathers of the English novel. They were among the first of their era to write long prose narratives that were wildly popular among the reading public. Their works were set in a recognizable, realistic time and place—the present-day England in which their readers lived. The characters were prone to be types rather than distinct individuals, but their motivations and actions were believable within that limitation. The plots often bordered on the improbable.

Many of these novels were coming-of-age tales, in which the protagonist begins as an immature young person, learns important lessons about life in the course of the plot, and ends as a mature adult. Although these early novels may seem stilted and artificial today, they laid a foundation for a marvelous flowering of the form in the next century.

The Nineteenth Century

The novel was maturing as a form. In the nineteenth century, characters became three-dimensional individuals with strong personalities. Plots became more realistic, often dealing with everyday events. Novelists explored universal human themes. When people read novels, they often found themselves in a realistic and recognizable world. Many nineteenth-century writers devoted dozens of pages to descriptive writing, portraying settings in great detail. A novel's setting added to its atmosphere, and readers in the nineteenth century were not in a hurry to finish a book.

The nineteenth century is generally considered to be the high point of the full-length novel. The English population was highly literate, and the middle and upper classes had enough leisure time to enjoy reading. Major English novelists included Jane Austen, George Eliot, the Brontë sisters, and Charles Dickens.

With the nation established and expanding, and with an educated population of its own, American authors began experimenting with the novel. James Fenimore Cooper found huge popular success with his historical novels of the American frontier. Other important American novelists of this century included Herman Melville, Mark Twain, Nathaniel Hawthorne, and Harriet Beecher Stowe, whose *Uncle Tom's Cabin* (1852) outsold every book except the Bible in the years leading up to the American Civil War.

Nineteenth-century writers wrote not only to entertain their readers but also to educate them about society. In this era before broadcast media existed, popular novelists were major celebrities, and they used their power to sway the public on important issues of the day. In novels such as *Oliver Twist* and *Hard Times*, Dickens wrote with such passion about the terrible conditions in prisons and boys' schools that he convinced his readers to support reform. *Uncle Tom's Cabin,* a detailed look at American slavery, painted an unsparing picture of a system that corrupted everyone it touched. Stowe's novel was so widely read and discussed that it played a major role in committing Northerners to the cause of abolition. When President Abraham Lincoln met Stowe at the White House in the 1860s, he is reported to have greeted her with the words, "So you're the little lady who started this great war!"

The Twentieth Century and Beyond

American prose fiction came into its own in the twentieth century with such authors as Henry James, Edith Wharton, Willa Cather, Ernest Hemingway, F. Scott Fitzgerald, and John Steinbeck. Notable British novelists of the era included Graham Greene, Evelyn Waugh, E. M. Forster, and D. H. Lawrence. Irish novelists included Elizabeth Bowen, and James Joyce—one of the greatest fiction writers of the modern era. Authors from other lands also wrote great works of English-language fiction. Joseph Conrad of Poland and

Vladimir Nabokov of Russia wrote numerous novels in English. Nabokov is best known for the notorious *Lolita*; Conrad, for the short novel *Heart of Darkness* and other tales of Southeast Asia.

Modern and contemporary novels have less of an emphasis on descriptive writing, and their prose is often more spare than that of their nineteenth-century counterparts. The novel was affected by the rise of technology, as other forms of entertainment (such as movies, professional sports, and eventually television and the Internet) competed for people's attention. Modern novels are perhaps more prone to imply important information about characters, rather to state it directly. They are also more likely than earlier novels to have open-ended or ambiguous resolutions.

Two highly popular forms of the novel that first appeared in the nineteenth century became enormously popular in the twentieth—the detective story and the science-fiction novel. Both are written almost solely for entertainment purposes, although detective novelists such as John le Carré and Raymond Chandler produced works of very high literary merit.

The Short Story

A **short story** is like a miniature novel. Short stories generally run from 2 or 3 to about 50 pages. Some stories run as long as 80 pages. When stories become much longer than this, they are usually considered novellas. Short stories are usually published in collections of 10 or 15—sometimes all by one author, sometimes by various authors. A novella may be published on its own or together with a few shorter stories by the same author.

Structure of the Short Story

The major differences between novels and short stories are dictated by their comparative length. In a short story, an author must use the same literary techniques to tell a story more concisely. There is much less time to develop a character or a conflict. A short story generally aims to produce a single effect on the reader. It has a much narrower focus than a novel.

Whereas a novel may have multiple plot and subplots, a short story usually has only one plot. A short story will develop only a few characters in detail. Although a novel constantly shifts its physical setting, a short story usually takes place entirely in one setting, or in a very few settings at most. A short story usually concentrates on only one major theme.

History of the Short Story's Development

The Ancient World

The world's first written short stories included the fables of Aesop (Greece, sixth century B.C.E.) and Chuang-Tzu (China, fourth century B.C.E.). Aesop's brief tales feature animal and sometimes human characters who, in the course of the story, learn lessons that the author sums up as morals, or good advice to the reader. Chuang-Tzu's fables feature peasants, artisans, and scholars debating the meaning of the natural phenomena they observe in the world around them.

The Middle Ages

As the ancient world gave way to the modern, authors began to imagine more sophisticated and complex plots featuring individual personalities. One of the earliest and most famous short-story collections dates to about 950 C.E. *The Thousand and One Nights,* also known as *The Arabian Nights,* appeared in Persia (modern-day Iran) at this time. *The Arabian Nights* begins with a frame story: the account of a sultan who is convinced that all women are faithless. He therefore makes love to a different woman every night, only to order her executed in the morning. When Scheherazade is brought in to spend the night with him, she tells him the beginning of an exciting tale. Wanting to hear the end of the story, the sultan decides to keep her alive for one more night. As the nights pass, Scheherazade breaks off each new story at some exciting point, and the sultan continues to postpone her execution until the whole idea of killing her is long forgotten. Each of Scheherazade's tales is a self-contained short story, but the overall framing device unifies the entire work.

Two famous fourteenth-century short-story collections, *The Decameron* and *The Canterbury Tales,* employ a similar structure. In *The Decameron* (1353), Giovanni Boccaccio created the story of ten young men and women fleeing the city of Florence to escape the plague. They settle in a country villa and pass the time by telling stories. Each character tells one story every day for 10 days, making a total of 100 tales. *The Decameron* is an unforgettable collection of romance, comedy, tragedy, and farce.

In England, Geoffrey Chaucer published *The Canterbury Tales* (c. 1386). Like *The Thousand and One Nights* and *The Decameron,* it is a collection of self-contained short stories linked by an overall framing device. Several religious pilgrims on their way to Canterbury Cathedral meet en route at the Tabard Inn. They agree to hold a storytelling contest to while away the tedium of the journey. Although all but two tales in the collection are written in verse, *The Canterbury Tales* is considered a short-story collection because of the length of each tale and its strong basis in the major elements of prose fiction: plot, character, setting, and theme.

The Nineteenth Century

The world's first literary and popular magazines began appearing in the early 1800s. The magazine was a perfect medium for publishing individual short stories. Many novelists of the era were also short-story writers. An author who took many months to finish a novel was glad to be able to earn money in the meantime by tossing off short stories for the magazines. To this day, magazines such as *The New Yorker* continue to publish short stories by the best-known writers.

The Twentieth Century

In the twentieth century, the best-known American short-story writers included O. Henry, Henry James, Edith Wharton, Ernest Hemingway, F. Scott Fitzgerald, Sherwood Anderson, and William Faulkner. Notable British short-story writers of the era included Graham Greene, D. H. Lawrence, and Elizabeth Bowen.

Collections of linked short stories remained popular. Sherwood Anderson's *Winesburg, Ohio* portrays an entire town by focusing each story in the collection on a different character, with several characters appearing in more than one story. In 1914, James Joyce published *Dubliners*, stories that provide a portrait of a city and its people by showing various aspects of contemporary Dublin.

Some writers create a popular character and write a series of self-contained short stories linked only by the fact that they feature this character. Saki (the pen name of H. H. Munro) wrote a collection of satirical stories about Reginald and another about Clovis. Sir Arthur Conan Doyle stumbled on an enormous success with his stories of Sherlock Holmes, who may be the best-known literary character ever created.

REVIEW QUESTIONS

Questions 1–4. Read the following passage carefully before you choose your answers.

While the mate was getting the hammer, Ahab, without speaking, was slowly rubbing the gold piece against the skirts of his jacket, as if to heighten its lustre, and without using any words was meanwhile lowly humming to himself, producing a sound so strangely muffled and inarticulate that it seemed the mechanical humming of the wheels of his vitality in him.

Receiving the top-maul from Starbuck, he advanced towards the main-mast with the hammer uplifted in one hand, exhibiting the gold with the other, and with a high raised voice exclaiming: "Whosoever of ye raises me a white-headed whale with a wrinkled brow and a crooked jaw; whosoever of ye raises me that white-headed whale, with three holes punctured in his starboard fluke—look ye, whosoever of ye raises me that same white whale, he shall have this gold ounce, my boys!"

"Huzza! huzza!" cried the seamen, as with swinging tarpaulins they hailed the act of nailing the gold to the mast.

"It's a white whale, I say," resumed Ahab, as he threw down the top-maul: "a white whale. Skin your eyes for him, men; look sharp for white water; if ye see but a bubble, sing out."

All this while Tashtego, Daggoo, and Queequeg had looked on with even more intense interest and surprise than the rest, and at the mention of the wrinkled brow and crooked jaw they had started as if each was separately touched by some specific recollection.

"Captain Ahab," said Tashtego, "that white whale must be the same that some call Moby Dick."

. . . "Captain Ahab," said Starbuck, who, with Stubb and Flask, had thus far been eyeing his superior with increasing surprise, but at last seemed struck with a thought which somewhat explained all the wonder. "Captain Ahab, I have heard of Moby Dick—but it was not Moby Dick that took off thy leg?"

"Who told thee that?" cried Ahab; then pausing, "Aye, Starbuck; aye, my hearties all round; it was Moby Dick that dismasted me; Moby Dick that brought me to this dead stump I stand on now. Aye, aye," he shouted with a terrific, loud, animal sob, like that of a heart-stricken moose; "Aye, aye! it was that accursed white whale that razeed me; made a poor pegging lubber of me for ever and a day!" Then tossing both arms, with measureless imprecations he shouted out: "Aye, aye! and I'll chase him round Good Hope, and round the Horn, and round the Norway Maelstrom, and round perdition's flames before I give him up. And this is what ye have shipped for, men! to chase that white whale on both sides of land, and over all sides of earth, till he spouts black blood and rolls fin out. What say ye, men, will ye splice hands on it, now? I think ye do look brave."

"Aye, aye!" shouted the harpooners and seamen, running closer to the excited old man: "A sharp eye for the White Whale; a sharp lance for Moby Dick!"

"God bless ye," he seemed to half sob and half shout. "God bless ye, men. Steward! go draw the great measure of grog. But what's this long face about, Mr. Starbuck; wilt thou not chase the white whale? art not game for Moby Dick?"

"I am game for his crooked jaw, and for the jaws of Death too, Captain Ahab, if it fairly comes in the way of the business we follow; but I came here to hunt whales, not my commander's vengeance. How many barrels will thy vengeance yield thee even if thou gettest it, Captain Ahab? it will not fetch thee much in our Nantucket market."

"Nantucket market! Hoot! But come closer, Starbuck; thou requirest a little lower layer. If money's to be the measurer, man, and the accountants have computed their great counting-house the globe, by girdling it with guineas, one to every three parts of an inch; then, let me tell thee, that my vengeance will fetch a great premium *here*!"

"He smites his chest," whispered Stubb, "what's that for? methinks it rings most vast, but hollow."

"Vengeance on a dumb brute!" cried Starbuck, "that simply smote thee from blindest instinct! Madness! To be enraged with a dumb thing, Captain Ahab, seems blasphemous."

"Hark ye yet again,—the little lower layer. All visible objects, man, are but as pasteboard masks. But in each event—in the living act, the undoubted deed—there, some unknown but still reasoning thing puts forth the mouldings of its features from behind the unreasoning mask. If man will strike, strike though the mask! How can the prisoner reach outside except by thrusting through the wall? To me, the white whale is that wall, shoved near to me. Sometimes I think there's naught beyond. But 'tis enough. He tasks me; he heaps me; I see in him outrageous strength, with an inscrutable malice sinewing it. That inscrutable thing is chiefly what I hate; and be the white whale agent, or be the white whale principal, I will wreak that hate upon him."

(1851)

1. Why does Starbuck question Ahab's plan to hunt down Moby Dick?

   (A) He is afraid Moby Dick will attack Ahab again.
   (B) He does not believe that they can catch Moby Dick.
   (C) He believes it is a sin to hunt down and kill an animal for revenge.
   (D) He does not want to chase whales because that is not the purpose of the ship's voyage.
   (E) He believes that Ahab is insane to hunt whales.

2. Given Ahab's statements in this excerpt, Moby Dick appears to symbolize for him

(A) his own desire for revenge against an evil force
(B) malicious and tyrannical God
(C) an elusive love who cannot be caught and held
(D) his own mysterious destiny or fate
(E) freedom from authority and fear

3. How does the shipboard setting affect the relationships among the characters?

(A) The ship is a setting that no one can escape except in death.
(B) The setting gives Ahab supreme authority, which the crew will not question except in an extreme situation.
(C) The crew members are packed together in a small space, so they all get along well.
(D) Captain Ahab would not be able to pursue Moby Dick except in a ship.
(E) The characters feel lost and uncertain on a ship, when they would be strong and sure of themselves on land.

4. Based on this excerpt, the novel deals with all of the following universal themes EXCEPT

(A) the conflict between conscience and professional duties
(B) the obsession with revenge against an enemy
(C) the battle between man and nature
(D) the temptation to sin in spite of warnings
(E) the pursuit of an unattainable love

ANSWERS AND EXPLANATIONS

1. **Correct Choice: C**

   Dialogue in the passage shows that the ship's business is to hunt and kill whales for their oil. Therefore, Starbuck would find it perfectly appropriate to kill Moby Dick if they came across him in the natural course of the voyage. However, Starbuck sees a tremendous difference between killing whales as a profession and chasing one particular whale to kill it for personal revenge. Starbuck describes this as "blasphemy." This makes choice C correct.

2. **Correct Choice: B**

   Ahab seems to believe that life in unknowable, consisting of mysterious enemy forces that wear masks. God has created these enemy forces and given them their masks, and humankind must constantly struggle to survive in this hostile environment. Moby Dick is a symbol of what Ahab sees as God's tyranny and his arbitrary creation of a dangerous world. This best matches choice B.

3. **Correct Choice: B**

   A nineteenth-century ship is a small world, floating by itself in an ocean. The captain is the ruler of this small universe, in which a chain of command is highly important. The setting gives Ahab a measure of authority and absolute power that he would not possess anywhere else. Starbuck does question him, but only in an extreme situation—because he believes the captain's plan is endangering the voyage. Ahab's word is law on the ship, and the other characters will have to obey him. This makes choice B correct. The other four choices are either untrue statements or they do not really address the question of character relationships.

4. **Correct Choice: E**

   Note the word *except* in the question. Choice E is correct because Moby Dick does not represent love. Ahab is chasing him from entirely different motives.

▰▰ REVIEW QUESTIONS

Questions 5–8. Read the following passage carefully before you choose your answers.

I did it—I should have known better. I persuaded Reginald to go to the McKillops' garden-party against his will.

We all make mistakes occasionally. "They know you're here, and they'll think it so funny if you don't go. And I want particularly to be in with Mrs. McKillop just now."

"I know, you want one of her smoke Persian kittens as a prospective wife for Wumples—or a husband, is it?" (Reginald has a magnificent scorn for details, other than sartorial.) "And I am expected to undergo social martyrdom to suit the connubial exigencies—"

"Reginald! It's nothing of the kind, only I'm sure Mrs. McKillop would be pleased if I brought you. Young men of your brilliant attractions are rather at a premium at her garden-parties."

"Should be at a premium in heaven," remarked Reginald complacently.

"There will be very few of you there, if that is what you mean. But seriously, there won't be any great strain upon your powers of endurance; I promise you that you shan't have to play croquet, or talk to the Archdeacon's wife, or do anything that is likely to bring on physical prostration. You can just wear your sweetest clothes and a moderately amiable expression, and eat chocolate-creams with the appetite of a *blasé* parrot. Nothing more is demanded of you."

Reginald shut his eyes. "There will be the exhaustingly up-to-date young women who will ask me if I have seen *San Toy*: a less progressive grade who will yearn to hear about the Diamond Jubilee—the historic event, not the horse. With a little encouragement, they will inquire if I saw the Allies march into Paris. Why are women so fond of raking up the past? They're as bad as tailors, who invariably remember what you owe them for a suit long after you've ceased to wear it."

"I'll order lunch for one o'clock; that will give you two and a half hours to dress in."

Reginald puckered his brow into a tortured frown, and I knew that my point was gained. He was debating what tie would go with which waistcoat.

Even then I had my misgivings.

5. Which best describes the author's purpose in writing this passage?

   (A) to entertain readers with an amusing tale
   (B) to persuade readers not to pressure their friends into accepting invitations against their wills
   (C) to inform readers what happens at a garden-party
   (D) to describe the modern up-to-date young society woman
   (E) to intrigue readers with a challenging puzzle

6. Based on this passage, what is the major conflict in the story?

   (A) Reginald's desire to remain in his comfortable chair versus his desire to go to the party
   (B) the narrator's desire that Reginald attend the party versus Reginald's desire to avoid it
   (C) Reginald's desire to dress well for the party versus the lack of time to get ready
   (D) the young women's desire to talk to Reginald versus his desire to keep to himself
   (E) Reginald's desire to behave well at the party versus the narrator's desire to make mischief

7. What literary technique does the writer use to describe the garden-party setting?

   (A) He lets readers imagine the setting from the simple term *garden-party*.
   (B) He has his two main characters discuss the party in detail in the dialogue.
   (C) He writes a detailed descriptive passage that allows the reader to experience the party through the five senses.
   (D) He indicates the social rank of the character who is hosting the party.
   (E) He has one character describe the garden to the other in detail.

8. The sentences "I did it—I should have known better" and "Even then I had my misgivings" can best be described as examples of

   (A) imagery
   (B) flashbacks
   (C) characterization
   (D) foreshadowing
   (E) verbal irony

ANSWERS AND EXPLANATIONS

5. **Correct Choice: A**

   The tone of the story is light, the subject matter is frivolous, and there is plenty of sarcastic humor in the dialogue. The story was clearly written mainly to entertain the reader, choice A.

6. **Correct Choice: B**

   The dialogue shows that the narrator wants Reginald to go to the party, and Reginald wants to stay away. This describes choice B—a basic literary conflict, in which one character pushes and the other one resists. The lines "I should have known better" and "We all make mistakes occasionally" further support this choice, showing that because Reginald does not want to go to the party, he will not behave well there.

7. **Correct Choice: B**

   In the dialogue, the narrator and Reginald discuss many details of the party. The reader knows there will be croquet and refreshments, that people will be well-dressed, and that there will be pleasant conversation. This supports choice B.

8. **Correct Choice: D**

   Foreshadowing means hinting to the reader about what is to come next. This matches choice D. Imagery is language that appeals to the five senses, a flashback occurs when the narration shifts to an earlier time, characterization helps to develop an individual's personality, and verbal irony is the difference between what is stated and what is meant.

CHAPTER 3
NONFICTION

NONFICTION

Nonfiction is the opposite of fiction—it is not imagined stories, but true ones. Nonfiction comes in two varieties: **narrative nonfiction** and **expository nonfiction.**

Narrative nonfiction resembles narrative fiction in its structure and its use of literary elements. Narrative **history, biography,** or **autobiography,** like narrative fiction, consist of characters acting out events in a specific setting. The difference is that in nonfiction, the **characters** are real people, the **settings** are the real times and places in which those people lived, and the **plot** consists of events that actually took place. **Historical novels** are outside the category of narrative nonfiction; they are based on real people and events, but they are works of fiction because the author retells the events in an imaginative way.

Expository nonfiction includes prose works written by authors who want to persuade, inform, and/or entertain readers by writing about their thoughts, ideas, and observations. **Essays** and **speeches** are the primary forms of expository nonfiction.

This chapter gives a brief overview of the three types of nonfiction you are most likely to see excerpted on the SAT Literature Test: the autobiography or memoir, the essay, and the speech. Use the sample passages and questions to test your ability to read and understand literary nonfiction.

The Autobiography

An **autobiography** or **memoir** is the story of the author's life. Autobiographies are usually written in the form of journal entries or prose narratives; a notable exception to this rule is the free-verse autobiography *Leaves of Grass* (Walt Whitman, United States, 1855). Writing about this work more than 30 years later, Whitman explained,

> *Leaves of Grass* indeed (I cannot too often reiterate) has mainly been the outcropping of my own emotional and other personal nature—an attempt, from first to last, to put *a Person*, a human being (myself, in the latter half of the Nineteenth Century, in America), freely, fully, and truly on record.

When studying or analyzing an autobiography, the reader must consider what is termed in fiction the **unreliable narrator**—a first-person narrator whose account of events the reader should accept only with caution. There are three reasons that autobiographies may be unreliable accounts, despite the fact that their authors were (obviously) eyewitnesses to everything they describe.

First, many autobiographers rely on their memories rather than looking up dates, names, and facts. This often leads to major and minor errors, because no one has a perfect memory of recent events, let alone those that happened many years ago. Second, few people are objective about themselves and their own motives. Like anyone else, the authors of autobiographies have the natural human temptation to portray themselves in the best possible light. Before the nineteenth century, authors often acknowledged their own bias by including the word *Apologia* (meaning "self-justification") in the titles of their memoirs.

Third, an autobiography represents only one point of view—the author's. A biographer is likely to consult numerous sources, all of which will give slightly different points of view about the subject. An autobiographer usually does not consult any sources, but instead writes from his or her memory.

Both ordinary and extraordinary individuals have been writing autobiographies since the beginning of recorded history. Notable literary autobiographies include *Confessions* (Saint Augustine, North Africa, 397–398 C.E.), *The Autobiography of Benvenuto Cellini* (Italy, 1556–1558), *Autobiography* (Benjamin Franklin, United States, 1771–1790), and *Narrative of the Life of Frederick Douglass* (United States, 1845). Douglass's autobiography is an example of a **slave narrative**—an autobiography that recounts the author's experiences as a slave in the United States. Many escaped slaves wrote and published slave narratives in the years between the American Revolution and the Civil War.

Two of the most famous twentieth-century autobiographies are *Good-bye to All That* (Robert Graves, England, 1929) and *The Autobiography of Alice B. Toklas* (Gertrude Stein, United States, 1933). Graves's memoir concentrates on his youth, particularly his combat experiences during World War I. It is a notable example of antiwar literature. Stein's work is typical of her delight in confounding readers' expectations; it may well be the only autobiography ever written from a point of view other than the author's. Despite its title, *The Autobiography of Alice B. Toklas* is the story of Stein's life, written by Stein from the point of view of her life's companion.

The Essay

An **essay** is a short piece of writing, from several paragraphs to several pages in length. It may defend an opinion, express a point of view, or discuss and describe ideas and observations. An essay is generally built around an **argument,** also called a **thesis statement** or a statement of the author's main idea. The argument or thesis is the focus of the essay. It is generally stated directly, rather than implied. The essayist then defends his or her opinion with facts and evidence.

The literary essay was first identified as such in 1580, when Michel de Montaigne published his *Les Essais* in France. The French verb *essayer* means "to attempt." Montaigne used this name for his short prose discussions to indicate that they were only attempts to explore certain subjects and ideas—that they bore the same relationship to finished works of philosophy that rough sketches would bear to a completed oil painting. Nearly 20 years later, Francis Bacon of England wrote a volume of *Essays* of his own, adopting Montaigne's title, style, and format. These two works are the fathers of the essay form.

The first literary magazines appeared in the early eighteenth century. The magazine provided a perfect opportunity for essay writers to publish their short works. Rather than having to write enough essays to fill a book, an author could submit each one to a magazine as soon as it was finished, thus earning a steady income. Because magazines were intended as light entertainment, essays published in them began to diverge somewhat from their serious philosophical beginnings. They became lighter, more humorous, and less formal.

In the late eighteenth century, the essay pendulum swung back again toward the more serious and substantial. One of the best-known collections of essays of this era is the *Federalist Papers*, which appeared serially in print from 1787 to 1788 and were later collected as a book. Written under the pseudonym "Publius" by Alexander Hamilton, James Madison, and John Jay, these 85 essays argue for the passage of the U.S. Constitution. One of the most famous of the essays, "Federalist No. 10," discusses the dangers of faction in a democratic government.

Serious essays continued to appear through the nineteenth century. The best-known American essayists of the time were Ralph Waldo Emerson and Henry David Thoreau. Emerson's essays are lengthy and thoughtful explorations of the human character, with such titles as "On Friendship" and "On Love." Thoreau's "Civil Disobedience" examines human motivations and what he saw as the evils of society.

In modern and contemporary times, essays are everywhere in print. The essay category is broad enough to include introductions and prefaces to literary works; movie, theater, and concert reviews; art criticism; newspaper editorials—in fact, almost any short piece of writing that proposes and defends a particular argument or point of view.

When analyzing or studying an essay, the reader should always ask, "Do I believe the thesis?" In an essay, the author's purpose is, above all, to persuade. The reader should consider whether the thesis seems reasonable and whether it is adequately supported with details and facts.

The Speech

A **speech** is a prose work delivered orally to a listening audience. Most speeches are written down first, so that the speaker can be sure to include all the necessary points and express him- or herself as memorably and clearly as possible. Most speeches are made by politicians and government officials or by candidates for government. In the past, public figures wrote their own speeches; today, most hire speechwriters to do it for them.

The purposes of a speech are to explain, inform, and persuade. To accomplish these purposes, a speech employs many **rhetorical devices**, such as **parallelism** (the repetition of a grammatical pattern) and **repetition** of words and phrases. Speechwriters use rhetorical devices so that their words and ideas will linger in a listener's memory.

A speech can be as brief as a few paragraphs or as long as several pages. One of the most effective speeches in history, Abraham Lincoln's Gettysburg Address, is only 10 sentences long.

When analyzing or studying a speech, the reader should first identify the speaker's purpose, then pay close attention to the literary devices the writer uses to accomplish that purpose.

REVIEW QUESTIONS

Questions 1–3. Read the following passage carefully before you choose your answers.

As I journeyed across France to Marseilles, and made thence a terribly rough voyage to Alexandria, I wrote my allotted number of pages every day . . . When I have commenced a new book, I have always prepared a diary, divided into weeks, and carried it on for the period which I
5   have allowed myself for the completion of the work. In this I have entered, day by day, the number of pages I have written, so that if at any time I have slipped into idleness for a day or two, the record of that idleness has been there, staring me in the face, and demanding of me increased labor, so that the deficiency might be supplied. According to
10   the circumstances of the time,—whether my other business might be then heavy or light, or whether the book which I was writing was or was not wanted with speed,—I have allotted myself so many pages a week . . .

I have been told that such appliances are beneath the notice of a man of
15   genius. I have never fancied myself to be a man of genius, but had I been so I think I might well have subjected myself to these trammels . . .

I have known authors whose lives have always been troublesome and painful because their tasks have never been done in time. They have ever been as boys struggling to learn their lessons as they entered the
20   school gates. Publishers have distrusted them, and they have failed to write their best because they have seldom written at ease. I have done double their work—though burdened with another profession,—and have done it almost without an effort. I have not once, through all my literary career, felt myself even in danger of being late with my task. I
25   have known no anxiety as to "copy." The needed pages far ahead—very far ahead—have almost always been in the drawer beside me. And that little diary, with its dates and ruled spaces, its record that must be seen, its daily, weekly demand upon my industry, has done all that for me.

30   There are those who would be ashamed to subject themselves to such a taskmaster, and who think that the man who works with his imagination should allow himself to wait till—inspiration moves him. When I have heard such doctrine preached, I have hardly been able to repress my scorn. To me it would not be more absurd if the shoemaker were to
35   wait for inspiration, or the tallow-chandler for the divine moment of melting. If the man whose business it is to write has eaten too many good things, or has drunk too much, or smoked too many cigars,—as men who write sometimes will do,—then his condition may be unfavorable for work; but so will be the condition of a shoemaker who has been
40   similarly imprudent. I have sometimes thought that the inspiration wanted has been the remedy which time will give to the evil results of such imprudence.—*Mens sana in corpore sano*.[1] The author wants that as does every other workman,—that and a habit of industry. I was once

[1] A sound mind in a healthy body.

45 told that the surest aid to the writing of a book was a piece of cobbler's wax on my chair. I certainly believe in the cobbler's wax much more than the inspiration.

It will be said, perhaps, that a man whose work has risen to no higher pitch than mine has attained, has no right to speak of the strains and impulses to which real genius is exposed. I am ready to admit the great 50 variations in brain power which are exhibited by the products of different men, and am not disposed to rank my own very high; but my own experience tells me that a man can always do the work for which his brain is fitted if he will give himself the habit of regarding his work as a normal condition of his life.

(1883)

1. Why is the author "hardly able to repress his scorn" when he hears people say that an artist should only write when "inspiration moves him" (lines 32–34)?

(A) He feels that he himself is an uninspired writer and cannot wait for such inspiration.
(B) He looks upon writing as a job that should be done on schedule like any other job.
(C) He is jealous of greater writers' bursts of creative imagination, knowing that he has little imagination of his own.
(D) He has worked as a publisher and knows how exasperating it is when an author does not deliver manuscript on time.
(E) He believes that there is no such thing as creative inspiration in literature.

2. The author feels that other authors he knows "have ever been as boys struggling to learn their lessons as they entered the school gates" (lines 18–20) because

(A) they do not know how to write well
(B) they have no imagination
(C) they use their writing time inefficiently
(D) they never get through their research on time
(E) they do not keep daily diaries of their progress

3. All these aspects of this passage suggest that the author is a reliable narrator, EXCEPT

(A) he draws reasonable conclusions that are based on personal observation and experience
(B) his description of his approach to writing is not intended to make him look glamorous or "artistic"
(C) he is not describing personal or emotional matters on which he is likely to write with a strong bias
(D) he does not claim to be a genius or an extraordinary talent
(E) he assumes that his approach to writing as a career is the best possible system

ANSWERS AND EXPLANATIONS

1. **Correct Choice: B**

   The author compares writing to two other jobs, shoemaker and chandler (maker of candles). He approaches his own writing not so much as a creative art but as a job that should be done in a professional manner, according to contracts made by businessmen. This matches choice B.

2. **Correct Choice: C**

   The schoolboys the author describes did not do their homework at a reasonable pace the night before and now have to cram an evening's study into a few minutes. Naturally, this is not a good way to learn a lesson thoroughly or well. By the same token, a writer should produce his work at an even, steady pace. He or she should not waste time for days or weeks, then frantically try to catch up in order to meet a looming deadline. Choice C summarizes the fault the author finds with other authors.

3. **Correct Choice: E**

   In the final paragraph, the author acknowledges that there may be other ways of working than his own, but he still feels that there is no author who could not profit by using his system. This describes Choice E, which is the only item that might make a reader question the author's reliability. Anyone who is convinced his or her own view is best is not necessarily making an objective evaluation.

REVIEW QUESTIONS

Questions 4–6. Read the following passage carefully before you choose your answers.

The ways by which you may get money almost without exception lead downward. To have done anything by which you earned money *merely* is to have been truly idle or worse. If the laborer gets no more than the wages which his employer pays him, he is cheated, he cheats himself. If you would get money as a writer or lecturer, you must be popular, which is to go down perpendicularly. Those services which the community will most readily pay for it is most disagreeable to render. You are paid for being something less than a man. The State does not commonly reward a genius any more wisely. Even the poet-laureate would rather not have to celebrate the accidents of royalty. He must be bribed with a pipe of wine; and perhaps another poet is called away from his muse to gauge that very pipe. As for my own business, even that kind of surveying which I could do with most satisfaction my employers do not want. They would prefer that I should do my work coarsely and not too well, ay, not well enough. When I observe that there are different ways of surveying, my employer commonly asks which will give him the most land, not which is most correct. I once invented a rule for measuring cord-wood, and tried to introduce it in Boston; but the measurer there told me that the sellers did not wish to have their wood measured correctly,—that he was already too accurate for them, and therefore they commonly got their wood measured in Charlestown before crossing the bridge.

The aim of the laborer should be, not to get his living, to get "a good job," but to perform well a certain work; and, even in a pecuniary sense, it would be economy for a town to pay its laborers so well that they would not feel that they were working for low ends, as for a livelihood merely, but for scientific, or even moral ends. Do not hire a man who does your work for money, but him who does it for love of it.

It is remarkable that there are few men so well employed, so much to their minds, but that a little money or fame would commonly buy them off from their present pursuit. I see advertisements for *active* young men, as if activity were the whole of a young man's capital. Yet I have been surprised when one has with confidence proposed to me, a grown man, to embark in some enterprise of his, as if I had absolutely nothing to do, my life having been a complete failure hitherto. What a doubtful compliment this is to pay me! As if he had met me half-way across the ocean beating up against the wind, but bound nowhere, and proposed to me to go along with him! If I did, what do you think the underwriters would say? No, no! I am not without employment at this stage of the voyage. To tell the truth, I saw an advertisement for able-bodied seamen, when I was a boy, sauntering in my native port, and as soon as I came of age I embarked.

The community has no bribe that will tempt a wise man. You may raise money enough to tunnel a mountain, but you cannot raise money 45 enough to hire a man who is minding *his own* business. An efficient and valuable man does what he can, whether the community pay him for it or not. The inefficient offer their inefficiency to the highest bidder, and are forever expecting to be put into office. One would suppose that they were rarely disappointed.

(1863)

4. Which of the following best encompasses the author's thesis or argument?

   (A) "The ways by which you may get money almost without exception lead downward." (lines 1–2)
   (B) "Those services which the community will most readily pay for it is most disagreeable to render." (lines 6–7)
   (C) "The aim of the laborer should be, not to get his living, to get 'a good job,' but to perform well a certain work." (lines 23–24)
   (D) "An efficient and valuable man does what he can, whether the community pay him for it or not." (lines 45–47)
   (E) "The inefficient offer their inefficiency to the highest bidder, and are forever expecting to be put into office." (lines 47–48)

5. When the author says "To have done anything by which you earned money *merely* is to have been truly idle or worse" (lines 2–3), he means

   (A) you never have to work hard to earn a lot of money
   (B) you should earn enough money to be able to retire and live idly
   (C) there is nothing more important in life than earning enough money
   (D) if you earn only money, not inner satisfaction, you have wasted your time
   (E) earning money is a waste of time because money is not essential for any reason

6. Why does the author believe that his employers do not want him to do his work too well?

   (A) They do not want his efficiency to make them look lazy by contrast.
   (B) They do not want to pay him as much as a better worker would demand.
   (C) They do not want to have to fire him for incompetence or laziness.
   (D) They do not want to lose his services to a better company.
   (E) They do not want him to impress their clients too much.

ANSWERS AND EXPLANATIONS

4. **Correct Choice: C**

   The author's main point is that people should choose the job they love for its own sake, not the job that pays the most money, because loving your job enriches your life. Choice C most closely expresses this idea.

5. **Correct Choice: D**

   The author believes that the true goal of work is, or should be, to acquire wisdom and experience while doing something you love. Money, in his view, is simply a by-product or a bonus; as long as you are earning what you need for self-support, you should be content with that. If you want to earn the most money possible simply for its own sake, you are wasting your time; given the number of hours most adults work, you are in fact wasting your life. Choice D best expresses the author's definition of "earning money *merely*."

6. **Correct Choice: A**

   The author observes that his employers are comfortable with their system exactly as it is. When he thinks he can make improvements, they discourage him. He realizes that they do not want to make the effort that would be involved in having everyone work more efficiently; they prefer to muddle along as they are, doing the least possible work for the maximum amount of money. If the author were allowed to be efficient, he would make everyone else look bad. This approximates choice A.

REVIEW QUESTIONS

Questions 7–9. Read the following speech carefully before you choose your answers.

First of all, let me assert my firm belief that the only thing we have to fear is fear itself—nameless, unreasoning, unjustified terror which paralyzes needed efforts to convert retreat into advance. In every dark hour of our national life, a leadership of frankness and vigor has met with that
5 understanding and support of the people themselves which is essential to victory. I am convinced that you will again give that support to leadership in these critical days.

In such a spirit on my part and on yours we face our common difficulties. They concern, thank God, only material things. Values have shrunk-
10 en to fantastic levels; taxes have risen; our ability to pay has fallen; government of all kinds is faced by serious curtailment of income; the means of exchange are frozen in the currents of trade; the withered leaves of industrial enterprise lie on every side; farmers find no markets for their produce; the savings of many years in thousands of families are gone.

15 More important, a host of unemployed citizens face the grim problem of existence, and an equally great number toil with little return. Only a foolish optimist can deny the dark realities of the moment.

Yet our distress comes from no failure of substance. We are stricken by no plague of locusts. Compared with the perils which our forefathers con-
20 quered because they believed and were not afraid, we have still much to be thankful for. Nature still offers her bounty and human efforts have multiplied it. Plenty is at our doorstep, but a generous use of it languishes in the very sight of the supply. Primarily this is because the rulers of the exchange of mankind's goods have failed, through their own stub-
25 bornness and their own incompetence, have admitted their failure, and abdicated. Practices of the unscrupulous moneychangers stand indicted in the court of public opinion, rejected by the hearts and minds of men.

True, they have tried, but their efforts have been cast in the pattern of an outworn tradition. Faced by failure of credit they have proposed only
30 the lending of more money. Stripped of the lure of profit by which to induce our people to follow their false leadership, they have resorted to exhortations, pleading tearfully for restored confidence. They know only the rules of a generation of self-seekers. They have no vision, and when there is no vision the people perish.

35 The moneychangers have fled from their high seats in the temple of our civilization. We may now restore that temple to the ancient truths. The measure of the restoration lies in the extent to which we apply social values more noble than mere monetary profit.

Happiness lies not in the mere possession of money; it lies in the joy of
40 achievement, in the thrill of creative effort. The joy and moral stimulation of work no longer must be forgotten in the mad chase of evanescent profits. These dark days will be worth all they cost us if they teach us that our true destiny is not to be ministered unto, but to minister to ourselves and to our fellow men.

45   Recognition of the falsity of material wealth as the standard of success
      goes hand in hand with the abandonment of the false belief that public
      office and high political position are to be valued only by the standards
      of pride of place and personal profit; and there must be an end to a con-
      duct in banking and in business which too often has given to a sacred
50   trust the likeness of callous and selfish wrongdoing. Small wonder that
      confidence languishes, for it thrives only on honesty, on honor, on the
      sacredness of obligations, on faithful protection, on unselfish perform-
      ance; without them it cannot live.

                                                                    (1933)

7. Which line(s) does the speaker use to imply that his listeners must play a
    major role in the struggle that is to come?

        I.   I am convinced that you will again give that support to leadership
             in these critical days.
        II. In such a spirit on my part and on yours we face our common
             difficulties.
        III. Practices of the unscrupulous moneychangers stand indicted
             in the court of public opinion, rejected by the hearts and minds
             of men.

    (A) I and II only
    (B) II only
    (C) II and III only
    (D) III only
    (E) I, II, and III

8. Which period of American history is the speaker describing in paragraphs
    2 and 3?

    (A) World War I
    (B) World War II
    (C) the Great Depression
    (D) the Civil Rights era
    (E) the Oklahoma land rush

9. The speaker uses the words in each pair to convey the same or nearly the
    same idea, EXCEPT

    (A) frankness and vigor (line 4)
    (B) understanding and support (line 5)
    (C) failure and substance (line 18)
    (D) stubbornness and incompetence (lines 24–25)
    (E) hearts and minds (line 27)

ANSWERS AND EXPLANATIONS

7. **Correct Choice: E**

   Option I suggests that the leader alone cannot end the financial crisis; the people must lend him their support. Option II mentions facing "our common difficulties" together with a determination to overcome them. Option III suggests that "the hearts and minds of men"—in other words, the hearts and minds of the listeners—are the opposite of the "unscrupulous moneychangers." All three options satisfy the question. Therefore choice E is correct.

8. **Correct Choice: C**

   The speaker refers to a financial crisis, a failure of credit, and the idea that financial profit should not be the basis of a society. The only choice that matches these references to an economic issue is choice C, the Great Depression. The fact that the speech is dated 1933 is another clue to the correct answer; the Great Depression began in 1929, when the stock market crashed, and continued through the 1930s.

9. **Correct Choice: C**

   The two words in choice C are opposite or nearly opposite in meaning. Therefore C is the correct answer.

CHAPTER 4
POETRY

POETRY

Poetry stands out from other forms of writing because it is written in verse, not prose. Of all forms of literature, poetry is most closely allied to music, because so much of poetry is dictated by consideration of sound effects. **Meter, rhyme,** and **rhythm** are the three major elements of verse (see Chapter 1 for definitions and examples).

This chapter gives a brief overview of poetry: its history, structural elements, and forms. Use the sample poems and questions in this chapter to test your ability to read and understand poetry.

Poetic Structure

The one thing all poems have in common is that they are written in verse. Poetry is written in rhymed or unrhymed lines in patterns of stressed and unstressed syllables, with a certain number of syllables per line. This gives poetry a unique appearance on a page; a poem takes up a block of space rather than reaching all the way to the right margin like prose. Free verse lacks the rhythm and meter of other poetry, but you can still identify it as poetry simply by the way it looks on the page. It does not look like prose.

The basic unit of prose is the paragraph; the basic unit of poetry is the line. Just as a new paragraph always begins on a new line of the page, so does a new line of poetry. A line of poetry may or may not equal a complete phrase, sentence, or thought. The ends of lines in poetry are dictated by sound, not by sense—the demands of the meter and rhythm, not the completion of the thought, mark the end of a line of verse. If a poet is writing in iambic pentameter, with ten syllables per line, each line will end with the tenth syllable, no matter where this occurs in the sentence or complete thought. A group of lines in a poem is called a **stanza;** you can identify the end of a stanza because there will be a blank space on the page between one stanza and the next.

Poets employ a great variety of meters and rhythms. Until modern times, most (not all) English and American poetry rhymed. This began to change in the mid-nineteenth century with the appearance of free verse. By the end of the twentieth century, unrhymed poetry and free verse were quite common, although rhyme had by no means disappeared altogether.

Types of Poems

Poems come in three varieties: **narrative, epic,** and **lyric.** The purpose of a **narrative poem** is to tell a story; like any work of fiction, it is built on the four elements of plot, character, setting, and theme. An **epic poem** is a book-length narrative poem focusing on the life of the **epic hero,** a man of extraordinary strength and courage. He is a leader of his people and undergoes a series of adventures that test his moral and physical strength. Like other types of mythology, an epic was considered by the listening audience to be something between fiction and nonfiction. People believed that the heroes existed and that their adventures were true, although they conceded that the tales told by poets were exaggerated versions of what really happened.

Although **lyric poems** can describe characters performing actions and can suggest or imply stories, their main purpose is to evoke a specific emotional reaction in the reader. Lyric poems capture a mood or feeling rather than recounting a plot. Although not all lyric poems are short, most short poems are lyric poems.

Lyric poems are much shorter than epics. A lyric poem aims at producing a single effect on the reader. It is usually a highly personal expression of the speaker's (and possibly also the poet's) emotions and experiences. The speaker and the poet are not necessarily the same person; they may be, but this should only be assumed based on factual knowledge of the poet's life. In general, it is best to assume that the speaker of a lyric poem is a first-person narrator, like any other fictional character, and does not necessarily represent the author.

Literary Elements in Poetry

Because lyric and narrative poems are more concise than most prose fiction, each word in the poem must be chosen with extra care. There is no room for anything extra or unnecessary. Because each individual word has to carry extra freight, poems are rich in **figurative language** and **imagery.** Poets use **similes, metaphors,** and other **figures of speech** with greater frequency than do prose writers.

Two other major elements for the poetry reader to consider are **speaker** and **mood.** The speaker is the poem's first-person narrator, a fictional character like any prose narrator. Comprehending the speaker's personality and character are of central importance to understanding a lyric poem. **Mood,** the total effect the poem has on the reader, is equally important. The reader must identify the poem's mood and analyze how the poet used language and literary elements to create this mood.

History of Poetry's Development

Ancient Times

In the ancient world, most poems were epics that were told or sung aloud. The earliest epics come from Iraq. *The Descent of Inanna* was first written down about 2000 B.C.E., although versions of the story go back another 1500 years before that. *The Epic of Gilgamesh,* though unknown to modern scholars until the mid-1800s, may date back equally far; the first written version dates to the seventh century B.C.E. Parts of the Bible, some of which (such as the story of David) can be considered epic poetry, first appeared as early as 1000 B.C.E.

The most ancient poetic works in Western literature are Homer's *Iliad* and *Odyssey* (Greece, c. 700 B.C.E.), two epics of the Trojan War and its heroes. In the Roman world, the *Aeneid* (Virgil, Italy, 19 C.E.) continued the epic tradition with its tales of Aeneas, the hero who founded Italy.

Lyric poetry dates back at least to the Bible, written between 1000 and 200 B.C.E. The works of Sappho of Lesbos (c. 550 B.C.E.) are considered the greatest of all Greek lyrics, though only a few examples of her poetry have survived. Lyric poetry later enjoyed great success in Rome, with poets such as Catullus and Ovid.

The Middle Ages to the Seventeenth Century

Epic poetry began to appear in northern Europe by the 700s C.E., with *Beowulf* (Anglo-Saxon, c. 750) and a variety of Irish sagas. In 1321, the Italian poet Dante Alighieri published *The Divine Comedy,* in which the spirit of Virgil guides the speaker through hell, purgatory, and paradise. *The Divine Comedy* can be regarded as the first modern epic, because it does not tell the story of a traditional epic hero. Instead, its central figure is a contemporary man—the poet himself—who is a cultural hero rather than a warrior, chieftain, or king.

Dante was not the only major Italian poet of the era. His contemporary Francesco Petrarch invented the **sonnet,** which quickly became a favorite form among poets of other countries as well. Sir Thomas Wyatt, Petrarch's translator and a poet in his own right, wrote the first English-language sonnets. English poets modified the **Petrarchan sonnet** by changing its rhyme scheme; this English sonnet form is called the **Shakespearean sonnet.** (See **sonnet,** Chapter 1.)

It was around the late 1500s that the English language achieved the form that we speak and read today. Apart from differences in spelling and in the use of the informal pronoun *thou/thee* and its verb forms, Elizabethan English is perfectly comprehensible to a modern English speaker—with a little practice to get used to the differences in writing style.

The Renaissance (the period between approximately 1400 and 1600 C.E.) was a true high point of English poetry. William Shakespeare, widely considered the greatest of all English-language writers, produced the world's most famous sonnet sequence and some longer narrative poems, in addition to his plays (see Chapter 5). Other great English poets of the era include John Milton, author of the epic *Paradise Lost* and many shorter poems; Christopher Marlowe, who like Shakespeare is also famous for his plays; Sir Philip Sidney; and John Donne.

Most British poetry of the era concentrated on one of four themes: love, religion, abstract philosophy, or descriptions of nature. Donne, for example, is famous for his secular love poems and also for a deeply religious series of sonnets called the *Holy Sonnets.* Plays on words, puns, and the use of words with double meanings are characteristic of Elizabethan poetry.

The first English-speaking American poets began writing in the seventeenth century. Many of their poems were religious in nature, due in part to the central importance of worship in their communities and, in part to the harsh realities of life in the original thirteen British colonies. Americans had to conquer a wilderness, combat extremes of weather, build or make everything they needed, and either make friends with the Indians or fight them off. Life was a struggle for survival, and Americans did what they could to make sure God was on their side, including dedicating much of their literature to Him. Americans also wrote poems about love and nature. Anne Bradstreet is one of the best-known American poets of this early colonial era.

The Nineteenth Century

The nineteenth century ushered in the Romantic era in poetry. William Wordsworth, Samuel Taylor Coleridge, Percy Bysshe Shelley, John Keats, and Lord Byron are the best-known of the British Romantics. Later in the century came Elizabeth Barrett Browning, Robert Browning, and Alfred Lord Tennyson. All of these authors produced both lyric and narrative poetry.

Epic poetry continued as a form. Byron wrote the modern epics *Childe Harold's Pilgrimage* and *Don Juan*. Tennyson wrote several book-length narrative poems, including *Idylls of the King* (tales of King Arthur and his knights), *The Princess,* and *Maud*.

American poets of the era included Walt Whitman, Herman Melville, Henry Wadsworth Longfellow, Emily Dickinson, and Edgar Allan Poe. Longfellow is dismissed as an artist by modern scholars but holds the distinction of being the first American to earn his living by writing poetry. Dickinson is almost as famous for her reclusive lifestyle as for her highly unusual poems. It was only in 1955 that readers finally saw Dickinson's work as she wrote it, with its unconventional capitalization, punctuation, and use of dashes; the few poems published during her lifetime and immediately after her death were heavily edited to bring them into line with accepted usage.

The nineteenth century saw the first **free-verse poems** (see Chapter 1). Whitman, unconventional and ahead of his time in many ways, published the free-verse collection *Leaves of Grass* in 1855. He continued to put out new editions until the 1890s, adding to the collection until it contained more than 400 poems, including the highly unconventional autobiographical epic *Song of Myself*. In 1894, Stephen Crane followed Whitman's example by publishing his own free-verse collection, *The Black Riders*.

The Romantic era is characterized by a new interest in expressing one's self. This was true across all forms of the creative arts. Poems were more likely to deal openly with, and even exaggerate, the speaker's emotions. There was less formal wordplay than in the Elizabethan era and less reliance on clever rhyme than in the eighteenth century. Romantic poetry was above all about emotion and individualism.

The Twentieth Century and Beyond

The first major twentieth-century event to affect the development of poetry was the outbreak of World War I in 1914. Several British soldiers and officers, known to history as the World War I poets, won immortality by publishing lyric poems about their experiences in the trenches. Siegfried Sassoon, Wilfred Owen, and Rupert Brooke are among them; neither Owen nor Brooke survived the war.

Irish poets came into their own in the twentieth century, including William Butler Yeats, Dylan Thomas, and Seamus Heaney. Intensity and a kind of wild ecstasy of language characterize their works.

American lyric poets include T. S. Eliot, Carl Sandburg, E. E. Cummings, and Sylvia Plath. Eliot is best known for *The Waste Land,* a set of four free-form dramatic lyrics filled with so many obscure literary allusions that Eliot included a list of endnotes so that readers could track them down and "decode" his work for themselves. Sandburg echoed Whitman's style and subject matter—the glorification of the common working man. Cummings developed a style all his own, dispensing with capital letters and punctuation and playing with rhythm and rhyme in ways that made his lyrics appear to dance right off the page. Plath wrote a highly praised, savage collection of lyrics called *Ariel* before she committed suicide at an early age, following the breakup of her marriage to fellow poet Ted Hughes.

Twentieth-century poets, like other writers and artists of their time, had few illusions left. Apart from light verse written strictly to amuse (such as the works of Ogden Nash), their poems tend to be darker in outlook, more ambiguous in tone, and more spare in imagery than verse of earlier times.

REVIEW QUESTIONS

Questions 1–3. Read the following poem carefully before you choose your answers.

Some lovers speak when they their muses entertain,
Of hopes begot by fear, of wot not what desires,
Of force of heav'nly beams, infusing hellish pain,
    Of living deaths, dear wounds, fair storms and freezing fires.
5   Some one his song in Jove, and Jove's strange tales, attires,
Broidered with bulls and swans, powdered with golden rain.
Another, humbler, wit to shepherd's pipe retires,
Yet hiding royal blood full oft in rural vein.
    To some a sweetest plaint a sweetest style affords,
10   While tears pour out his ink, and sighs breathe out his words,
His paper, pale despair, and pain his pen doth move.
    I can speak what I feel, and feel as much as they,
    But think that all the map of my state I display,
When trembling voice brings forth, that I do Stella love.

(c. 1581)

1. This poem meets all the usual standards for a sonnet EXCEPT

   (A) meter
   (B) number of lines
   (C) subject matter
   (D) rhythm
   (E) imagery

2. Which best sums up the speaker's main point?

   (A) Others write long poems and use a lot of figurative language to express their feelings; I express just as much feeling when I say simply "I love Stella."
   (B) I wish that I could express my love as others do, by writing beautiful and elaborate poems about Stella whom I love so much.
   (C) Since my muse is paying so much attention to other lovers, who spend all their time writing poems to their ladies, I can only say "I love Stella."
   (D) I cannot compare my love for Stella to the love felt by poets who write beautiful poetry, because I can only say directly that I love Stella.
   (E) I think it is much better to say directly "I love Stella" than to cry because I am unable to write beautiful poetry about her.

3. When the speaker says "Another, humbler, wit to shepherd's pipe retires, / Yet hiding royal blood full oft in rural vein" (lines 7–8), he means

   (A) A humble shepherd may write a love poem pretending that he is really a prince in disguise.
   (B) If a prince is clever and witty, he may ask a shepherd to change places with him.
   (C) A royal prince may write a love poem suggesting that he is a humble shepherd.
   (D) A poet may give up writing altogether, and serenade his beloved with the music of a shepherd's pipe.
   (E) When a prince goes into the country, he often amuses himself by pretending he is a common shepherd.

ANSWERS AND EXPLANATIONS

1. **Correct Choice: D**

   The meter is iambic, which is standard for sonnets. The number of lines is 14, which is standard. A sonnet can address almost any topic, but love is certainly one of the most common. This sonnet is full of imagery, like most sonnets. The correct answer is D; most sonnets have five iambic feet (10 syllables) per line, while this sonnet has six feet (12 syllables).

2. **Correct Choice: A**

   The speaker spends the first 11 lines of the sonnet describing all the elaborate poems that other lovers write about their ladies. In the last 3 lines, he explains that in order to show the same feeling, all he has to say is "I love Stella." A simple "I love you" is as good as bushels of carefully written poetry. This best matches choice A.

3. **Correct Choice: D**

   "Hiding royal blood" is the key phrase. It shows that the prince is disguising his royal rank by pretending to be a shepherd. This eliminates choice A. Choice B is wrong because there is nothing here about the shepherd pretending to be the prince. Choice C is wrong because the phrase "to shepherd's pipe retires" means that the prince has given up on poetry altogether; his wit is too humble to write. He has turned to music instead. Choice E leaves out the reason for the prince's disguise: to win the love of the lady. Choice D is the correct explanation: the prince's wit is too humble to write clever poetry, so he gives up the attempt and plays music to his lady instead.

REVIEW QUESTIONS

Questions 4–6. Read the following poem carefully before your choose your answers.

Ode to Memory

I

Thou who stealest fire,
From the fountains of the past,
To glorify the present; oh, haste,
    Visit my low desire!
5   Strengthen me, enlighten me!
I faint in this obscurity,
Thou dewy dawn of memory.

II

Come not as thou camest of late,
Flinging the gloom of yesternight
10 On the white day; but robed in soften'd light
        Of orient state.
Whilome thou camest with the morning mist,
    Even as a maid, whose stately brow
The dew-impearled winds of dawn have kiss'd,
15   When she, as thou,
Stays on her floating locks the lovely freight
Of overflowing blooms, and earliest shoots
Of orient green, giving safe pledge of fruits,
Which in wintertide shall star
20 The black earth with brilliance rare.

(1830)

4. The lines "Thou who stealest fire, / From the fountains of the past, / To glorify the present" (lines 1–3) are an example of

    (A) personification
    (B) verbal irony
    (C) simile
    (D) theme
    (E) slant rhyme

5. The imagery throughout the poem appeals most strongly to the sense of

    (A) hearing
    (B) sight
    (C) taste
    (D) touch
    (E) smell

6. What does the speaker mean by "obscurity" (line 6)?

    (A) He cannot see in the dark.
    (B) He is desperately ill and afraid to die.
    (C) He cannot remember something important.
    (D) He cannot understand something.
    (E) He is angry about something.

ANSWERS AND EXPLANATIONS

4. **Correct Choice: A**

   The lines are an example of personification. The speaker endows memory, an abstract concept, with the human ability to steal. Choice A is the correct answer.

5. **Correct Choice: B**

   Most of the sensory details in the poem are visual. There are several references to light and dark and a physical description of memory as a beautiful young girl. Choice B is the correct answer.

6. **Correct Choice: C**

   The speaker pleads for memory to visit him because he is "fainting in obscurity"—in other words, he has lost his memories of the past and needs to find them again for the sake of their comfort. Choice C is correct.

▬▬ REVIEW QUESTIONS

Questions 7–9. Read the following poem carefully before you choose your answers.

The Leaders of the Crowd

    They must to keep their certainty accuse
    All that are different of a base intent;
    Pull down established honor; hawk for news
    Whatever their loose phantasy invent
5   And murmur it with bated breath, as though
    The abounding gutter had been Helicon
    Or calumny a song. How can they know
    Truth flourishes where the student's lamp has shone,
    And there alone, that have no solitude?
10 So the crowd come they care not what may come.
    They have loud music, hope every day renewed
    And heartier loves; that lamp is from the tomb.

                                                    (1921)

7. Who are the "they" the poet mentions in line 1?

   (A) journalists
   (B) politicians
   (C) poets
   (D) lovers
   (E) entertainers

8. By saying that "they" "have no solitude" (line 9), the poet implies that "they"

       I.   avoid spending any time by themselves
       II. never sit quietly alone thinking about anything serious
       III. would feel frightened and nervous if they found themselves alone

   (A) I and II only
   (B) I and III only
   (C) II and III only
   (D) II only
   (E) I, II, and III

9. The word "calumny" (line 7) is best defined as

   (A) music
   (B) slander
   (C) insult
   (D) noise
   (E) information

ANSWERS AND EXPLANATIONS

7. **Correct Choice: B**

   The poem's title suggests that choice B, politicians, is the correct answer. This is supported by a careful reading of the poem's long first sentence (lines 1–7).

8. **Correct Choice: E**

   In the first half of the poem, the poet describes a group of people who are so insecure that they attack everyone who disagrees with them; people who make things up and pass them off to journalists as news; people who do not care what happens as long as the crowd follows them. People like this avoid spending time alone because they only feel important if surrounded by a cheering crowd. They do not want any time to think quietly, because they do not know how to think in a serious way. They would be frightened if they were alone, because they do not know who they are. All three options are reasonable answers, so choice E is correct.

9. **Correct Choice: B**

   The poet uses *song* in contrast to *calumny*, so A is wrong. "They" are making stories up and selling them to the press as news, which suggests that *calumny* is something false. You can therefore eliminate choices D and E. *Slander* and *insult* are relatively close in meaning—they are both malicious statements about others—but while an insult may be true, slander is by definition false. This is the closest in meaning to *calumny*, which means "a false accusation" (it comes from a Latin root meaning "to deceive"). Choice B is correct.

CHAPTER 5
DRAMA

DRAMA

Drama is a special kind of literature that is written to be performed by actors. Once a **play** has been produced on stage for the first time, it is published in book form as a play or a **playscript**.

This chapter contains a brief overview of the structural elements and history of drama. Use the sample dramatic excerpt and questions at the end of the chapter to test your ability to read and interpret drama.

Structural Elements of Drama

Playscripts consist primarily of two structural elements: **dialogue** and **stage directions.** A playwright may also include a **foreword** or **preface, introduction, afterword,** or **notes.**

Dialogue refers to the words the actors speak. This is the part of the play the audience members hear when they go to the theater. Dialogue in a play contains a full range of literary elements: **figurative language, imagery, irony, humor,** and so on. Dialogue may be written in verse or in prose. The entire story of the play is told solely through the dialogue.

Dialogue is written by the playwright, but unlike prose writers and poets, a playwright has a group of collaborators. Since the Elizabethan era, playwrights have been, and continue to be, a central part of the production process, in which the play is prepared for its first performance. During rehearsals, as they see the effects of their work on stage for the first time, playwrights make both substantial and minor changes to their scripts. Depending on the historical period and the individuals involved, the director and the leading actors involved in the first production may have considerable input into the final version of the script.

Stage directions note the following information:

1. when the characters enter and exit the stage, and how they move about during the scene
2. the location and appearance of each scene
3. the tone of voice in which the actor is to read the line or speech
4. any details or information the playwright wishes to share with readers

The audience in the theater does not hear, read, or see stage directions. These are provided in published scripts primarily to help the reader visualize the way the play would look on stage.

Playwrights do not write stage directions in categories 1 and 2 in the list above. In most cases, these stage directions are simply the stage manager's record of how the actors moved about the stage during the play's first production. When the play was published in print, the stage directions were included as a record of the first production and as a guide to actors and directors of future productions.

Stage directions in categories 3 and 4 in the list above did not begin to appear in playscripts until the late nineteenth century. These stage directions are written by the playwright.

A play may also include a preface, introduction, afterword, or notes. Again, these materials are not part of the audience's experience of seeing the play performed. The playwright includes these elements for the reader.

Plays are written primarily to entertain, but many playwrights also write to comment on and reform society. George Bernard Shaw (Ireland), Henrik Ibsen (Norway), and Bertolt Brecht (Germany) are examples of major playwrights who believed that social reform was an important part of their task as writers.

History of the Drama's Development

Ancient Times

The earliest Western dramas were religious ceremonies held in honor of the god Dionysus. Ceremonies dealing with life, death, and resurrection led to the development of **tragedy,** while **comedy** has its roots in fertility rites.

A comedy is a play written to make people laugh; a tragedy is more likely to make them cry, although it may be uplifting. Comedies often feature mistaken identities, disguised characters, misunderstandings, and a variety of silly plot complications. In a comedy, the characters generally straighten out all misunderstandings in the final scene, and a happy ending is achieved.

A tragedy generally features a **tragic hero** or **heroine,** usually someone who occupies a high place at the beginning of the story and is brought down by a central flaw in his or her own character.

The drama as we understand it today—that is, an imagined or historical story acted out on a stage—dates back to the fifth century B.C.E. The playwrights Aeschylus, Euripides, and Sophocles were the pillars of Greek tragedy, and their works are still performed today. Aristophanes was the outstanding comic writer of the ancient era. Plautus was an important Roman writer of comedy; one of his works, as adapted into the book of the musical *A Funny Thing Happened on the Way to the Forum,* continues to amuse today's audiences.

The Middle Ages

Medieval drama began to develop around the ninth century and reached its pinnacle around the fourteenth century. Like ancient drama, its roots were religious—in this case, Christian. Strolling troops of players performed miracle, passion, and morality plays that grew directly from the text of the church service. Miracle plays dramatized the lives of Christ, his mother Mary, and the saints. Passion plays depicted the story of Christ's death. Morality plays were allegories that dramatized the consequences of sin and the rewards of virtue. Morality plays were the direct precursors of Elizabethan drama.

The Renaissance

The Renaissance was one of the great eras for English drama. At this point, drama moved away from its medieval basis in religion and once again became a medium for telling secular stories. Elizabethan playwrights made up their own original stories or borrowed them from earlier sources. Audiences could choose among comedies, tragedies, romances, and histories. Plays were generally presented in five acts that corresponded to the five stages of a plot: Act I introduced the characters and conflicts; in Act II, the action rose to the Act III climax; Acts IV and V contained the falling action that led to the Act V resolution.

Elizabethan plays are written in a mix of **blank verse** (see Chapter 1), rhymed verse, and prose. In general, upper-class characters speak in verse, and commoners speak in prose; blank verse is allied with tragedy, whereas other verse forms and prose are associated with comedy. However, authors often played with these conventions to create dramatic interest. For example, in Shakespeare's *Henry V,* the king speaks in prose during a scene when he is disguised as a common soldier.

In Renaissance era scripts, stage directions are the bare minimum; they specify a location and give the characters' entrances and exits. Shakespeare and his contemporaries did not write these stage directions; they were added at the time of publication. Their purpose is simply to help the reader follow the action on the page.

Elizabethan dialogue, in contrast to the stage directions, is extraordinarily elaborate, making full use of poetic techniques such as figurative language, imagery, and rhetorical devices. Imagery was especially important on the Elizabethan stage, because there were no theatrical illusions such as we have today. Plays were performed outdoors in the daylight; costumes were hastily thrown together, often consisting of contemporary street clothes; and there were no sets, apart from an occasional bench, bed, or table if needed. The power of language helped the audiences imagine a great variety of exotic and elaborate settings.

William Shakespeare was the most important playwright of the English Renaissance (he can safely be called the most important English-language writer in history). His colleagues included Christopher Marlowe, Ben Jonson, John Webster, and John Ford.

The most important element of a Shakespearean play is **character.** Every generation has marveled at Shakespeare's ability to create believable human individuals with whom audiences can empathize and identify. Even the minor characters are so strong and individual that they are great favorites with both actors and audiences.

The Seventeenth and Eighteenth Centuries

The years 1642 to 1666 are known in English history as the Interregnum (meaning "between monarchs"). As the result of a civil war, commoner Oliver Cromwell deposed the hereditary monarch and took over the throne in 1642. Cromwell, a Puritan, thought theater was sinful and banned it altogether. In 1666, the monarchy was restored to the throne, and the theaters were reopened.

During this period, known as the Restoration, plays became much more artificial. Light comedy and farce were the order of the day. Shakespeare's plays were still performed, but they were substantially rewritten to reflect the current taste for lighter fare. Irishman Richard Brinsley Sheridan is the best-known British playwright of the era.

The plots of Restoration and eighteenth-century comedies and dramas were elaborate and full of improbable twists and coincidences. Characters were archetypes—the frivolous young girl, the cantankerous older man, and the bawdy serving maid. The purpose of these plays was strictly to amuse the audiences and to poke fun at social customs without having any serious reforming spirit.

The Nineteenth Century to the Present

Since the late nineteenth century, plays have usually been written in speech appropriate to what the characters might say in reality. Dialogue no longer needs to fill in visual details for the audience; designers provide lighting, sound effects, costumes, and scenery to help create the theatrical illusion.

During this era, stage directions became much more detailed, often describing sets, giving an idea of a character's physical appearance, and specifying how the actors were to read their lines (i.e., happily, with a puzzled expression, angrily). Irish playwright George Bernard Shaw is known for extraordinarily meticulous stage directions. Shaw also wrote long prefaces to his plays, discussing his opinions on the social issues that each play was about. These prefaces were not part of the performance in the theater; Shaw wrote them for the reading public.

Two of the most important playwrights of the modern era, Henrik Ibsen and Bertolt Brecht, were not English-language writers, but their work had an enormous influence on their British and American colleagues. Ibsen of Norway is considered the father of modern drama. His plays feature middle-class and working-class characters in ordinary settings, dealing with serious personal problems such as infidelity, old family grievances, lost love, and similar conflicts. When audiences went to see an Ibsen play, they were watching characters like themselves and their neighbors in dramatic situations that might well occur in real life. Major English-language playwrights of the time followed Ibsen's lead, bringing a welcome new realism to the stage.

Like Ibsen and Shaw, German writer Brecht was a passionate social critic. Brecht believed that the primary purpose of a play was to hold up a mirror to the audience and shake them out of their complacency. He not only wrote many plays but also created an entirely new style of design and production known as *Brechtian*, loosely meaning "detached." Most people believed that theater's purpose was to create an illusion of reality; Brecht believed it was his job always to remind the audience that they were watching actors performing on a stage. He did not want audiences to identify with his characters as though they were real individuals; he wanted people to think about the overall social message of the piece. Brecht is the father of all political theater.

Important English-language playwrights of the era included Eugene O'Neill, Tennessee Williams, Arthur Miller, and Thornton Wilder in the United States; and Shaw, T. S. Eliot, Oscar Wilde, William Butler Yeats, and John Millington Synge in Britain.

Verse plays had not entirely disappeared; major authors of verse plays in this era include Yeats (*The Land of Heart's Desire*, 1894), W. H. Auden (*The Dance of Death*, 1933), Eliot (*Murder in the Cathedral*, 1935), and Archibald MacLeish (*J.B*, 1956).

After World War II, a movement called **theater of the absurd** arose. Its two best-known practitioners are Harold Pinter and Samuel Beckett. Beckett's *Waiting for Godot* (1952), originally written in French and translated into English by Beckett himself, is the best-known play of this school; many people believe it to be the most influential play of its time. In a typical theater-of-the-absurd play, the characters exchange short and banal lines of dialogue, and nothing much happens. Theater of the absurd is intended to emphasize the meaninglessness, banality, and random cruelty of everyday life.

Perhaps, the most important English-language playwright of the present day is Tom Stoppard. Born in Czechoslovakia and raised in India and England, Stoppard is considered a British playwright. His works range from a theater-of-the-absurd retelling of Shakespeare's *Hamlet* (*Rosencrantz and Guildenstern Are Dead*, 1966) to a somber trilogy about nineteenth-century Russian philosophers (*The Coast of Utopia*, 2002). Other major contemporary playwrights include David Mamet, Edward Albee, Peter Shaffer, and August Wilson. Wilson's plays portray the African American experience in the twentieth century, with one play set in each decade.

REVIEW QUESTIONS

Questions 1–3. Read the following dramatic excerpt carefully before you choose your answers.

(In Act I, Serbians and Bulgarians are fighting in the streets. A soldier (Captain Bluntschli) in enemy uniform appears at Raina Petkoff's window, demanding refuge. Raina takes pity on him, gives him a night's shelter, and lends him an old coat of her father's in which to escape. Soon after, peace is declared. In Act II, Bluntschli comes by to return the borrowed coat. In the Act III excerpt below, he and Raina find themselves alone for the first time since their encounter in Act I.)

1   RAINA *[going to the table, and leaning over it towards him].* It must have made a lovely story for them: all that about me and my room.

BLUNTSCHLI. Capital story. But I only told it to one of them: a particular friend.

RAINA. On whose discretion you could absolutely rely?

5   BLUNTSCHLI. Absolutely.

RAINA. Hmm! He told it all to my father and Sergius[1] the day you exchanged the prisoners. *[She turns away and strolls carelessly across to the other side of the room.]*

BLUNTSCHLI *[deeply concerned, and half incredulous].* No! you don't mean that, do you?

RAINA *[turning, with sudden earnestness].* I do indeed. But they don't know that it was in this
10   house you took refuge. If Sergius knew, he would challenge you and kill you in a duel.

BLUNTSCHLI. Bless me! then don't tell him.

RAINA. Please be serious, Captain Bluntschli. Can you realize what it is to me to deceive him? I want to be quite perfect with Sergius: no meanness, no smallness, no deceit. My relation to him is the one really beautiful and noble part of my life. I hope you can understand that.

15   BLUNTSCHLI *[skeptically].* You mean that you wouldn't like him to find out that the story about the ice pudding was a—a—a—You know.

RAINA *[wincing].* Ah, don't talk of it in that flippant way. I lied: I know it. But I did it to save your life. He would have killed you. That was the second time I ever uttered a falsehood . . .

BLUNTSCHLI *[dubiously].* There's reason in everything. You said you'd told only two lies in your
20   whole life. Dear young lady: isn't that rather a short allowance? I'm quite a straightforward man myself; but it wouldn't last me a whole morning.

RAINA *[staring haughtily at him].* Do you know, sir, that you are insulting me?

BLUNTSCHLI. I can't help it. When you strike that noble attitude and speak in that thrilling voice, I admire you; but I find it impossible to believe a single word you say.

25   RAINA *[superbly].* Captain Bluntschli!

BLUNTSCHLI *[unmoved].* Yes?

RAINA *[standing over him, as if she could not believe her senses].* Do you mean what you said just now? Do you *know* what you said just now?

BLUNTSCHLI. I do.

30   RAINA *[gasping].* I! I!!! *[She points to herself incredulously, meaning "I, Raina Petkoff, tell lies!" He meets her gaze unflinchingly. She suddenly sits down beside him, and adds, with a complete change of manner from the heroic to a babyish familiarity.]* How did you find me out?

BLUNTSCHLI *[promptly].* Instinct, dear young lady. Instinct, and experience of the world.

RAINA *[wonderingly].* Do you know, you are the first man I ever met who did not take me seriously?

35   BLUNTSCHLI. You mean, don't you, that I am the first man that has ever taken you quite seriously?

RAINA. Yes: I suppose I do mean that. *[Cosily, quite at her ease with him]* How strange it is to be talked to in such a way! You know, I've always gone on like that . . . I mean the noble attitude and

---

[1] Raina's fiancé

the thrilling voice. *[They laugh together]* I did it when I was a tiny child to my nurse. *She* believed in it. I do it before my parents. *They* believe in it. I do it before Sergius. *He* believes in it.

40   BLUNTSCHLI. Yes: he's a little in that line himself, isn't he?

RAINA *[startled]*. Oh! Do you think so?

BLUNTSCHLI. You know him better than I do.

RAINA. I wonder—I wonder, is he? If I thought that—! *[Discouraged]* Ah, well, what does it matter? I suppose, now that you've found me out, you despise me.

45   BLUNTSCHLI *[warmly, rising]*. No, my dear young lady, no, no, no a thousand times. It's part of your youth: part of your charm. I'm like all the rest of them: the nurse, your parents, Sergius: I'm your infatuated admirer.

RAINA *[pleased]*. Really?

BLUNTSCHLI *[slapping his breast smartly with his hand, German fashion]*. *Hand aufs Herz!*[2]
50   Really and truly.

RAINA *[very happy]*. But what did you think of me for giving you my portrait?

BLUNTSCHLI *[astonished]*. Your portrait! You never gave me your portrait.

RAINA *[quickly]*. Do you mean to say you never got it?

BLUNTSCHLI. No. *[He sits down beside her, with renewed interest, and says, with some compla-*
55   *cency]* When did you send it to me?

RAINA *[indignantly]*. I did not send it to you. *[She turns her head away, and adds, reluctantly]* It was in the pocket of that coat.

(1898)

---

[2] Cross my heart!

1. What does Bluntschli mean by telling Raina he is "the first person who has ever taken you quite seriously" (line 35)?

    (A) He admires her grand manner and the ideals she expresses.
    (B) He appreciates the real person beneath the act she puts on.
    (C) He finds her beautiful, attractive, and charming.
    (D) He is very grateful to her for saving his life in Act I.
    (E) He is intrigued by her confession that she gave him her portrait.

2. Why has Raina "always gone on like that . . . I mean, the noble attitude and the thrilling voice" (lines 37–38)?

    (A) She acts like the person she wishes she truly were.
    (B) She is a liar and a faker by nature.
    (C) She enjoys the admiration and attention she gets.
    (D) She does not trust any of the people around her.
    (E) She wants to make Sergius fall in love with her.

3. What does Bluntschli's statement, "I'm quite a straightforward man, myself; but [two lies] wouldn't last me a whole morning" (lines 20–21) imply about him?

    (A) He thinks he is honest, but his frequent lies show that he is really dishonest.
    (B) He is only careful to tell the truth in certain situations.
    (C) He wants to make Raina feel better about having told a lie.
    (D) He is horrified by any evidence that another person is a liar.
    (E) He often tells polite lies, but does not regard this as true dishonesty.

ANSWERS AND EXPLANATIONS

1. **Correct Choice: B**
   Bluntschli tells Raina frankly that he does not believe in her "noble attitude and thrilling voice"; that he doesn't mind her telling lies because it is "part of your youth, part of your charm." He sees through her pose, and he likes her anyway. This best matches choice B. Choice C does not go far enough, because by "taking you quite seriously," Bluntschli means "liking you for who you really are." It is not just that he finds her charming, but that he sees through her act and still finds her charming.

2. **Correct Choice: C**
   Choice A is wrong because Raina does not genuinely wish to be as noble as the act she puts on; some of her dialogue in this scene shows she finds the act rather tiresome. Choice B is wrong because she seems to be quite frank when she drops the act. Choice C fits best; she sees that people admire and look up to her when she puts on the "noble attitude and thrilling voice," and naturally she enjoys the attention. Choice D is wrong because distrust of others does not seem to be an issue. Choice E is wrong because she has been putting on this act all her life, since long before she met Sergius.

3. **Correct Choice: E**
   The dialogue in this scene shows clearly that Bluntschli is blunt by nature as well as by name. Therefore you can eliminate any choices that suggest that he is dishonest. If Bluntschli is really in the habit of telling more than two lies every morning, it suggests that he spends a lot of time in business or social situations where one always utters certain polite lies, such as saying automatically, "Fine, thank you," when someone asks how you are. Bluntschli regards such polite lies as social necessities and does not blame himself for them. This best fits choice E.

PART III
SIX FULL-LENGTH PRACTICE TESTS

PRACTICE TEST 1
LITERATURE

The following practice test is designed to be just like the real SAT Literature Test. It matches the actual test in content coverage and degree of difficulty.

Once you finish the practice test, determine your score. Carefully read the answer explanations of the questions you answered incorrectly. Identify any weaknesses in your literature skills by determining the areas in which you made the most errors. Review those sections of this book first. Then, as time permits, go back and review your strengths.

Allow one hour to take the test. Time yourself and work uninterrupted. If you run out of time, take note of where you stopped when time ran out. Remember that you lose a quarter point for each incorrect answer, but you do not lose points for questions you leave blank. Therefore, unless you can eliminate one or more of the five choices, it is best to leave a question unanswered.

Use the following formula to calculate your score:

(number of correct answers) – ¼ (number of incorrect answers)

If you treat this practice test just like the actual exam, it will accurately reflect how you are likely to perform on test day. Here are some hints on how to create test-taking conditions similar to those of the actual exam:

- Complete the test in one sitting. On test day, you will not be allowed to take a break.
- Tear out the answer sheet and fill in the ovals just as you will on the actual test day.
- Have a good eraser and more than one sharp pencil handy. On test day, you will not be able to go get a new pencil if yours breaks.
- Do not allow yourself any extra time; put down your pencil after exactly one hour, no matter how many questions are left to answer.
- Become familiar with the directions on the test. If you go in knowing what the directions say, you will not have to waste time reading and thinking about them on the actual test day.

PRACTICE TEST 1
LITERATURE

ANSWER SHEET

Tear out this answer sheet and use it to mark your answers.

1. Ⓐ Ⓑ Ⓒ Ⓓ Ⓔ	16. Ⓐ Ⓑ Ⓒ Ⓓ Ⓔ	31. Ⓐ Ⓑ Ⓒ Ⓓ Ⓔ	46. Ⓐ Ⓑ Ⓒ Ⓓ Ⓔ
2. Ⓐ Ⓑ Ⓒ Ⓓ Ⓔ	17. Ⓐ Ⓑ Ⓒ Ⓓ Ⓔ	32. Ⓐ Ⓑ Ⓒ Ⓓ Ⓔ	47. Ⓐ Ⓑ Ⓒ Ⓓ Ⓔ
3. Ⓐ Ⓑ Ⓒ Ⓓ Ⓔ	18. Ⓐ Ⓑ Ⓒ Ⓓ Ⓔ	33. Ⓐ Ⓑ Ⓒ Ⓓ Ⓔ	48. Ⓐ Ⓑ Ⓒ Ⓓ Ⓔ
4. Ⓐ Ⓑ Ⓒ Ⓓ Ⓔ	19. Ⓐ Ⓑ Ⓒ Ⓓ Ⓔ	34. Ⓐ Ⓑ Ⓒ Ⓓ Ⓔ	49. Ⓐ Ⓑ Ⓒ Ⓓ Ⓔ
5. Ⓐ Ⓑ Ⓒ Ⓓ Ⓔ	20. Ⓐ Ⓑ Ⓒ Ⓓ Ⓔ	35. Ⓐ Ⓑ Ⓒ Ⓓ Ⓔ	50. Ⓐ Ⓑ Ⓒ Ⓓ Ⓔ
6. Ⓐ Ⓑ Ⓒ Ⓓ Ⓔ	21. Ⓐ Ⓑ Ⓒ Ⓓ Ⓔ	36. Ⓐ Ⓑ Ⓒ Ⓓ Ⓔ	51. Ⓐ Ⓑ Ⓒ Ⓓ Ⓔ
7. Ⓐ Ⓑ Ⓒ Ⓓ Ⓔ	22. Ⓐ Ⓑ Ⓒ Ⓓ Ⓔ	37. Ⓐ Ⓑ Ⓒ Ⓓ Ⓔ	52. Ⓐ Ⓑ Ⓒ Ⓓ Ⓔ
8. Ⓐ Ⓑ Ⓒ Ⓓ Ⓔ	23. Ⓐ Ⓑ Ⓒ Ⓓ Ⓔ	38. Ⓐ Ⓑ Ⓒ Ⓓ Ⓔ	53. Ⓐ Ⓑ Ⓒ Ⓓ Ⓔ
9. Ⓐ Ⓑ Ⓒ Ⓓ Ⓔ	24. Ⓐ Ⓑ Ⓒ Ⓓ Ⓔ	39. Ⓐ Ⓑ Ⓒ Ⓓ Ⓔ	54. Ⓐ Ⓑ Ⓒ Ⓓ Ⓔ
10. Ⓐ Ⓑ Ⓒ Ⓓ Ⓔ	25. Ⓐ Ⓑ Ⓒ Ⓓ Ⓔ	40. Ⓐ Ⓑ Ⓒ Ⓓ Ⓔ	55. Ⓐ Ⓑ Ⓒ Ⓓ Ⓔ
11. Ⓐ Ⓑ Ⓒ Ⓓ Ⓔ	26. Ⓐ Ⓑ Ⓒ Ⓓ Ⓔ	41. Ⓐ Ⓑ Ⓒ Ⓓ Ⓔ	56. Ⓐ Ⓑ Ⓒ Ⓓ Ⓔ
12. Ⓐ Ⓑ Ⓒ Ⓓ Ⓔ	27. Ⓐ Ⓑ Ⓒ Ⓓ Ⓔ	42. Ⓐ Ⓑ Ⓒ Ⓓ Ⓔ	57. Ⓐ Ⓑ Ⓒ Ⓓ Ⓔ
13. Ⓐ Ⓑ Ⓒ Ⓓ Ⓔ	28. Ⓐ Ⓑ Ⓒ Ⓓ Ⓔ	43. Ⓐ Ⓑ Ⓒ Ⓓ Ⓔ	58. Ⓐ Ⓑ Ⓒ Ⓓ Ⓔ
14. Ⓐ Ⓑ Ⓒ Ⓓ Ⓔ	29. Ⓐ Ⓑ Ⓒ Ⓓ Ⓔ	44. Ⓐ Ⓑ Ⓒ Ⓓ Ⓔ	59. Ⓐ Ⓑ Ⓒ Ⓓ Ⓔ
15. Ⓐ Ⓑ Ⓒ Ⓓ Ⓔ	30. Ⓐ Ⓑ Ⓒ Ⓓ Ⓔ	45. Ⓐ Ⓑ Ⓒ Ⓓ Ⓔ	60. Ⓐ Ⓑ Ⓒ Ⓓ Ⓔ

PRACTICE TEST 1
Time: 60 minutes

Directions: This test consists of selections from literary works and questions on their content, form, and style. After reading each passage or poem, choose the best answer to each question and then fill in the corresponding oval on the answer sheet.

Note: Pay particular attention to the requirements of questions that contain the words NOT or EXCEPT.

Questions 1–9. Read the following poem carefully before you choose your answers.

I died for Beauty—but was scarce
Adjusted in the Tomb
When One who died for Truth, was lain
In an adjoining Room—

5 He questioned softly "Why I failed"?
"For Beauty," I replied—
"And I—for truth—Themself are One—
We Bretheren, are," He said—

And so, as Kinsmen, met a Night—
10 We talked between the Rooms—
Until the Moss had reached our lips—
And covered up—our names—

(1862)

1. The word "Themself" (line 7) refers to

   (A) the dead man and the other character
   (B) truth and beauty
   (C) beauty and failure
   (D) kinsmen and bretheren
   (E) truth and bretheren

2. Which of the following might the speaker mean by saying "I died for Beauty" (line 1)?

   (A) I died fighting for a cause in whose beauty and justice I believed.
   (B) I died because I was a woman of great physical beauty.
   (C) I died because I knew I would be beautiful to look at only in death.
   (D) I died of a disease that disfigured me and destroyed my beauty.
   (E) I died of old age, having lost the beauty of my youth.

3. What does the statement "We Bretheren are" (line 8) suggest?

   (A) that lonely people should turn to one another for companionship
   (B) that the two characters in the poem loved the same person
   (C) that the two characters in the poem died at the same time
   (D) that the speaker and the dead man are brothers
   (E) that people who believe in the same things are kindred spirits

4. The mood of the poem is best described as

   (A) philosophical
   (B) melancholy
   (C) eerie
   (D) bitter
   (E) passionate

5. The word "softly" (line 5) implies which of the following about the dead man?

   (A) He died for Truth.
   (B) His voice is beautiful.
   (C) He knew the other character in life.
   (D) His manner is gentle.
   (E) He is delighted not to be buried alone.

6. Lines 11–12 suggest that the speaker and the dead man

   (A) continued talking for many years
   (B) talked throughout the night
   (C) talked together until they died
   (D) could not talk because they were dead
   (E) had nothing to say to one another

GO ON TO THE NEXT PAGE

PRACTICE TEST—*Continued*

7. All of the following words are used metaphorically in this poem EXCEPT

   (A) Beauty (line 1)
   (B) Tomb (line 2)
   (C) Truth (line 3)
   (D) Bretheren (line 8)
   (E) Kinsmen (line 9)

8. The poem is an example of which of the following?

   (A) ballad
   (B) free verse
   (C) quatrain
   (D) couplet
   (E) narrative poem

9. Why do the two characters feel that they are "Kinsmen" and "Bretheren"?

     I. They are both dead.
    II. They died for similar reasons.
   III. They care about the same things.

   (A) I and III
   (B) II only
   (C) II and III only
   (D) III only
   (E) I, II, and III

Questions 10–17. Read the following poem carefully before you choose your answers.

Mamie

Mamie beat her head against the bars of a little Indiana
       town and
dreamed of romance and big things off somewhere the
way the railroad trains all ran.
She could see the smoke of the engines get lost down
       where the
5   streaks of steel flashed in the sun and when the
newspapers came in on the morning mail she knew
       there
was a big Chicago far off, where all the trains ran.
She got tired of the barber shop boys and the post office
       chatter
and the church gossip and the old pieces the band
       played
10 on the Fourth of July and Decoration Day
And sobbed at her fate and beat her head against the
       bars and
was going to kill herself
When the thought came to her that if she was going to
       die she
might as well die struggling for a clutch of romance
15 among the streets of Chicago.

She has a job now at six dollars a week in the basement
       of the
Boston Store
And even now she beats her head against the bars in the
       same old
way and wonders if there is a bigger place the railroads
20 run to from Chicago where maybe there is
       romance
       and big things
       and real dreams
       that never go smash.

           (1916)

10. Which best describes the poet's attitude toward Mamie?

   (A) He pities her for her unhappiness.
   (B) He thinks she is silly.
   (C) He loves and admires her.
   (D) Her behavior amuses him.
   (E) She reminds him of himself.

11. The repetition of the phrase "beat(s) her head against the bars" accomplishes which of the following?

     I. emphasizes the strength of Mamie's despair and helplessness
    II. suggests that Mamie will never get through the "bars," no matter how far she travels
   III. makes the reader feel that Mamie is ridiculous and contemptible

   (A) I only
   (B) I and II only
   (C) II only
   (D) III only
   (E) I, II, and III

12. The poet includes the list of things Mamie is tired of (lines 8–10) for all the following reasons EXCEPT

   (A) to give the reader a picture of her everyday life
   (B) to help the reader understand why she wants to escape
   (C) to contrast the life she has with the romance she longs for
   (D) to show his own impatience with small-town life
   (E) to help the reader get a mental picture of her character

GO ON TO THE NEXT PAGE

13. Which best defines the word "romance" as it is used in this poem?

    (A) lies and exaggerations
    (B) a love affair
    (C) exciting adventures
    (D) everyday reality
    (E) a work of unrealistic fiction

14. For Mamie, Chicago symbolizes

    (A) excitement and glamour
    (B) sin and wickedness
    (C) noise and confusion
    (D) anonymity and solitude
    (E) community and home

15. The phrase "Mamie beat her head against the bars" means that Mamie

    (A) is in reform school because she ran away
    (B) is in a mental hospital because she tried to kill herself
    (C) feels like an animal in a zoo because people always stare at her
    (D) feels trapped and confined like a caged animal
    (E) has to be locked in her room because she can't be trusted

16. Why does the poet set off the final four lines of the poem, both by their brevity and their visual placement on the page?

    (A) to show that what Mamie wants from life is permanently beyond her reach
    (B) to reveal what made Mamie unhappy enough to leave Indiana
    (C) to keep the last stanza of the poem from being too long
    (D) to emphasize the intangibles that Mamie longs for
    (E) to leave the reader with some hope that Mamie will find happiness

17. Why is Mamie no happier in Chicago than she was in the little Indiana town?

    (A) She misses her home town in a way she did not anticipate.
    (B) She is unable to earn any money in Chicago.
    (C) She has discovered that life in a big city is as routine as in a small town.
    (D) She does not know where the Chicago trains might take her.
    (E) She has no one to talk to or spend her free time with.

Questions 18–25. Read the following passage carefully before you choose your answers.

In my preceding chapters I have tried, by going into the minutiae of the science of piloting, to carry the reader step by step to a comprehension of what the science consists
5   of; and at the same time I have tried to show him that it is a very curious and wonderful science, too, and very worthy of his attention. If I have seemed to love my subject, it is no surprising thing, for I loved the profession
10 far better than any I have followed since, and I took a measureless pride in it. The reason is plain: a pilot, in those days, was the only unfettered and entirely independent human being that lived in the earth. Kings are but
15 the hampered servants of parliament and people; parliaments sit in chains forged by their constituency; the editor of a newspaper cannot be independent, but must work with one hand tied behind him by party and
20 patrons, and be content to utter only half or two-thirds of his mind; no clergyman is a free man and may speak the whole truth, regardless of his parish's opinions; writers of all kinds are manacled servants of the public. We write
25 frankly and fearlessly, but then we "modify" before we print. In truth, every man and woman and child has a master, and worries and frets in servitude; but in the day I write of, the Mississippi pilot had *none*. The captain
30 could stand upon the hurricane-deck, in the pomp of a very brief authority, and give him five or six orders while the vessel backed into the stream, and then that skipper's reign was over. The moment that the boat was under
35 way in the river, she was under the sole and unquestioned control of the pilot. He could do with her exactly as he pleased, run her when and whither he chose, and tie her up to the bank whenever his judgment said that that
40 course was best. His movements were entirely free; he consulted no one, he received commands from nobody, he promptly resented even the merest suggestions. Indeed, the law of the United States forbade him to listen to
45 commands or suggestions, rightly considering

GO ON TO THE NEXT PAGE

PRACTICE TEST—*Continued*

that the pilot necessarily knew better how to handle the boat than anybody could tell him. So here was the novelty of a king with-
50 out a keeper, an absolute monarch who was absolute in sober truth and not by a fiction of words. I have seen a boy of eighteen tak-ing a great steamer serenely into what seemed almost certain destruction, and the aged captain standing mutely by, filled with
55 apprehension but powerless to interfere. His interference, in that particular instance, might have been an excellent thing, but to permit it would have been to establish a most pernicious precedent. It will easily be
60 guessed, considering the pilot's boundless authority, that he was a great personage in the old steamboating days. He was treated with marked courtesy by the captain and with marked deference by all the officers
65 and servants; and this deferential spirit was quickly communicated to the passengers, too. I think pilots were about the only peo-ple I ever knew who failed to show, in some degree, embarrassment in the presence of
70 traveling foreign princes. But then, people in one's own grade of life are not usually embarrassing objects.

(1896)

18. The metaphor "parliaments sit in chains forged by their constituency" (lines 16–17) is best para-phrased as

(A) Only the voters can decide who will hold elec-tive office.
(B) Parliament must convene for a specific number of months each year.
(C) Voters are always eager to catch politicians behaving dishonestly.
(D) Government representatives must obey the will of the voters.
(E) Members of government are often jailed for improper behavior.

19. The author compares the steamboat pilot to a king, an absolute monarch, and a traveling foreign prince in order to

(A) explain why he wanted so badly to become a pilot
(B) show how much he loved piloting a steamboat professionally
(C) demonstrate his bias in favor of republicanism over monarchy
(D) make the reader understand the extent of the pilot's authority
(E) emphasize the glamour of a steamboat pilot's life on the river

20. The word "pernicious" (line 59) is best defined as

(A) unwise
(B) calming
(C) irritating
(D) important
(E) destructive

21. All these details support the author's statement that the Mississippi pilot had no master, EXCEPT

(A) "I loved the profession far better than any I have followed since"
(B) "the boat . . . was under the sole and unques-tioned control of the pilot"
(C) "the law of the United States forbade him to listen to commands"
(D) "he consulted no one, he received commands from nobody"
(E) "He could do with her exactly as he pleased . . . when and whither he chose"

GO ON TO THE NEXT PAGE

PRACTICE TEST—*Continued*

22. The writer suggests that he prefers the profession of steamboat pilot to that of writer because

    (A) pilots make more money than writers
    (B) a pilot is his own boss, while a writer must please his employers
    (C) pilots work outdoors and writers work indoors
    (D) pilots work in dangerous situations, while writers are always safe
    (E) a pilot need not obey the laws, but a writer must obey them

23. The tone of the last two sentences of the passage is best described as

    (A) earnest
    (B) satirical
    (C) thoughtful
    (D) humorous
    (E) serious

24. The phrase "marked deference" (line 64) means that the crew showed the pilot

    (A) nervous fear
    (B) warm friendliness
    (C) unquestioning obedience
    (D) sullen anger
    (E) kindness and compassion

25. The fact that a pilot's authority is determined by law implies which of the following?

    I.   Steamboat pilots are government employees.
    II. River traffic is a matter of national importance.
    III. There are many steamboat accidents every year.

    (A) I only
    (B) II only
    (C) I and II only
    (D) I and III only
    (E) II and III only

Questions 26–34. Read the following poem carefully before you choose your answers.

On Time

Fly envious Time, till thou run out thy race,
Call on the lazy leaden-stepping hours,
Whose speed is but the heavy Plummet's[1] pace;
And glut thyself with what thy womb devours,
5 Which is no more than what is false and vain,
And merely mortal dross;
So little is our loss,
So little is thy gain.
For when as each thing bad thou hast entomb'd,
10 And, last of all, thy greedy self consum'd,
Then long Eternity shall greet our bliss
With an individual kiss;
And Joy shall overtake us as a flood,
When every thing that is sincerely good
15 And perfectly divine,
With Truth, and Peace, and Love, shall ever shine
About the supreme Throne
Of him, t'whose happy-making sight alone,
When once our heav'nly-guided soul shall clime,
20 Then all this Earthy grossness quit,
Attir'd with Stars, we shall for ever sit,
    Triumphing over Death, and Chance, and thee
    O Time.

                                              (1633)

[1] A weight regulating the movement of a clock's hands.

26. Why does the speaker call Time "envious" (line 1)?

    (A) Time resents the poet's dismissive attitude toward it.
    (B) Time wants to be able to pass more quickly.
    (C) Time wants to become a creative, not a destructive, force.
    (D) Time wants human beings to pay more attention to it.
    (E) Time resents its lack of real power over human beings.

GO ON TO THE NEXT PAGE

PRACTICE TEST—*Continued*

27. When the poet says Time devours "what is false and vain, / And merely mortal dross" (lines 5–6), you can conclude that he means

    (A) the passage of time cannot destroy anything of real importance
    (B) time can only be measured at the pace of the Plummet
    (C) living people do not worry about the passage of time
    (D) time can only destroy life; it cannot create or build anything
    (E) no harm can come to anyone solely because of the passage of time

28. The speaker implies that people triumph over Death, Chance, and Time by

    (A) being extraordinarily lucky throughout their mortal lives
    (B) achieving salvation and eternal life after death
    (C) saving their material goods for a comfortable old age
    (D) "living" forever in one's children, grandchildren, and descendants
    (E) dying when they are young, healthy, and beautiful

29. "Attir'd with stars, we shall for ever sit" (line 21) is best paraphrased as

    (A) we shall wear robes decorated with the stars of heaven
    (B) we shall sit under the stars and await eternal life
    (C) our bodies will be wrapped in star-spangled shrouds
    (D) our souls shall live in heaven, among the stars
    (E) we shall be buried under a starry sky

30. "The supreme Throne / Of him" (lines 17–18) refers to

    (A) the seat of God in heaven
    (B) the throne of the King of England
    (C) the poet's chair in his study or library
    (D) the clock in which Time is "enthroned"
    (E) the tomb in which the dead lie in state

31. Which of the following best states the argument of the poem?

    (A) Time will eventually take the poet's life, but his poems are immortal.
    (B) The poet has the power to create, but time can only destroy.
    (C) Things that are truly worth having come only with the passage of time.
    (D) Human beings should spend their time preparing for life after death.
    (E) Time can kill the mortal body, but the soul achieves eternal life in heaven.

32. Which of the following is NOT personified in the poem?

    (A) Time (line 1)
    (B) Plummet (line 3)
    (C) Eternity (line 11)
    (D) Truth (line 16)
    (E) Peace (line 16)

33. The poet employs an irregular meter in order to emphasize which of the following?

    I. the mystery of eternal life
    II. the powerlessness of time
    III. his pleasure in his own creative powers

    (A) I only
    (B) I and II only
    (C) II only
    (D) II and III only
    (E) I and III only

34. The phrase "our heav'nly guided soul" (line 19) is best paraphrased as

    (A) a dead person who is resurrected to life
    (B) the soul we have helped guide to heaven
    (C) our soul that has been guided to heaven
    (D) our soul that heaven has guided to eternity
    (E) the way that guides help our soul to heaven

GO ON TO THE NEXT PAGE

Questions 35–42. Read the following speech carefully before you choose your answers.

Two thousand years ago the proudest boast was "Civis Romanus sum."[1] Today, in the world of freedom, the proudest boast is "Ich bin ein Berliner."[2]

5 I appreciate my interpreter translating my German!

There are many people in the world who really don't understand, or say they don't, what is the great issue between the free
10 world and the Communist world. Let them come to Berlin. There are some who say that communism is the wave of the future. Let them come to Berlin. And there are some who say in Europe and elsewhere we can
15 work with the Communists. Let them come to Berlin. And there are some who say that it is true that communism is an evil system, but it permits us to make economic progress. Lass' sie nach Berlin kommen.[3] Let them
20 come to Berlin.

Freedom has many difficulties and democracy is not perfect, but we have never had to put a wall up to keep our people in, to prevent them from leaving us. I want to say, on
25 behalf of my countrymen, who live many miles away on the other side of the Atlantic, who are far distant from you, that they take the greatest pride that they have been able to share with you, even from a distance, the
30 story of the last 18 years. I know of no town, no city, that has been besieged for 18 years that still lives with the vitality and the force, and the hope and the determination of the city of West Berlin. While the wall is the most
35 obvious and vivid demonstration of the failures of the Communist system, for all the world to see, we take no satisfaction in it, for it is, as your Mayor has said, an offense not only against history but an offense against
40 humanity, separating families, dividing husbands and wives and brothers and sisters, and dividing a people who wish to be joined together . . .

Freedom is indivisible, and when one man is
45 enslaved, all are not free. When all are free, then we can look forward to that day when this city will be joined as one and this country and this great Continent of Europe in a peaceful and hopeful globe. When that day
50 finally comes, as it will, the people of West Berlin can take sober satisfaction in the fact that they were in the front lines for almost two decades.

All free men, wherever they may live, are cit-
55 izens of Berlin, and, therefore, as a free man, I take pride in the words "Ich bin ein Berliner."

(1963)

35. The speaker uses two German phrases in an otherwise largely English-language speech in order to

(A) refer to his early life and education in Germany
(B) show his German audience that he identifies with them
(C) ensure that his audience understands what he is saying
(D) prove to his audience that he speaks fluent German
(E) explain to his audience that he is of German descent

36. The comment "I appreciate my interpreter translating my German!" (lines 5–6) shows the speaker's

(A) sense of humor
(B) impatience
(C) discourtesy
(D) uncertainty
(E) intensity

37. What does the speaker mean when he says "All free men, wherever they may live, are citizens of Berlin" (lines 54–55)?

(A) that all people in the world were born in Berlin
(B) that Germany rules an empire of many nations
(C) that all free people support a free Berlin and a free Germany
(D) that it is easy for anyone to acquire German citizenship
(E) that the United States and West Germany are permanent allies

[1] I am a Roman citizen.
[2] I am from Berlin.
[3] Let them come to Berlin.

GO ON TO THE NEXT PAGE

PRACTICE TEST—*Continued*

38. The speaker's tone is best described as

    (A) pensive, introspective, and dreamy
    (B) neutral, objective, and matter-of-fact
    (C) intense, scholarly, and thoughtful
    (D) excited, hysterical, and passionate
    (E) forceful, determined, and confident

39. The metaphor "in the front lines" (line 52) suggests that the speaker regards the people of Berlin as

    (A) free men and women
    (B) soldiers
    (C) citizens
    (D) Communists
    (E) victims

40. Why does the speaker believe that "Ich bin ein Berliner" is "the proudest boast" of the day?

    (A) The fact that West Berlin maintains a free society shows the moral courage of its people.
    (B) West Berlin's existence is proof that a Communist system will succeed.
    (C) The Berlin Wall isolates West Berlin in the middle of Communist East Germany.
    (D) West Berliners are permitted to travel freely between West and East Berlin.
    (E) Although West Berlin is an occupied city, it is one of the wealthiest cities in Europe.

41. What does the speaker imply will happen if the people he describes in the third paragraph take up his challenge and "come to Berlin"?

    (A) They will realize they were right to support Communism.
    (B) They will learn to speak German.
    (C) They will try to find a way to combine Communism with freedom.
    (D) They will see that democracy is a better system than Communism.
    (E) They will become citizens of Berlin.

42. The speaker uses both words in each pair to emphasize the same idea, EXCEPT

    (A) "Europe and elsewhere" (line 14)
    (B) "Freedom . . . and democracy" (lines 21–22)
    (C) "the vitality and the force" (line 32)
    (D) "the hope and the determination" (line 33)
    (E) "peaceful and hopeful" (line 49)

Questions 43–49. Read the following dramatic excerpt carefully before you choose your answers.

(Earlier in the play, Macbeth and Lady Macbeth murdered the King of Scotland and seized his throne. Guilt has driven Lady Macbeth insane. In this scene, Macbeth prepares to face the army who is coming to avenge Duncan's death.)

Macbeth

            Seyton!—I am sick at heart,
When I behold—Seyton, I say!—This push
Will cheer me ever, or disseat me now.
I have lived long enough: my way of life
5 Is fall'n into the sere, the yellow leaf;
And that which should accompany old age,
As honor, love, obedience, troops of friends,
I must not look to have; but, in their stead,
Curses, not loud but deep, mouth-honor, breath,
10 Which the poor heart would fain deny, and dare not.
Seyton!

(*Enter Seyton*)

Seyton

What is your gracious pleasure?

Macbeth

                What news more?

Seyton

All is confirm'd, my lord, which was reported.

Macbeth

I'll fight till from my bones my flesh be hack'd.
15 Give me my armor.

Seyton

'Tis not needed yet.

Macbeth

             I'll put it on.
Send out more horses; skirr the country round;
Hang those that talk of fear. Give me mine armor.
How does your patient,[1] doctor?

---

[1] Lady Macbeth

GO ON TO THE NEXT PAGE

PRACTICE TEST—*Continued*

Doctor

20 Not so sick, my lord,
   As she is troubled with thick coming fancies,
   That keep her from her rest.

Macbeth

                              Cure her of that.
   Canst thou not minister to a mind diseas'd,
   Pluck from the memory a rooted sorrow,
25 Raze out the written troubles of the brain
   And with some sweet oblivious antidote
   Cleanse the stuff'd bosom of that perilous stuff
   Which weighs upon the heart?

Doctor

                              Therein the patient
   Must minister to himself.

Macbeth

30 Throw physic to the dogs; I'll none of it.
   Come, put mine armor on; give me my staff.
   Seyton, send out. Doctor, the thanes fly from me.—
   Come, sir, dispatch.—If thou couldst, doctor, cast
   The water of my land, find her disease,
35 And purge it to a sound and pristine health,
   I would applaud thee to the very echo,
   That should applaud again.

                              (C. 1607)

43. In this context, the word "oblivious" (line 26) means

   (A) unaware of
   (B) causing forgetfulness
   (C) bitter-tasting
   (D) long-lasting
   (E) insensitive

44. The statement "I'll fight till from my flesh my bones be hack'd" (line 14) shows that Macbeth is

   (A) afraid
   (B) resigned
   (C) courageous
   (D) enraged
   (E) brutal

45. The questions Macbeth asks the Doctor show that he feels which of the following for Lady Macbeth?

   I.   love and concern
   II. guilt and shame
   III. pity and sorrow

   (A) I and II only
   (B) II and III only
   (C) I and III only
   (D) I only
   (E) III only

46. "This push / Will cheer me ever, or disseat me now" (lines 2–3) is best paraphrased as

   (A) If the army marching toward me does not cheer me up, it will take my throne away from me.
   (B) If Lady Macbeth does not soon recover her health and good cheer, I will have to give up the throne.
   (C) I have been so unhappy since taking the throne that I think I should allow the army to defeat me.
   (D) If the Doctor brings good news of Lady Macbeth, it will cheer me up enough to win the battle.
   (E) The coming attack will fail and leave me permanently safe, or succeed and seize my throne from me.

47. You can infer from Seyton's words and the way Macbeth speaks to him that Seyton is a

   (A) doctor
   (B) prince
   (C) warrior
   (D) servant
   (E) priest

48. When Macbeth says he will receive "mouth-honor" (line 9), he means

   (A) people will address him by the title "Your Majesty"
   (B) the Scots will think and speak well of him
   (C) his subjects will give him only an outward show of respect
   (D) he will be honored for being a brave soldier
   (E) he will say what he pleases to anyone in his kingdom

PRACTICE TEST—*Continued*

49. Which of the following is NOT a reasonable inference to make about the Doctor?

    (A) He is adequate, no more, as a physician.
    (B) He feels little sympathy for Lady Macbeth's suffering.
    (C) He does not like Macbeth, nor want to serve him.
    (D) He is afraid he may be killed in the coming battle.
    (E) He is not qualified or able to treat mental illness.

Questions 50–60. Read the following passage carefully before you choose your answers.

She was fast asleep.

Gabriel, leaning on his elbow, looked for a few moments unresentfully on her tangled hair and half-open mouth, listening to her
5 deep-drawn breath. So she had had that romance in her life: a man had died for her sake. It hardly pained him now to think how poor a part he, her husband, had played in her life. He watched her while she
10 slept as though he and she had never lived together as man and wife. His curious eyes rested long upon her face and on her hair: and, as he thought of what she must have been then, in that time of her first girlish
15 beauty, a strange friendly pity for her entered his soul. He did not like to say even to himself that her face was no longer beautiful but he knew that it was no longer the face for which Michael Furey had braved
20 death.

Perhaps she had not told him all the story. His eyes moved to the chair over which she had thrown some of her clothes. A petticoat string dangled to the floor. One boot stood
25 upright, its limp upper fallen down: the fellow of it lay upon its side. He wondered at his riot of emotions of an hour before. From what had it proceeded? From his aunt's supper, from his own foolish speech, from
30 the wine and dancing, the merry-making when saying good-night in the hall, the pleasure of the walk along the river in the snow. Poor Aunt Julia! She, too, would soon be a shade with the shade of Patrick
35 Morkan and his horse. He had caught that haggard look upon her face for a moment when she was singing *Arrayed for the Bridal*. Soon, perhaps, he would be sitting in that same drawing-room, dressed in black, his
40 silk hat on his knees. The blinds would be drawn down and Aunt Kate would be sitting beside him, crying and blowing her nose and telling him how Julia had died. He would cast about in his mind for some
45 words that might console her, and would find only lame and useless ones. Yes, yes: that would happen very soon.

The air of the room chilled his shoulders. He stretched himself cautiously along under the
50 sheets and lay down beside his wife. One by one they were all becoming shades. Better pass boldly into that other world, in the full glory of some passion, than fade and wither dismally with age. He thought of how she
55 who lay beside him had locked in her heart for so many years that image of her lover's eyes when he had told her that he did not wish to live.

Generous tears filled Gabriel's eyes. He had
60 never felt like that himself towards any woman but he knew that such a feeling must be love. The tears gathered more thickly in his eyes and in the partial darkness he imagined he saw the form of a
65 young man standing under a dripping tree. Other forms were near. His soul had approached that region where dwell the vast hosts of the dead. He was conscious of, but could not apprehend, their wayward
70 and flickering existence. His own identity was fading out into a grey impalpable world: the solid world itself which these dead had one time reared and lived in was dissolving and dwindling.

75 A few light taps upon the pane made him turn to the window. It had begun to snow again. He watched sleepily the flakes, silver and dark, falling obliquely against the lamplight. The time had come for him to
80 set out on his journey westward. Yes, the newspapers were right: snow was general all over Ireland. It was falling on every part of the dark central plain, on the treeless hills,

GO ON TO THE NEXT PAGE

PRACTICE TEST—*Continued*

falling softly upon the Bog of Allen and, far-
85 ther westward, softly falling into the dark
mutinous Shannon waves. It was falling,
too, upon every part of the lonely church-
yard on the hill where Michael Furey lay
buried. It lay thickly drifted on the crooked
90 crosses and headstones, on the spears of the
little gate, on the barren thorns. His soul
swooned slowly as he heard the snow falling
faintly through the universe and faintly
falling, like the descent of their last end,
95 upon all the living and the dead.

(1916)

50. The word "shade" as used in this passage means

(A) shadow
(B) ghost
(C) snowfall
(D) death
(E) curtain

51. Which of the following best describes Gabriel's feeling toward his wife in these paragraphs?

(A) sympathetic
(B) romantic
(C) jealous
(D) angry
(E) amused

52. Which of the following best describes the tone of the
passage?

(A) merry
(B) hopeless
(C) ominous
(D) resigned
(E) elegiac

53. What happens to Gabriel in the final paragraph?

(A) He dies of a broken heart.
(B) He ponders the meaning of his existence.
(C) He decides to ask his wife for a divorce.
(D) He falls asleep while watching the snow fall.
(E) He resolves to be a better person hereafter.

54. Which of the following literary elements appears in
the final sentence?

(A) rhyme
(B) alliteration
(C) hyperbole
(D) comedy
(E) allusion

55. The author uses snow throughout the passage to
symbolize

(A) death
(B) winter
(C) passion
(D) sleep
(E) cold

56. The writer describes Gabriel's tears as "generous"
(line 59) in order to

(A) show that Gabriel's wife has never loved him
(B) reveal Gabriel's sorrow at the death of his
friend Michael Furey
(C) foreshadow Gabriel's grief over the death of
Aunt Julia
(D) emphasize Gabriel's sympathy with his wife's
grief over her loss
(E) underline Gabriel's bitterness over his wife's
deception

57. Gabriel's thoughts and emotions in this passage
enable the reader to characterize him as

(A) intellectual and detached
(B) credulous and naive
(C) petty and jealous
(D) kind and unselfish
(E) stodgy and dull

58. The sentence beginning "It lay thickly drifted" in the
final paragraph (lines 88–91) contains three images
that allude to the

(A) death of Michael Furey
(B) poetry of Shakespeare
(C) history of Ireland
(D) cycle of seasons
(E) crucifixion of Jesus

GO ON TO THE NEXT PAGE

59. In the paragraph beginning "The air of the room chilled his shoulders," Gabriel concludes that it is better to

    (A) die young than to live a long life
    (B) die of a broken heart than to live with one
    (C) experience both passion and pain than to experience neither
    (D) live without love than to die of love
    (E) kill oneself rather than to wait for a natural death

60. Which of the following does the author achieve with the repetition of the word "falling" in the final paragraph?

    I. lulls the reader to sleep with the repetition
    II. helps the reader visualize the gently falling snow
    III. emphasizes the warmth of the room

    (A) I only
    (B) I and II only
    (C) II only
    (D) II and III only
    (E) III only

STOP
IF YOU FINISH BEFORE TIME IS CALLED, YOU MAY CHECK YOUR WORK ON THIS TEST ONLY.
DO NOT TURN TO ANY OTHER TEST IN THIS BOOK.

ANSWER KEY

1. B	21. A	41. D
2. A	22. B	42. A
3. E	23. D	43. B
4. A	24. C	44. C
5. D	25. B	45. C
6. A	26. E	46. E
7. B	27. A	47. D
8. E	28. B	48. C
9. C	29. D	49. D
10. A	30. A	50. B
11. B	31. E	51. A
12. D	32. B	52. E
13. C	33. D	53. D
14. A	34. C	54. B
15. D	35. B	55. A
16. D	36. A	56. D
17. C	37. C	57. D
18. D	38. E	58. E
19. D	39. B	59. C
20. E	40. A	60. B

ANSWERS AND EXPLANATIONS

1. **Correct Choice: B**
   The two characters say the following: "Why did you fail?" "For Beauty." "And I for truth; Themself are one." The pronoun clearly refers to "truth and beauty."

2. **Correct Choice: A**
   "I died for Beauty" is a metaphor. Beauty in this context is not a reference to the speaker's own literal, physical beauty or lack thereof. If a person fights and dies for a glorious cause, that person might say he or she "died for Beauty."

3. **Correct Choice: E**
   Since Truth and Beauty "are One," both characters died for the same thing. They both believed in the same cause and shared the same values. This makes them kindred spirits. D is wrong because the word "bretheren" is used metaphorically.

4. **Correct Choice: A**
   The mood is one of mystery because the atmosphere is hushed and still, and the poet leaves the reader wondering about many questions. The two characters seem calm, safe, and happy, which makes the other four choices wrong.

5. **Correct Choice: D**
   The dead man speaks softly because he feels gentle and compassionate toward the other character. By itself, speaking softly does not imply any of the other four choices.

6. **Correct Choice: A**
   If they talked until the moss grew up the sides of their coffins, they talked for many years. Moss grows slowly. D is obviously wrong; although they are dead, they still have the power of speech. C is wrong because they only meet and talk after death.

7. **Correct Choice: B**
   The tomb appears to be a literal tomb—a place in which dead people are buried. The other four words are not used literally. Beauty and Truth might mean any number of things; and the two characters are kinsmen or brothers only in the metaphorical sense of being alike in character.

8. **Correct Choice: E**
   Although this is very short for a narrative poem, it has the necessary elements of characters, a setting, and a plot. A sonnet is a 14-line poem in iambic pentameter, free verse lacks a rhyme scheme and metric structure, a quatrain has only four lines, and a couplet has only two.

9. **Correct Choice: C**
   The fact of being dead, by itself, would not make the two characters feel that they share a common bond of sympathy, so Option I is wrong. They are drawn to each other because they died for truth and beauty, which they believe are the same thing, and their values are alike.

10. **Correct Choice: A**
    The poet seems to feel a gentle pity for Mamie, without any expectation that she will find what she wants.

11. **Correct Choice: B**
    The phrase is repeated three times in a short poem. The author's focus is on Mamie's feeling of being trapped, her unhappiness, and her desire to escape the metaphorical "bars" of her situation. Option III is incorrect because the author shows no contempt for Mamie; he regards her as an object of compassion.

12. **Correct Choice: D**
    The poet does not give his own opinion of life in the little Indiana town. He understands that Mamie hates it, and he shows compassion for her, but he gives no hint of his own feeling about places like this town.

13. **Correct Choice: C**
    Choices A, B, C, and E are all accurate definitions of *romance*, but only choice C makes sense in this context. Mamie is looking for an exciting life in which adventures will happen. Choice D is wrong because it means the opposite of romance.

14. **Correct Choice: A**
    Mamie is looking for a place more exciting than her little home town in Indiana—a place of romance and adventure.

15. **Correct Choice: D**
    Mamie is not literally beating her head against actual bars. She is not physically locked up anywhere. The "bars" are the lack of opportunity, the conventions, and a lack of money that keep her in a certain socioeconomic situation. She feels trapped, like an animal in a cage at the zoo that wants its freedom.

16. **Correct Choice: D**
    Repeating Mamie's desires and setting them off visually emphasizes them so that the reader will remember them.

17. **Correct Choice: C**
    Mamie went to Chicago to escape a dreary everyday routine. All she finds in Chicago is a different dreary routine—this time a full-time job in a basement where she can't even look out a window.

18. **Correct Choice: D**
    Constituency means "voters." In a representative government like the parliamentary system, the representatives are bound to pass laws supported by the people who voted for them. The chains are not literal.

19. **Correct Choice: D**
The main idea of the entire passage is that the pilot has total authority over his boat, in the same way that an absolute monarch has total command of his kingdom.

20. **Correct Choice: E**
Pernicious is derived from a French word meaning "destruction." The other choices are inaccurate definitions.

21. **Correct Choice: A**
Choices B, C, D, and E all give specific examples of a steamboat pilot's authority. Choice A is not relevant.

22. **Correct Choice: B**
The writer says that writers have to modify what they write. By contrast, a pilot has unquestioned authority and can always do exactly what he wants. Choices A, C, and D might be true statements, but the writer does not suggest they are why he loves the profession of pilot the most. Choice E is a false statement.

23. **Correct Choice: D**
In any literal sense, a steamboat pilot is many social grades below a foreign prince; the comparison is exaggerated for humor. There is humor in the mental image of a common working man like a pilot greeting a prince with perfect unconcern, as if they were of the same rank.

24. **Correct Choice: C**
To defer to someone means to yield to his wishes or commands.

25. **Correct Choice: B**
Because the government regulates traffic on the river, it must be a matter of importance to the nation. Option I is wrong because all citizens, not just government employees, must obey laws. Option III is wrong because a rise in steamboat accidents would likely lead to laws that lessened the pilot's authority.

26. **Correct Choice: E**
The main idea of the poem is that Time can only destroy what has no value. Time is "envious" because it wants more power.

27. **Correct Choice: A**
The poet states that one's mortal, physical life is of no importance compared to the eternal life of the soul. Time can only destroy "mortal dross," meaning youth, health, wealth, and physical beauty; it has no power over the immortal soul.

28. **Correct Choice: B**
The argument of the poem is that Time is "envious" because it has no power over the eternal life of the soul. What is true of Time is also true of Death and Chance; they can kill the body but not the soul.

29. **Correct Choice: D**
Renaissance-era Christians believed that heaven was in the sky; therefore the souls of the dead will live among the stars. The other choices are either too literal in meaning or they miss the point of the line.

30. **Correct Choice: A**
Christians believe that Heaven is God's kingdom, where He sits on a throne just as an earthly king would. The context makes it clear that the poet is describing the soul's eternal life in God's kingdom.

31. **Correct Choice: E**
The first sentence of the poem (lines 1–8) states that Time can only kill "mortal dross" for "little gain." The rest of the poem explains that the soul escapes Time's power when it achieves eternal life.

32. **Correct Choice: B**
The poet does not give the Plummet any human attributes. The other four words are given human attributes: Time is characterized throughout the poem, Eternity "shall greet our bliss / With a kiss," Truth and Peace "shall ever shine / About the supreme Throne."

33. **Correct Choice: D**
Time itself is characterized by a regular rhythm, *tick tock, tick tock,* and an unchanging pace. The poet's decision NOT to use a fixed meter and rhythm underscores how little power Time has over anything of value in life. Therefore Option II is correct. The poet's choice of an irregular meter was conscious, and he most likely enjoyed defying Time in this witty way; therefore Option III is also correct.

34. **Correct Choice: C**
The poet refers to the soul that has been guided to heaven.

35. **Correct Choice: B**
The speaker is clearly addressing a German-speaking audience. He speaks to them in their own language to underline his fellow-feeling with them, which he discusses in detail in the text of the speech. If he spoke fluent German, he would need no interpreter; and since he has an interpreter, he need not speak German to be sure his audience understands him.

36. **Correct Choice: A**
The speech is evidently being simultaneously translated into German, and the interpreter repeated the phrase "Ich bin ein Berliner." The speaker is amused, perhaps at his own possibly faulty pronunciation, perhaps because it was not necessary for the interpreter to repeat German words in German.

37. **Correct Choice: C**
The speaker does not mean this statement literally. He is telling the people of West Berlin "the rest of the free world is behind you, supports you, and identifies with you."

38. **Correct Choice: E**
The speaker uses many short declarative and imperative sentences, which contribute to the forceful and confident tone. He also says "When all are free" rather than "If all ever become free," showing his firm belief that this will happen.

39. **Correct Choice: B**
The "front lines" is a metaphor drawn from battle, referring to the troops who are positioned closest to the enemy. The speaker refers to the people of Berlin, his audience, as soldiers in the front lines because they are the people most directly and nearly threatened by the Communist enemy.

40. **Correct Choice: A**
The speaker admires West Berliners for insisting on maintaining a free and democratic society in spite of the fact that they face serious threats from Communist East Germany. Choice C is a true statement, but not in itself a reason for pride.

41. **Correct Choice: D**
The speaker addresses those people who believe that Communism is a good system. He challenges them to come to Berlin so they can see what a terrible system it is, by looking at the wall that physically prevents East Germans from choosing to leave.

42. **Correct Choice: A**
Both words in each pair have similar meaning and connotations, except "Europe and elsewhere." This pair shows a contrast—it lists two opposite ideas.

43. **Correct Choice: B**
Oblivious usually means *unaware*, but in this case Shakespeare uses it to mean "causing oblivion" or "causing forgetfulness." The lines "pluck from the memory a rooted sorrow" and "raze out the written troubles of the brain" show that the only antidote that will cure Lady Macbeth is to forget the horrors of the past. Therefore choice B is the only one that makes sense.

44. **Correct Choice: C**
Anyone who refuses to give in, no matter how high the odds are against him, is brave.

45. **Correct Choice: C**
Macbeth does not show any sense of guilt for his wife's sad condition. He does show pity, love, concern, and a great desire for her to be cured.

46. **Correct Choice: E**
Macbeth knows that the coming battle will mean either a final victory or a final defeat for him.

47. **Correct Choice: D**
Seyton addresses Macbeth by his title, while Macbeth calls Seyton by his name. This shows that Macbeth is of higher rank. Macbeth asks Seyton to help him with his armor and to carry out other orders. All these things show that Seyton is a servant. Seyton and the Doctor are two separate characters, so choice A is wrong.

48. **Correct Choice: C**
The expression "mouth-honor" means the same as the contemporary "lip service." Macbeth has just stated that he will receive only the outward show of the respect due to his position as king; this outward show will not reflect what his subjects truly feel about him.

49. **Correct Choice: D**
The Doctor's tone in speaking to Macbeth is almost curt; his brief answers make it reasonable to infer that he does not like Macbeth. He expresses little concern or sympathy for Lady Macbeth. He says that a mentally ill patient "must minister to himself," showing that he is not capable of treating such a patient. A dedicated doctor would try to be of more help. This leaves choice D, which is NOT a reasonable inference because the Doctor expresses no fear of the battle and because as a doctor, he would not be likely to take any part in the fighting.

50. **Correct Choice: B**
This definition of *shade* is no longer common usage, but the context of the passage makes it clear that Gabriel is referring to ghosts.

51. **Correct Choice: A**
The phrase "a strange friendly pity for her entered his soul" makes it clear that he feels sympathy rather than any of the other choices.

52. **Correct Choice: E**
An elegy is a speech made over the dead. Gabriel is pondering the subject of death, of those who have died and those who will soon die, and he thinks of his marriage and his life and being "dead" because they both lack intense emotion. The tenderness Gabriel expresses throughout the passage make "hopeless" and "resigned" inappropriate answers.

53. **Correct Choice: D**
"His soul swooned slowly" is a poetical, metaphorical way of saying he has fallen asleep. Although writers commonly compare sleep metaphorically to death, it is only a metaphor; Gabriel has not actually died; and although he

is moved by his wife's story and shares her grief, he is not heartbroken.

54. **Correct Choice: B**

"Soul swooned slowly," "faintly falling," and "falling faintly" are examples of alliteration, series of words beginning with the same sound.

55. **Correct Choice: A**

Throughout the passage, Gabriel is preoccupied with thoughts of death, of those who are dead and are soon to die, and of the living death of people who feel no intense emotions. Snow and winter are common symbols for death because they represent the "death" or sleep of plants and animals during the cycle of the seasons.

56. **Correct Choice: D**

Sympathy and generosity go together better than any of the other choices. Gabriel is described as feeling "a strange friendly pity" for his wife.

57. **Correct Choice: D**

The writer applies the words "generous" and "friendly" to Gabriel and makes it clear that he thinks only of his wife's grief as she shares her memories of the boy who died for love of her. Many people would be jealous, petty, or bitter in this situation, but Gabriel is sympathetic.

58. **Correct Choice: E**

The crooked cross, the spears, and the thorns all allude to the Crucifixion. Jesus was crowned with thorns and nailed to a crooked cross; soldiers poked spears in his side to see if he was dead.

59. **Correct Choice: C**

Michael Furey experienced the glory of passionate love and also the anguish of losing his beloved. The pain of the separation is what killed him. Gabriel feels it is better to have felt the passion, in spite of the pain it can bring, than to live a quiet, uneventful life that contains neither a great passion nor any anguish.

60. **Correct Choice: B**

Gabriel is falling asleep during the last paragraph, and the repetition helps the reader "become" Gabriel as he or she too is lulled. So Option I is correct. Option II is also correct because the word repeatedly draws attention to the falling snow, reminding the reader of it and helping the reader to picture it. Option III is incorrect: The repetition of "falling" does not evoke feelings of the cold weather or the warmth of the room.

![ ] **HOW TO CALCULATE YOUR SCORE**

Count the number of correct answers and enter the total below.
Count the number of wrong answers. Do NOT include any questions you did not answer.
Multiply the number of wrong answers by 0.25 and enter the total below.
Do the subtraction. The answer is your raw score. Use the scoring scale to find your scaled score.

$$\underset{\text{(number of correct answers)}}{\text{[short WOL]}} - \underset{\text{(number of wrong answers} \times 0.25)}{\text{[short WOL]}} = \underset{\text{(raw score)}}{\text{[short WOL]}}$$

Raw Score	Scaled Score	Raw Score	Scaled Score	Raw Score	Scaled Score	Raw Score	Scaled Score	Raw Score	Scaled Score
60	800	44	710	28	560	12	420	−4	260
59	800	43	700	27	550	11	410	−5	250
58	800	42	690	26	540	10	400	−6	240
57	800	41	690	25	530	9	390	−7	230
56	800	40	680	24	520	8	380	−8	220
55	800	39	670	23	510	7	370	−9	210
54	790	38	660	22	500	6	360	−10	200
53	790	37	650	21	500	5	350	−11	200
52	780	36	640	20	490	4	340	−12	200
51	770	35	630	19	490	3	330	−13	200
50	760	34	620	18	480	2	320	−14	200
49	750	33	610	17	470	1	310	−15	200
48	740	32	600	16	460	0	300		
47	740	31	590	15	450	−1	290		
46	730	30	580	14	440	−2	280		
45	720	29	570	13	430	−3	270		

Note: This is only a sample scoring scale. Scoring scales differ from exam to exam.

PRACTICE TEST 2
LITERATURE

The following practice test is designed to be just like the real SAT Literature Test. It matches the actual test in content coverage and degree of difficulty.

Once you finish the practice test, determine your score. Carefully read the answer explanations of the questions you answered incorrectly. Identify any weaknesses in your literature skills by determining the areas in which you made the most errors. Review those sections of this book first. Then, as time permits, go back and review your strengths.

Allow one hour to take the test. Time yourself and work uninterrupted. If you run out of time, take note of where you stopped when time ran out. Remember that you lose a quarter point for each incorrect answer, but you do not lose points for questions you leave blank. Therefore, unless you can eliminate one or more of the five choices, it's best to leave a question unanswered.

Use the following formula to calculate your score:

(number of correct answers) − ¼ (number of incorrect answers)

If you treat this practice test just like the actual exam, it will accurately reflect how you are likely to perform on test Day. Here are some hints on how to create test-taking conditions similar to those of the actual exam:

- Complete the test in one sitting. On test day, you will not be allowed to take a break.
- Tear out the answer sheet and fill in the ovals just as you will on the actual test day.
- Have a good eraser and more than one sharp pencil handy. On test day, you will not be able to go get a new pencil if yours breaks.
- Do not allow yourself any extra time; put down your pencil after exactly one hour, no matter how many questions are left to answer.
- Become familiar with the directions on the test. If you go in knowing what the directions say, you will not have to waste time reading and thinking about them on the actual test day.

PRACTICE TEST 2
LITERATURE

ANSWER SHEET

Tear out this answer sheet and use it to mark your answers.

1. A B C D E	16. A B C D E	31. A B C D E	46. A B C D E
2. A B C D E	17. A B C D E	32. A B C D E	47. A B C D E
3. A B C D E	18. A B C D E	33. A B C D E	48. A B C D E
4. A B C D E	19. A B C D E	34. A B C D E	49. A B C D E
5. A B C D E	20. A B C D E	35. A B C D E	50. A B C D E
6. A B C D E	21. A B C D E	36. A B C D E	51. A B C D E
7. A B C D E	22. A B C D E	37. A B C D E	52. A B C D E
8. A B C D E	23. A B C D E	38. A B C D E	53. A B C D E
9. A B C D E	24. A B C D E	39. A B C D E	54. A B C D E
10. A B C D E	25. A B C D E	40. A B C D E	55. A B C D E
11. A B C D E	26. A B C D E	41. A B C D E	56. A B C D E
12. A B C D E	27. A B C D E	42. A B C D E	57. A B C D E
13. A B C D E	28. A B C D E	43. A B C D E	58. A B C D E
14. A B C D E	29. A B C D E	44. A B C D E	59. A B C D E
15. A B C D E	30. A B C D E	45. A B C D E	60. A B C D E

PRACTICE TEST 2
Time: 60 minutes

Directions: This test consists of selections from literary works and questions on their content, form, and style. After reading each passage or poem, choose the best answer to each question and then fill in the corresponding oval on the answer sheet.

Note: Pay particular attention to the requirements of questions that contain the words NOT or EXCEPT.

Questions 1–9. Read the following speech carefully before you choose your answers.

My loving people, we have been persuaded
by some, that are careful of our safety, to
take heed how we commit ourselves to
armed multitudes, for fear of treachery; but
5 I assure you, I do not desire to live to distrust
my faithful and loving people. Let tyrants
fear; I have always so behaved myself that,
under God, I have placed my chiefest
strength and safeguard in the loyal hearts
10 and good will of my subjects. And therefore I
am come amongst you at this time, not as for
my recreation or sport, but being resolved, in
the midst and heat of the battle, to live or die
amongst you all; to lay down, for my God,
15 and for my kingdom, and for my people, my
honor and my blood, even the dust. I know I
have but the body of a weak and feeble
woman; but I have the heart of a king, and of
a king of England, too; and think foul scorn
20 that Parma or Spain, or any prince of
Europe, should dare to invade the borders of
my realms: to which, rather than any dishon-
or should grow by me, I myself will take up
arms; I myself will be your general, judge,
25 and rewarder of every one of your virtues in
the field. I know already, by your forwardness, that you have deserved rewards and
crowns; and we do assure you, on the word
of a prince, they shall be duly paid you. In the
30 mean my lieutenant general shall be in my
stead, than whom never prince commanded
a more noble and worthy subject; not doubt-
ing by your obedience to my general, by your
concord in the camp, and by your valor in the
35 field, we shall shortly have a famous victory
over the enemies of my God, of my kingdom,
and of my people.

(1588)

1. The speaker uses the word "forwardness" (lines 26–27) to mean

   (A) demonstration of bravery on the battlefield
   (B) promptness in volunteering for military duty
   (C) disrespectful, familiar, or brazen behavior
   (D) high rank in the nobility or aristocracy
   (E) eagerness among the crowd to get close enough to hear

2. The tone of the speech is best described as

   (A) ironic
   (B) anguished
   (C) solemn
   (D) ominous
   (E) inspiring

3. What is the source of the potential treachery the speaker refers to in the opening sentence?

   (A) her close advisers
   (B) her family members
   (C) her volunteer soldiers
   (D) the enemy army
   (E) the opposing political party

4. By saying "Let tyrants fear" (lines 6–7), the speaker implies which of the following?

   (A) that her enemies are tyrants
   (B) that she is not a tyrant
   (C) that subjects fear a tyrant
   (D) that tyrants cannot be trusted
   (E) that she is abdicating the throne

5. In which sense does the speaker use the word "mean" (line 30)?

   (A) interval
   (B) average
   (C) miserly
   (D) spiteful
   (E) intend

GO ON TO THE NEXT PAGE

PRACTICE TEST—*Continued*

6. Why does the speaker repeat the phrase "for/of my God, my kingdom, and my people" (lines 14–15 and 36–37)?

    I. to lull her audience into a calmer mood
    II. to emphasize the rightness of her cause
    III. to arouse her listeners' patriotism

    (A) I only
    (B) II only
    (C) II and III only
    (D) III only
    (E) I, II, and III

7. Which best describes the character of the speaker?

    (A) determined and courageous
    (B) cautious and prudent
    (C) cynical and bitter
    (D) manipulative and dishonest
    (E) brutal and fierce

8. The final sentence of the speech contains two examples of which literary technique?

    (A) rhetoric
    (B) parallelism
    (C) enjambment
    (D) simile
    (E) hyperbole

9. The word "crowns" (line 28) is a metaphor for

    (A) coin of the realm
    (B) rewards
    (C) medals and honors
    (D) royal headgear
    (E) ceremonies

Questions 10–17. Read the following poem carefully before you choose your answers.

Remembrance

Cold in the earth—and the deep snow piled above thee—
Far, far removed, cold in the dreary grave!
Have I forgot, my only love, to love thee,
Severed at last by time's all-severing wave?

5 Now, when alone, do my thoughts no longer hover
Over the mountains on that northern shore;
Resting their wings where heath and fern-leaves cover
Thy noble heart for ever, ever more?

Cold in the earth—and fifteen wild Decembers
10 From those brown hills have melted into spring—
Faithful, indeed, is the spirit that remembers
After such years of change and suffering!

Sweet love of youth, forgive if I forget thee
While the world's tide is bearing me along—
15 Other desires and other hopes beset me,
Hopes which obscure but cannot do thee wrong.

No later light has lightened up my heaven,
No second morn has ever shone for me:
All my life's bliss from thy dear life was given—
20 All my life's bliss is in the grave with thee.

But when the days of golden dreams had perished
And even despair was powerless to destroy,
Then did I learn how existence could be cherished,
Strengthened and fed without the aid of joy.

25 Then did I check my tears of useless passion—
Weaned my young soul from yearning after thine—
Sternly denied its burning wish to hasten
Down to that tomb already more than mine!

And even yet I dare not let it languish,
30 Dare not indulge in memory's rapturous pain—
Once drinking deep of that divinest anguish,
How could I seek the empty world again?

                                    (1845)

10. In the second stanza, the speaker compares her thoughts to

    (A) a faithful dog
    (B) a bird
    (C) the sun
    (D) a clock
    (E) the darkness

11. Which best sums up the speaker's message to the beloved?

    (A) She has moved on from her loss and achieved peace and serenity.
    (B) Her greatest wish is to be buried by the side of her beloved.
    (C) She refuses to think about her lost love because if she does she will lose her will to live.
    (D) She is grateful to have known happiness with her lost love, even though it was brief.
    (E) She has found another love, but promises always to remember the beloved who has died.

GO ON TO THE NEXT PAGE

PRACTICE TEST—*Continued*

12. By "Severed at last by time's all-severing wave" (line 4), the speaker implies that

    (A) in time, she will forget her beloved
    (B) her lover died of old age
    (C) the passage of time can destroy love
    (D) her beloved drowned in the ocean
    (E) her lover has been away for a long time

13. What consequences does the speaker anticipate from the act of writing/narrating this poem?

    (A) She will cease to care about living.
    (B) The act of expressing her feelings will lessen them.
    (C) The world will learn her most precious secret.
    (D) She will be reunited with her lover in heaven.
    (E) She will make her love immortal in a work of art.

14. Remembering her beloved causes the speaker to feel all of the following EXCEPT

    (A) dread
    (B) anguish
    (C) passion
    (D) serenity
    (E) emptiness

15. Which line from the poem seems to contradict the fact of the poem's existence?

    (A) "Faithful, indeed, is the spirit that remembers" (line 11)
    (B) "Other desires and other hopes beset me" (line 15)
    (C) "No later light has lightened up my heaven" (line 17)
    (D) "All my life's bliss is in the grave with thee" (line 20)
    (E) "[I] Dare not indulge in memory's rapturous pain" (line 30)

16. Which of the following has NOT happened to the speaker since the death of the beloved?

    (A) She has found another lover.
    (B) She has tried to forget her dead lover.
    (C) She has been tempted to commit suicide.
    (D) She has found reasons besides love to go on living.
    (E) She has lost all her happiness.

17. The fact that the speaker decided to go on living despite her loss implies that she is

    (A) frustrated and angry
    (B) listless and apathetic
    (C) disciplined and determined
    (D) romantic and dreamy
    (E) haughty and proud

Questions 18–24. Read the following passage carefully before you choose your answers.

Mrs. Ballinger was one of the ladies who pursue Culture in bands, as though it were dangerous to meet alone. To this end she had founded the Lunch Club, an association
5   composed of herself and several other indomitable huntresses of erudition. The Lunch Club, after three or four winters of lunching and debate, had acquired such local distinction that the entertainment of distin-
10 guished strangers became one of its accepted functions; in recognition of which it duly extended to the celebrated "Osric Dane," on the day of her arrival in Hillbridge, an invitation to be present at the next meeting.

15 The Club was to meet at Mrs. Ballinger's. The other members, behind her back, were of one voice in deploring her unwillingness to cede her rights in favor of Mrs. Plinth, whose house made a more impressive setting
20 for the entertainment of celebrities; while, as Mrs. Leveret observed, there was always the picture-gallery to fall back on.

Mrs. Plinth made no secret of sharing this view. She had always regarded it as one of
25 her obligations to entertain the Lunch Club's distinguished guests. Mrs. Plinth was almost as proud of her obligations as she was of her picture-gallery; she was in fact fond of implying that the one possession implied the
30 other, and that only a woman of her wealth could afford to live up to a standard as high as that which she had set herself. An all-round sense of duty, roughly adaptable to various ends, was, in her opinion, all that
35 Providence exacted of the more humbly stationed; but the power which had predestined Mrs. Plinth to keep footmen clearly

GO ON TO THE NEXT PAGE →

PRACTICE TEST—*Continued*

intended her to maintain an equally special-
ized staff of responsibilities. It was the more
40 to be regretted that Mrs. Ballinger, whose
obligations to society were bounded by the
narrow scope of two parlor-maids, should
have been so tenacious of the right to entertain Osric Dane.

45 The question of that lady's reception had for
a month past profoundly moved the members of the Lunch Club. It was not that they
felt themselves unequal to the task, but that
their sense of the opportunity plunged them
50 into the agreeable uncertainty of the lady
who weighs the alternatives of a well-stocked
wardrobe. If such subsidiary members as
Mrs. Leveret were fluttered by the thought of
exchanging ideas with the author of "The
55 Wings of Death," no forebodings of the kind
disturbed the conscious adequacy of Mrs.
Plinth, Mrs. Ballinger and Miss Van Vluyck.
"The Wings of Death" had, in fact, at Miss
Van Vluyck's suggestion, been chosen as the
60 subject of discussion at the last club meeting,
and each member had thus been enabled to
express her own opinion or to appropriate
whatever seemed most likely to be of use in
the comments of the others.

(1911)

18. The author of the passage thinks the Lunch Club
members are

   I. pretentious
   II. insincere
   III. intellectual

(A) I only
(B) I and II only
(C) II only
(D) III only
(E) I, II, and III

19. The fact that Mrs. Plinth owns the most impressive
of the club members' houses is an example of

(A) enjambment
(B) verbal irony
(C) metaphor
(D) hyperbole
(E) foreshadowing

20. The LEAST powerful and important member of the
Lunch Club is

(A) Mrs. Ballinger
(B) Mrs. Plinth
(C) Miss Van Vluyck
(D) Osric Dane
(E) Mrs. Leveret

21. The phrase "indomitable huntresses of erudition"
(line 6) is striking because

(A) it suggests that the ladies would rather hunt
than read books
(B) the Lunch Club members have become famous
in Hillbridge
(C) literature is meant to be enjoyed, not conquered
with weapons
(D) hunting is an outdoor activity and reading an
indoor one
(E) Osric Dane has written a novel about hunting

22. The name of "Osric Dane" (line 12), is an allusion to
a character in which of the following?

(A) Hamlet
(B) Othello
(C) King Lear
(D) Romeo and Juliet
(E) A Midsummer Night's Dream

23. The author implies that the Lunch Club's true purpose is

(A) to read and discuss interesting new books
(B) to meet and talk to famous authors
(C) to enjoy exploring Mrs. Plinth's picture gallery
(D) to make its members more important in their
own eyes
(E) to find out whose cook can provide the best
lunch

GO ON TO THE NEXT PAGE

PRACTICE TEST—*Continued*

24. The phrase "deploring her unwillingness to cede her rights" (lines 17–18) means

    (A) laughing at her for thinking she has any rights
    (B) thinking worse of her for sacrificing her rights
    (C) praying that she will hold fast to her rights
    (D) criticizing her for wanting to give up her rights
    (E) regretting her refusal to give up her rights

Questions 25–34. Read the following poem carefully before you choose your answers.

In Cabin'd Ships at Sea

In cabin'd ships at sea,
The boundless blue on every side expanding,
With whistling winds and music of the waves, the large
             imperious waves,
Or some lone bark buoy'd on the dense marine,
5 Where joyous full of faith, spreading white sails,
She cleaves the ether, mid the sparkle and the foam of day,
    or under many a star at night,
By sailors young and old haply will I, a reminiscence of
          the land, be read,
In full rapport at last.

10 Here are our thoughts, voyagers' thoughts,
Here not the land, firm land, alone appears, may then by
          them be said,
The sky o'erarches here, we feel the undulating deck
         beneath our feet,
We feel the long pulsation, ebb and flow of endless motion,
The tones of unseen mystery, the vague and vast suggestions
15   of the briny world, the liquid-flowing syllables,
The perfume, the faint creaking of the cordage, the
         melancholy rhythm,
The boundless vista and the horizon far and dim are all here,
And this is ocean's poem.

Then falter not O book, fulfil your destiny,
20 You not a reminiscence of the land alone,
You too as a lone bark cleaving the ether, purpos'd I know
         not whither,
    yet ever full of faith,
Consort to every ship that sails, sail you!
Bear forth to them folded my love, (dear mariners, for
         you I fold it here in every leaf;)
25 Speed on my book! spread your white sails my little bark
    athwart the imperious waves,
Chant on, sail on, bear o'er the boundless blue from me
         to every sea,
This song for mariners and all their ships.

                        (c. 1892)

25. The speaker of this poem is

    (A) an author
    (B) a traveler
    (C) a sailor
    (D) a voyager
    (E) a ship's captain

26. What is the effect of the alliteration in the line "With whistling winds and music of the waves, the large imperious waves" (line 3)?

    I. It echoes the wash of the ocean water.
    II. It suggests the ocean water because so many words begin with *w*.
    III. It shows how much the speaker loves the sound of the ocean.

    (A) I only
    (B) I and II only
    (C) II only
    (D) III only
    (E) I, II, and III

27. What does the speaker hope the mariners will find in his book?

    (A) happy memories of their lives on shore
    (B) religious inspiration and guidance
    (C) a sense of fellowship with a poet who understands them
    (D) blank pages on which they can write their own poems
    (E) entertainment that will help them pass the time

28. Which pair of words does the poet use to create a contrast?

    (A) winds and music (line 3)
    (B) sparkle and foam (line 6)
    (C) ebb and flow (line 13)
    (D) vague and vast (line 14)
    (E) far and dim (line 17)

29. The metaphor "white sails" (line 25) refers to

    (A) the sails of the "cabin'd ships"
    (B) the pages of the speaker's book
    (C) the white caps on the waves
    (D) the clouds in the sky
    (E) the mariners' letters to their families

GO ON TO THE NEXT PAGE

PRACTICE TEST—*Continued*

30. This poem is an example of which of the following?

 (A) sonnet
 (B) elegy
 (C) epic
 (D) free verse
 (E) limerick

31. The speaker directly addresses his book in which of the following stanzas?

 I.   stanza 1
 II.   stanza 2
 III   stanza 3

 (A) I only
 (B) I and III only
 (C) II only
 (D) II and III only
 (E) III only

32. The word "haply" (line 8) means

 (A) happily
 (B) eagerly
 (C) perhaps
 (D) easily
 (E) aloud

33. Which of the following is personified in the poem?

 (A) "the boundless blue" (line 2)
 (B) "some lone bark" (line 4)
 (C) "many a star" (line 4)
 (D) "the undulating deck" (line 12)
 (E) "the briny world" (line 15)

34. What quality does the speaker believe the mariners will respond to when they read his book?

 (A) the rhythm, rhymes, and meter
 (B) the allusions to mythology
 (C) the speaker's love for the ocean
 (D) the visual images
 (E) the practical advice

Questions 35–41. Read the following passage carefully before you choose your answers.

I have had to work hard; I have been often cheated, insulted, abused and injured; yet a black man, if he will be industrious and hon-est, can get along here as well as any one who
5   is poor and in a situation to be imposed on. I have been very unfortunate in life in this respect. Notwithstanding all my struggles, and sufferings, and injuries, I have been an honest man. There is no one who can come
10 forward and say he knows anything against Grimes. This I know, that I have been pun-ished for being suspected of things of which some of those who were loudest against me were actually guilty . . .

15 I have forebore to mention names in my his-tory where it might give the least pain; in this I have made it less interesting, and injured myself.

I may sometimes be a little mistaken, as I
20 have to write from memory, and there is a great deal I have omitted from want of recol-lection at the time of writing. I cannot speak as I feel on some subjects. If those who read my history think I have not led a life of trial,
25 I have failed to give a correct representation. I think I must be forty years of age, but don't know; I could not tell my wife my age. I have learned to read and write pretty well; if I had an opportunity I could learn very fast. My
30 wife has had a tolerable good education, which has been a help to me.

I hope some will buy my books from charity; but I am no beggar. I am now entirely desti-tute of property; where and how I shall live I
35 don't know; where and how I shall die I don't know; but I hope I may be prepared. If it were not for the stripes on my back which were made while I was a slave, I would in my will leave my skin as a legacy to the govern-
40 ment, desiring that it might be taken off and made into parchment, and then bind the Constitution of glorious, happy and *free* America. Let the skin of an American slave bind the charter of American liberty!

(1824)

35. The information in the second paragraph allows you to conclude that Grimes

 (A) cares more for the facts than for anyone's feelings
 (B) hates everyone from his past life
 (C) does not want to praise anyone too highly
 (D) is a person of ethics and integrity
 (E) cannot remember the names of his enemies

GO ON TO THE NEXT PAGE

PRACTICE TEST—*Continued*

36. The tone of the sentence beginning "If it were not for the stripes on my back" (line 36) is best described as

    (A) bitter and angry
    (B) resigned and weary
    (C) neutral and calm
    (D) noble and majestic
    (E) proud and confident

37. Why does Grimes include the final sentence when its ideas were already expressed one sentence earlier?

    (A) to demonstrate that he is a free citizen
    (B) to support his claim that he is an honest man
    (C) to emphasize his rage at his past treatment
    (D) to make sure his readers remember his words
    (E) to urge the government to free all slaves

38. Which is NOT a likely reason for Grimes to have written and published his life story?

    (A) to earn enough money to support himself and his family
    (B) to avenge himself on those who treated him badly
    (C) to persuade his readers to oppose slavery and support abolition
    (D) to make his readers aware of the evils of slavery
    (E) to put his true story on record so that he will be remembered accurately

39. This passage is an example of which of the following?

    (A) political satire
    (B) editorial
    (C) confession
    (D) slave narrative
    (E) biography

40. All of the following seem to characterize Grimes accurately EXCEPT

    (A) bitterness
    (B) cynicism
    (C) impatience
    (D) rage
    (E) self-pity

41. Which of the following suggest that Grimes is a reliable narrator?

    (A) He is writing about experiences he lived through.
    (B) He provides supporting details from other eye-witnesses.
    (C) His poverty and suffering are the common lot of a slave.
    (D) He is unable to remember all the events of his past.
    (E) He refuses to give the names of many people from his past.

Questions 42–49. Read the following poem carefully before you choose your answers.

The Dream

Dear love, for nothing less than thee
Would I have broke this happy dream;
    It was a theme
For reason, much too strong for fantasy.
5 Therefore thou wakd'st me wisely; yet
My dream thou brok'st not, but continued'st it.
Thou art so true that thoughts of thee suffice
To make dreams truths, and fables histories;
Enter these arms, for since thou thought'st it best
10 Not to dream all my dream, let's do the rest.

As lightning, or a taper's light,
Thine eyes, and not thy noise, waked me;
    Yet I thought thee
(For thou lov'st truth) an angel, at first sight,
15 But when I saw thou sawest my heart,
And knew'st my thoughts, beyond an angel's art,
When thou knew'st what I dreamt, when thou knew'st when
Excess of joy would wake me, and cam'st then,
I must confess it could not choose but be
20 Profane to think thee anything but thee.

Coming and staying show'd thee, thee,
But rising makes me doubt, that now
    Thou art not thou.
That love is weak, where Fear's as strong as he;
25 'Tis not all spirit, pure, and brave
If mixture it of *fear, shame, honor* have.
Perchance, as torches, which must ready be,
Men light and put out, so thou deal'st with me.
Thou cam'st to kindle, goest to come: then I
30 Will dream that hope again, but else would die.

(1633)

42. What happened just before the beginning of this poem?

    (A) The speaker was awakened from a nightmare.
    (B) The speaker received a visit from his lover.
    (C) The speaker's lover woke him up from a dream.
    (D) The speaker was unable to get his lover to wake up.
    (E) The speaker dropped something on the floor and broke it.

GO ON TO THE NEXT PAGE →

PRACTICE TEST—*Continued*

43. What causes the speaker to wake up?

    (A) a glance from his beloved's eyes
    (B) the thought of his beloved
    (C) being shaken awake by his beloved
    (D) the light of the bedside candles
    (E) his beloved's whisper in his ear

44. The lines "Thou art so true that thoughts of thee suffice / To make dreams truths, and fables histories" (lines 7 and 8) represent or include all of the following EXCEPT

    (A) slant rhyme
    (B) hyperbole
    (C) allusion
    (D) enjambment
    (E) heroic couplet

45. Why does the speaker say he is "profane" (line 20) for mistaking his beloved for an angel?

    (A) because comparing a mortal to an angel is blasphemy
    (B) because his beloved is higher and better than an angel
    (C) because he does not believe in angels, God, or heaven
    (D) because he saw an angel in his dream before he woke up
    (E) because only a dead mortal can join the ranks of the angels

46. By "It was a theme / For reason, much too strong for fantasy" (lines 3 and 4), the speaker means

    (A) the reason for his dream was his desire to escape into a fantasy
    (B) in the morning, he will write a logical argument about his dream
    (C) only in a dream could he understand this topic so clearly
    (D) he cannot explain the subject of his dream to his beloved
    (E) he was dreaming about a topic that required serious, conscious thought

47. Which quality does the speaker seem to value most in his beloved?

    (A) her beauty
    (B) her humor
    (C) her intelligence
    (D) her perceptiveness
    (E) her loyalty

48. Which is the best paraphrase of the phrase "Coming and staying show'd thee, thee" (line 21)?

    (A) Coming and staying shows you to yourself.
    (B) Your coming to me and staying proved to me that it really was you.
    (C) I know that only you would ever come to me and stay with me.
    (D) You saw your reflection when you came to me and looked into my eyes.
    (E) When I first woke up I knew right away that it was you.

49. Which is the best explanation of the comparison in the poem's last four lines?

    (A) The beloved kindles the speaker's desire just as a man lights a torch.
    (B) The beloved's eyes are like a torch that lights up a room.
    (C) The love of the two characters is as bright as a torch.
    (D) The lovers are so happy they don't notice when the torch goes out.
    (E) The speaker would recognize his lover even without the light of the torch.

Questions 50–60. Read the following passage carefully before you choose your answers.

The one opened the door with a latch-key and went in, followed by a young fellow who awkwardly removed his cap. He wore rough clothes that smacked of the sea, and he was
5 manifestly out of place in the spacious hall in which he found himself. He did not know what to do with his cap, and was stuffing it into his coat pocket when the other took it from him. The act was done quietly and nat-
10 urally, and the awkward young fellow appreciated it. "He understands," was his thought. "He'll see me through all right."

He walked at the other's heels with a swing to his shoulders, and his legs spread unwit-
15 tingly, as if the level floors were tilting up and sinking down to the heave and lunge of the sea. The wide rooms seemed too narrow for his rolling gait, and to himself he was in terror lest his broad shoulders should collide

GO ON TO THE NEXT PAGE

PRACTICE TEST—*Continued*

20 with the doorways or sweep the bric-a-brac from the low mantel. He recoiled from side to side between the various objects and multiplied the hazards that in reality lodged only in his mind. Between a grand piano and a
25 centre-table piled high with books was space for a half a dozen to walk abreast, yet he essayed it with trepidation. His heavy arms hung loosely at his sides. He did not know what to do with those arms and hands, and
30 when, to his excited vision, one arm seemed liable to brush against the books on the table, he lurched away like a frightened horse, barely missing the piano stool. He watched the easy walk of the other in front of him,
35 and for the first time realized that his walk was different from that of other men. He experienced a momentary pang of shame that he should walk so uncouthly. The sweat burst through the skin of his forehead in tiny
40 beads, and he paused and mopped his bronzed face with his handkerchief.

"Hold on, Arthur, my boy," he said, attempting to mask his anxiety with facetious utterance. "This is too much all at once for yours
45 truly. Give me a chance to get my nerve. You know I didn't want to come, an' I guess your fam'ly ain't hankerin' to see me neither."

"That's all right," was the reassuring answer. "You mustn't be frightened at us. We're just
50 homely people—Hello, there's a letter for me."

He stepped back to the table, tore open the envelope, and began to read, giving the stranger an opportunity to recover himself.
55 And the stranger understood and appreciated. His was the gift of sympathy, understanding; and beneath his alarmed exterior that sympathetic process went on. He mopped his forehead dry and glanced about
60 him with a controlled face, though in the eyes there was an expression such as wild animals betray when they fear the trap. He was surrounded by the unknown, apprehensive of what might happen, ignorant of what
65 he should do, aware that he walked and bore himself awkwardly, fearful that every attribute and power of him was similarly afflicted. He was keenly sensitive, hopelessly self-conscious, and the amused glance that the
70 other stole privily at him over the top of the letter burned into him like a dagger-thrust. He saw the glance, but he gave no sign, for among the things he had learned was discipline. Also, that dagger-thrust went to his
75 pride. He cursed himself for having come, and at the same time resolved that, happen what would, having come, he would carry it through. The lines of his face hardened, and into his eyes came a fighting light. He looked
80 about more unconcernedly, sharply observant, every detail of the pretty interior registering itself on his brain. His eyes were wide apart; nothing in their field of vision escaped; and as they drank in the beauty before them
85 the fighting light died out and a warm glow took its place. He was responsive to beauty, and here was cause to respond.

(1909)

50. Arthur is an example of which of the following?

(A) a protagonist
(B) a foil
(C) a main character
(D) an anti-hero
(E) a narrator

51. Which of the following can you conclude about Arthur's guest?

(A) He has been at sea for a very long time.
(B) He is clumsy and awkward by nature.
(C) He tries too hard to impress other people.
(D) He resents Arthur's attempts to set him at ease.
(E) He is from an intellectual and artistically inclined family.

52. The guest's response to the "amused glance that the other stole at him" (lines 69–70) shows that the guest is

(A) cowardly
(B) good-natured
(C) unselfconscious
(D) courageous
(E) temperamental

GO ON TO THE NEXT PAGE

PRACTICE TEST—*Continued*

53. The author compares the guest to "wild animals" (lines 61–62) and "a frightened horse" (line 32) for all of the following reasons EXCEPT

    (A) to show that he reacts by instinct alone
    (B) to emphasize how out-of-place he feels
    (C) to describe the strength of his uncertainty
    (D) to demonstrate his awkwardness
    (E) to show that he has no self-control

54. In which respect are Arthur and his guest alike?

    (A) Each wants to reassure the other.
    (B) Each is secretly amused at the other's behavior.
    (C) Each is aware of how the other one feels.
    (D) Each feels awkward in a strange setting.
    (E) Each wants to be a good host.

55. Which line from the passage suggests that in the end, the guest will overcome his discomfort?

    (A) "The wide rooms seemed too narrow for his rolling gait" (lines 17–18)
    (B) "He did not know what to do with those arms and hands" (lines 28–29)
    (C) "[He] realized that his walk was different from that of other men" (lines 35–36)
    (D) "[He] resolved that, happen what would, having come, he would carry it through" (lines 76–78)
    (E) "His eyes were wide apart; nothing in their field of vision escaped" (lines 82–83)

56. In this passage, the author concentrates on

    (A) describing a character
    (B) developing a conflict
    (C) introducing his plot
    (D) foreshadowing the resolution
    (E) analyzing the main theme

57. Why does the author have the guest speak in dialect at the end of the third paragraph?

    (A) to arouse the reader's contempt for him
    (B) to suggest that he is not very smart
    (C) to show that he has not been formally educated
    (D) to indicate where he comes from
    (E) to show that he is a foreigner

58. When Arthur says "We're just homely people" (line 49–50), he means

    (A) We are plain in appearance.
    (B) Welcome to our home.
    (C) We are rude and unrefined.
    (D) We are simple and ordinary.
    (E) Our home is a nice place.

59. The phrase "facetious utterance" (lines 43–44) means

    (A) a joking comment
    (B) a cry for help
    (C) a shout
    (D) a speech in dialect
    (E) a plea

60. The description of his home suggests that Arthur is

    (A) extremely wealthy
    (B) cultured and educated
    (C) careless and untidy
    (D) sociable and fun-loving
    (E) active and athletic

STOP

IF YOU FINISH BEFORE TIME IS CALLED, YOU MAY CHECK YOUR WORK ON THIS TEST ONLY.

DO NOT TURN TO ANY OTHER TEST IN THIS BOOK.

ANSWER KEY

1. B	21. C	41. C
2. E	22. A	42. C
3. C	23. D	43. A
4. B	24. E	44. C
5. A	25. A	45. B
6. C	26. E	46. E
7. A	27. C	47. D
8. B	28. C	48. B
9. C	29. B	49. A
10. B	30. D	50. B
11. C	31. E	51. A
12. C	32. C	52. D
13. A	33. B	53. E
14. D	34. C	54. C
15. E	35. D	55. D
16. A	36. A	56. A
17. C	37. C	57. C
18. B	38. B	58. D
19. B	39. D	59. A
20. E	40. C	60. B

ANSWERS AND EXPLANATIONS

1. **Correct Choice: B**
The context shows that this is a speech to the troops before a major battle. The speaker praises her troops for being so ready and eager to fight; "forwardness" means they have come forward to volunteer.

2. **Correct Choice: E**
The speaker says she has complete faith in her subjects' loyalty and the rightness of their cause, and she vows to lead the troops herself if need be. These words are intended to instill courage and determination in her hearers.

3. **Correct Choice: C**
The speaker's advisers warn her against "armed multitudes," which refers to her own soldiers. They believe that if she gives weapons to a citizen army, the citizens may turn against the government.

4. **Correct Choice: B**
The speaker contrasts herself with a tyrant, saying in effect "Let tyrants fear; I need not fear because I am not a tyrant."

5. **Correct Choice: A**
The phrase "in the mean" refers to the interval of time between the delivery of this speech and the end of the battle, when the soldiers will receive "rewards and crowns." All five choices define *mean* accurately, but only choice A makes sense in the context.

6. **Correct Choice: C**
Option I is wrong because the intent of the speech is not to lull, but to call soldiers to action. The mention of kingdom and people is likely to arouse the listeners' patriotic instincts, and the mention of God suggests that the speaker is fighting on the side of justice and right.

7. **Correct Choice: A**
The speaker shows her determination to protect her kingdom. Her decision to lead her troops herself, if necessary, shows great courage, particularly as she is a woman and thus lacks military experience.

8. **Correct Choice: B**
"By your obedience / by your concord / by your valor" and "of my God / of my kingdom / of my people" are examples of parallelism or parallel structure—a repetition of a given grammatical pattern for emphasis.

9. **Correct Choice: C**
The speaker says "rewards and crowns," which suggests that they are two different things. The most likely meaning is "medals and honors," because these are what a monarch would most likely give soldiers after a battle.

10. **Correct Choice: B**
Of the five choices, only birds have the ability to hover and rest their wings.

11. **Correct Choice: C**
The speaker explains that she has chosen to "cherish, strengthen and feed" her existence, even though her whole happiness is dead in the lover's grave. She dare not look back at her memories, because if she does, she will not want to "seek the empty world again."

12. **Correct Choice: C**
The speaker asks her beloved if her love for him has finally been destroyed by time. The phrase "all-severing" implies that time has unlimited power to destroy.

13. **Correct Choice: A**
The speaker thinks along these lines: "It is dangerous to remember you, because the act of remembering shows me how empty my life is now compared to how rich and full it was when you were alive." By narrating / writing this poem about her lover, she is remembering him. Therefore, this act will make her lose interest in life.

14. **Correct Choice: D**
The speaker's memories do *not* bring her peace, calm, or serenity. They bring the opposite—violent, unsettling feelings that she describes throughout the poem.

15. **Correct Choice: E**
The act of narrating and/or writing this poem shows that the speaker *does* dare to "indulge in memory's rapturous pain."

16. **Correct Choice: A**
When the speaker says "No later light has lightened up my heaven, / No second morn has ever shone for me," she means that she has not fallen in love again. The phrase "my only love" (line 3) also supports this answer.

17. **Correct Choice: C**
Stanzas 6 and 7 show that the speaker has made a conscious decision to move forward. Phrases like "sternly denied" and "check the tears of passion" show that it takes both self-control and determination to conquer a great sorrow like hers.

18. **Correct Choice: B**
The author pokes fun at the Lunch Club throughout the passage, showing that the ladies are both pretentious and insincere for pretending that they love books, when all they really

want to do is impress themselves and others with a show of interest in literature.

19. **Correct Choice: B**
It is ironic that the lady who owns the finest house is named for an architectural element; a *plinth* is a block used to support the decorative molding over a door or arch.

20. **Correct Choice: E**
Mrs. Leveret is described as being a "subsidiary" member, which means she is of less importance than the others. Osric Dane is not a member at all, but the author who is to be the next guest of honor.

21. **Correct Choice: C**
The image of huntresses, along with the phrase "ladies who pursue Culture in bands," suggests that the Lunch Club members have a basically hostile attitude toward reading; that it is a battle they are determined to win. The image is striking because one expects people who form a book club to do it because they enjoy reading. *Indomitable* means "unconquerable," and *erudition* means "learning."

22. **Correct Choice: A**
Allusion is the correct answer because the author's mention of a character, Osric the Dane, in the play *Hamlet* is a literary reference that the reader is expected to recognize.

23. **Correct Choice: D**
What the ladies truly care about is impressing each other, themselves, and Hillbridge society with their pretensions to being well-read and intellectual. Choices A and B are wrong because these are only the ostensible purposes of the club; these ladies are not genuinely interested in reading and thinking about interesting new books, nor in hearing what the authors have to say. Their interest in literature is a sham.

24. **Correct Choice: E**
Deploring means "lamenting or sorrowing over." To *cede* means "to give up." Choice E closely matches these definitions.

25. **Correct Choice: A**
The speaker has written a book which he hopes sailors will read on their voyages.

26. **Correct Choice: E**
Option I is correct because the repeated *w* sound in the line does echo the wash of the ocean waves. Option II is correct because the repetition of the word *waves* and the *w* sound does remind the reader of water, which also begins with *w*. Option III is correct because the speaker echoes the sound of the ocean so successfully it is clear that he has listened to it and loves it.

27. **Correct Choice: C**
In stanza 2, the mariners are looking at the book and saying it reflects not only the lives and experiences of the landsman but also the experiences and images of the ocean. Therefore, they feel that the book's author is a kindred spirit. The poet's belief that he and the mariners will achieve "full rapport" (line 9) through his book also supports this answer choice.

28. **Correct Choice: C**
When the ocean *ebbs*, it retreats from the shore. When it *flows*, it washes up on the shore. The other pairs of words are not opposites.

29. **Correct Choice: B**
The line "Speed on my book!" (line 25) shows that the speaker is directly addressing his book. The book is his "little bark," and its paper pages are the "white sails" that will carry it over the ocean.

30. **Correct Choice: D**
The lack of regular rhyme, meter, and rhythmic structure make this a free-verse poem.

31. **Correct Choice: E**
The line "Then falter not O book" shows that the speaker is addressing the book in stanza 3. In stanza 1, the speaker is talking to himself; in stanza 2, he is imagining what the mariners will say when they read his book.

32. **Correct Choice: C**
Haply is an archaic way of saying "perhaps." *Haply will I* means "perhaps I will." The speaker is imagining what *may* happen when "sailors young and old" read his book.

33. **Correct Choice: B**
The phrase "joyous full of faith" attributes human emotions to the bark.

34. **Correct Choice: C**
In every line of the poem, the sound effects, alliteration, imagery, and word choice reflect the speaker's deep love for the ocean's power, mystery, and beauty. He is sure the sailors will respond to this because they share the feeling.

35. **Correct Choice: D**
Grimes protects his enemies by not naming them, and he does this at some cost to himself. Only an ethical, honorable man would make this choice.

36. **Correct Choice: A**
There is an almost palpable sneer in the words "a glorious, happy and *free* America"— deeply ironic words when written by a former slave.

37. **Correct Choice: C**
The deeply angry tone of the two sentences shows that choice C is the best response. For

choice D to be true, Grimes should have used the same words twice, rather than repeating the same idea in different words.

38. **Correct Choice: B**
The line "I have forbore to mention names in my history where it might give the least pain" suggests that Grimes is not seeking revenge. Details in the passage and a general knowledge of slave narratives and their contents show that the other four choices are likely reasons for publication.

39. **Correct Choice: D**
A slave narrative is an autobiography dealing with the writer's life as a slave. The final sentence of the passage proves that Grimes was once a slave, and the first-person point of view shows that the selection is an autobiography.

40. **Correct Choice: C**
Grimes displays self-pity in his frequent allusions to his troubles—for example, "I am now entirely destitute of property." The final two sentences show both cynicism and open rage; bitterness appears in many references to past injuries. The only quality of the five that he does not display is impatience.

41. **Correct Choice: C**
It is a given that a slave narrative will describe terrible abuse and suffering. Choice A is wrong because people frequently rewrite their lives inaccurately (in the passage, Grimes refers to his faulty memory.) Choice B is wrong because Grimes does not provide any evidence for his statements. Choice D is wrong because an inability to remember does not suggest that he is reliable. Choice E is wrong because Grimes says he is concealing names to protect people, not because he cannot remember them.

42. **Correct Choice: C**
The lines "Dear love, for nothing less than thee / Would I have broke this happy dream" (lines 1 and 2) make it clear that he was dreaming and his lover woke him up. Because it was a "happy dream," choice A is wrong.

43. **Correct Choice: A**
The speaker says "Thine eyes, and not thy noise, waked me" (line 12). He compares her eyes to the light of a taper, or candle, but this is only a simile; the actual bedside taper did not wake him.

44. **Correct Choice: C**
Suffice / histories is a slant rhyme, not an exact rhyme. The idea that thoughts of someone can make true histories out of fables is hyperbole, or exaggeration. Line 7 continues without pause into line 8, an example of enjambment. Two rhymed lines of iambic pentameter make a

heroic couplet. The lines contain no allusions to any outside source, so choice C is the only one that does not apply.

45. **Correct Choice: B**
In lines 15–18, the speaker explains that an angel would not be able to see his heart, know his thoughts, know what he was dreaming, or know when to wake him up. Because his lover *does* know all these things, she is a higher form of creation than any angel, and he was *profaning*, or insulting, her by thinking she was "only" an angel.

46. **Correct Choice: E**
The theme, or subject, of the dream deserves the logical reasoning that the speaker might bring to it awake. It is less appropriate for the fleeting, sensory impressions he feels when he is asleep and dreaming.

47. **Correct Choice: D**
The speaker praises his beloved at length for her perceptiveness; she is better than an angel because unlike an angel, she can see into his heart and know what he is thinking. The other choices are wrong because he only implies that she has beauty and loyalty, and he says nothing about her humor or intelligence.

48. **Correct Choice: B**
The action in the poem can be described as follows: The speaker awakens. Confused for a moment, he thinks an angel has awakened him. When his beloved embraces him and remains by his side, he realizes that she is not an angel, but herself. In effect he says to her, "The fact that you came to me and stayed with me showed me that you were indeed you."

49. **Correct Choice: A**
The speaker says that just as a man can light or douse a torch, his lover can kindle or quench his desire by entering or leaving the room.

50. **Correct Choice: B**
A foil is a character who serves as a contrast to the main character of a literary work, as Arthur and his guest are contrasted in this passage. The guest, not Arthur, is apparently the main character or protagonist, since his actions and thoughts are described in detail and Arthur's are not.

51. **Correct Choice: A**
The fact that the guest's clothes "smacked of the sea" and that he walks as if he were on the heaving deck of a ship suggest that he has been away at sea for a very long time. Choice B is wrong because it takes considerable physical grace to be a successful sailor, and the guest seems only afraid of awkwardness because he doesn't yet have his "land legs."

52. **Correct Choice: D**
When the guest sees that Arthur is laughing at him, it pricks his pride and puts a "fighting light" into his eyes. His feelings are hurt, but he conceals this and determines not to run away. This response shows courage.

53. **Correct Choice: E**
The guest's fears of breaking something are instinctive, not logical. The guest feels out of place on land in a nice house, because he is so accustomed to being on a ship. He is almost as unsure of himself in this setting as an animal would be. The guest's fear of breaking something emphasizes his awkwardness in his surroundings. Only choice E is untrue; the final paragraph shows that the guest does have self-control and self-discipline.

54. **Correct Choice: C**
Choices A, B, and E are only true of Arthur. Choice D is only true of the guest. Choice C is true of both; the guest is aware of Arthur's understanding, and observes Arthur's "amused glance." Arthur knows how awkward his guest feels, and he tries to reassure him and give him time to recover.

55. **Correct Choice: D**
The guest's resolve and his vow to "carry it through" suggest, with other details in the passage that show his determination, that he will not give in to his desire to run away.

56. **Correct Choice: A**
This passage concentrates almost exclusively on introducing the reader to the character of Arthur's guest.

57. **Correct Choice: C**
The author indicates that the guest is a "young fellow" who has nonetheless been at sea for several years. This suggests, along with the dialect, that he has had little formal schooling. The author shows sympathy and respect for the guest throughout the passage, so choice A is wrong. Details in the last paragraph show that the guest is observant and aware, so choice B is wrong. Readers could not identify a region from such a short dialogue, so choice D is wrong. A foreigner would speak much more formal English, so choice E is wrong.

58. **Correct Choice: D**
Arthur tries to put his guest at ease with the word *homely*, meaning that he and his family are "just plain folks," simple, friendly, nothing to be alarmed about. Choices A and C are both accurate definitions of *homely*, but they do not fit this context.

59. **Correct Choice: A**
The word *facetious* means "witty." The guest is trying to be clever in a funny way, so that Arthur won't see how scared he feels underneath.

60. **Correct Choice: B**
The presence of the piano and the table "piled high with books," plus the visual beauty that the guest responds to, suggest that Arthur and his family appreciate literature and music. Because Arthur says "we're just homely people" and there are no servants in evidence, they are probably not extremely wealthy. Nothing in the passage supports the other three choices.

HOW TO CALCULATE YOUR SCORE

Count the number of correct answers and enter the total below.
Count the number of wrong answers. Do NOT include any questions you did not answer.
Multiply the number of wrong answers by 0.25 and enter the total below.
Do the subtraction. The answer is your raw score. Use the scoring scale to find your scaled score.

$$\frac{\text{[short WOL]}}{\text{(number of correct answers)}} - \frac{\text{[short WOL]}}{\text{(number of wrong answers} \times 0.25)} = \frac{\text{[short WOL]}}{\text{(raw score)}}$$

Raw Score	Scaled Score	Raw Score	Scaled Score	Raw Score	Scaled Score	Raw Score	Scaled Score	Raw Score	Scaled Score
60	800	44	710	28	560	12	420	−4	260
59	800	43	700	27	550	11	410	−5	250
58	800	42	690	26	540	10	400	−6	240
57	800	41	690	25	530	9	390	−7	230
56	800	40	680	24	520	8	380	−8	220
55	800	39	670	23	510	7	370	−9	210
54	790	38	660	22	500	6	360	−10	200
53	790	37	650	21	500	5	350	−11	200
52	780	36	640	20	490	4	340	−12	200
51	770	35	630	19	490	3	330	−13	200
50	760	34	620	18	480	2	320	−14	200
49	750	33	610	17	470	1	310	−15	200
48	740	32	600	16	460	0	300		
47	740	31	590	15	450	−1	290		
46	730	30	580	14	440	−2	280		
45	720	29	570	13	430	−3	270		

Note: This is only a sample scoring scale. Scoring scales differ from exam to exam.

PRACTICE TEST 3

LITERATURE

The following practice test is designed to be just like the real SAT Literature Test. It matches the actual test in content coverage and degree of difficulty.

Once you finish the practice test, determine your score. Carefully read the answer explanations of all the questions you answered incorrectly. Identify any weaknesses in your literature skills by determining the areas in which you made the most errors. Review those sections of this book first. Then, as time permits, go back and review your strengths.

Allow one hour to take the test. Time yourself and work uninterrupted. If you run out of time, take note of where you stopped when time ran out. Remember that you lose a quarter point for each incorrect answer, but you do not lose points for questions you leave blank. Therefore, unless you can eliminate one or more of the five choices, it is best to leave a question unanswered.

Use the following formula to calculate your score:

(number of correct answers) – $\frac{1}{4}$ (number of incorrect answers)

If you treat this practice test just like the actual exam, it will accurately reflect how you are likely to perform on test day. Here are some hints on how to create test-taking conditions similar to those of the actual exam:

- Complete the test in one sitting. On test day, you will not be allowed to take a break.
- Do not allow yourself any extra time; put down your pencil after exactly one hour, no matter how many questions are left to answer.
- Tear out the answer sheet and fill in the ovals just as you will on the actual test day.
- Have a good eraser and more than one sharp pencil handy. On test day, you will not be able to go get a new pencil if yours breaks.
- Become familiar with the directions on the test. If you go in knowing what the directions say, you will not have to waste time reading and thinking about them on the actual test day.

PRACTICE TEST 3
LITERATURE

ANSWER SHEET

Tear out this answer sheet and use it to mark your answers.

1. Ⓐ Ⓑ Ⓒ Ⓓ Ⓔ	16. Ⓐ Ⓑ Ⓒ Ⓓ Ⓔ	31. Ⓐ Ⓑ Ⓒ Ⓓ Ⓔ	46. Ⓐ Ⓑ Ⓒ Ⓓ Ⓔ
2. Ⓐ Ⓑ Ⓒ Ⓓ Ⓔ	17. Ⓐ Ⓑ Ⓒ Ⓓ Ⓔ	32. Ⓐ Ⓑ Ⓒ Ⓓ Ⓔ	47. Ⓐ Ⓑ Ⓒ Ⓓ Ⓔ
3. Ⓐ Ⓑ Ⓒ Ⓓ Ⓔ	18. Ⓐ Ⓑ Ⓒ Ⓓ Ⓔ	33. Ⓐ Ⓑ Ⓒ Ⓓ Ⓔ	48. Ⓐ Ⓑ Ⓒ Ⓓ Ⓔ
4. Ⓐ Ⓑ Ⓒ Ⓓ Ⓔ	19. Ⓐ Ⓑ Ⓒ Ⓓ Ⓔ	34. Ⓐ Ⓑ Ⓒ Ⓓ Ⓔ	49. Ⓐ Ⓑ Ⓒ Ⓓ Ⓔ
5. Ⓐ Ⓑ Ⓒ Ⓓ Ⓔ	20. Ⓐ Ⓑ Ⓒ Ⓓ Ⓔ	35. Ⓐ Ⓑ Ⓒ Ⓓ Ⓔ	50. Ⓐ Ⓑ Ⓒ Ⓓ Ⓔ
6. Ⓐ Ⓑ Ⓒ Ⓓ Ⓔ	21. Ⓐ Ⓑ Ⓒ Ⓓ Ⓔ	36. Ⓐ Ⓑ Ⓒ Ⓓ Ⓔ	51. Ⓐ Ⓑ Ⓒ Ⓓ Ⓔ
7. Ⓐ Ⓑ Ⓒ Ⓓ Ⓔ	22. Ⓐ Ⓑ Ⓒ Ⓓ Ⓔ	37. Ⓐ Ⓑ Ⓒ Ⓓ Ⓔ	52. Ⓐ Ⓑ Ⓒ Ⓓ Ⓔ
8. Ⓐ Ⓑ Ⓒ Ⓓ Ⓔ	23. Ⓐ Ⓑ Ⓒ Ⓓ Ⓔ	38. Ⓐ Ⓑ Ⓒ Ⓓ Ⓔ	53. Ⓐ Ⓑ Ⓒ Ⓓ Ⓔ
9. Ⓐ Ⓑ Ⓒ Ⓓ Ⓔ	24. Ⓐ Ⓑ Ⓒ Ⓓ Ⓔ	39. Ⓐ Ⓑ Ⓒ Ⓓ Ⓔ	54. Ⓐ Ⓑ Ⓒ Ⓓ Ⓔ
10. Ⓐ Ⓑ Ⓒ Ⓓ Ⓔ	25. Ⓐ Ⓑ Ⓒ Ⓓ Ⓔ	40. Ⓐ Ⓑ Ⓒ Ⓓ Ⓔ	55. Ⓐ Ⓑ Ⓒ Ⓓ Ⓔ
11. Ⓐ Ⓑ Ⓒ Ⓓ Ⓔ	26. Ⓐ Ⓑ Ⓒ Ⓓ Ⓔ	41. Ⓐ Ⓑ Ⓒ Ⓓ Ⓔ	56. Ⓐ Ⓑ Ⓒ Ⓓ Ⓔ
12. Ⓐ Ⓑ Ⓒ Ⓓ Ⓔ	27. Ⓐ Ⓑ Ⓒ Ⓓ Ⓔ	42. Ⓐ Ⓑ Ⓒ Ⓓ Ⓔ	57. Ⓐ Ⓑ Ⓒ Ⓓ Ⓔ
13. Ⓐ Ⓑ Ⓒ Ⓓ Ⓔ	28. Ⓐ Ⓑ Ⓒ Ⓓ Ⓔ	43. Ⓐ Ⓑ Ⓒ Ⓓ Ⓔ	58. Ⓐ Ⓑ Ⓒ Ⓓ Ⓔ
14. Ⓐ Ⓑ Ⓒ Ⓓ Ⓔ	29. Ⓐ Ⓑ Ⓒ Ⓓ Ⓔ	44. Ⓐ Ⓑ Ⓒ Ⓓ Ⓔ	59. Ⓐ Ⓑ Ⓒ Ⓓ Ⓔ
15. Ⓐ Ⓑ Ⓒ Ⓓ Ⓔ	30. Ⓐ Ⓑ Ⓒ Ⓓ Ⓔ	45. Ⓐ Ⓑ Ⓒ Ⓓ Ⓔ	60. Ⓐ Ⓑ Ⓒ Ⓓ Ⓔ

PRACTICE TEST 3

Time: 60 minutes

Directions: This test consists of selections from literary works and questions on their content, form, and style. After reading each passage or poem, choose the best answer to each question and then fill in the corresponding oval on the answer sheet.

Note: Pay particular attention to the requirements of questions that contain the words NOT or EXCEPT.

Questions 1–9. Read the following poem carefully before you choose your answers.

When most I wink, then do mine eyes best see,
For all the day they view things unrespected;
But when I sleep, in dreams they look on thee,
And darkly bright are bright in dark directed.
5 Then thou, whose shadow shadows doth make bright,
How would thy shadow's form form happy show
To the clear day with thy much clearer light,
When to unseeing eyes thy shade shines so!
How would, I say, mine eyes be blessed made
10 By looking on thee in the living day,
When in dead night thy fair imperfect shade
Through heavy sleep on sightless eyes doth stay!
   All days are nights to see till I see thee,
   And nights bright days when dreams do show thee me.

(1609)

1. Metaphorically, the speaker sees his beloved as a source of

   (A) inspiration
   (B) strength
   (C) light
   (D) love
   (E) shadow

2. When the speaker says that his eyes "view things unrespected" (line 2), he means

   (A) he sees without noticing or observing
   (B) he feels contempt for what he sees
   (C) he cannot see because his eyes are closed
   (D) his love has robbed him of the ability to see
   (E) he feels that he is invisible to others

3. Which of the following can you conclude about the relationship between the speaker and the beloved?

     I. They are in love with each other and happy together.
     II. They were in love long ago but no longer see one another.
     III. They have not seen one another for some time.

   (A) I only
   (B) I and II only
   (C) II only
   (D) III only
   (E) II and III only

4. Which is the best paraphrase of the lines "How would thy shadow's form form happy show / To the clear day with thy much clearer light, / When to unseeing eyes thy shade shines so!" (lines 6–8)?

   (A) You were very beautiful when alive, but your ghost that I see in the darkness is even more beautiful.
   (B) Given how beautiful your image looks to me in my sleep, think how much more beautiful you would be in the light of day!
   (C) How beautiful you would look in the light of day, if people were not too blind to recognize your beauty!
   (D) You would look so beautiful in the light of day that you should not be afraid to show yourself.
   (E) Even though you have never thought you were beautiful, the admiring stares you draw prove that you are.

5. Which literary element does the poet use most extensively in this sonnet?

   (A) contrast
   (B) hyperbole
   (C) parody
   (D) simile
   (E) allusion

GO ON TO THE NEXT PAGE

PRACTICE TEST—*Continued*

6. The phrase "thy fair imperfect shade" (line 11) implies which of the following about the beloved?

(A) The speaker does not find her truly beautiful to look at.

(B) She has no existence outside the speaker's imagination.

(C) The beloved is dead and her ghost haunts the speaker.

(D) She is under a magic spell that makes her hard to see.

(E) Her image is hazy because he sees her only in his mind's eye.

7. How do lines 13–14 differ from the first 12 lines?

　I. They form a rhymed couplet.
　II. They restate and summarize the main idea of the poem.
　III. They do not rhyme with any of the other lines.

(A) I only

(B) I and III only

(C) II and III only

(D) I and II only

(E) III only

8. The imagery in this poem appeals most directly to the sense of

(A) sight

(B) hearing

(C) touch

(D) smell

(E) taste

9. By saying "All days are nights" (line 14), the speaker means

(A) days and nights are the same to him

(B) days are dark and overcast

(C) days offer him no pleasure or fun

(D) he can see nothing during the day

(E) he does not like to see people during the day

Questions 10–17. Read the following passage carefully before you choose your answers.

　At the upper end of the Fair Ground, in Winesburg, there is a half decayed old grand-stand. It has never been painted and the boards are all warped out of shape. The Fair Ground
5　stands on top of a low hill rising out of the valley of Wine Creek and from the grand-stand one can see at night, over a cornfield, the lights of the town reflected against the sky.

　George and Helen climbed the hill to the Fair
10　Ground, coming by the path past Waterworks Pond. The feeling of loneliness and isolation that had come to the young man in the crowded streets of his town was both broken and intensified by the presence of
15　Helen. What he felt was reflected in her.

　In youth there are always two forces fighting in people. The warm unthinking little animal struggles against the thing that reflects and remembers, and the older, the more sophisti-
20　cated thing had possession of George Willard. Sensing his mood, Helen walked beside him filled with respect. When they got to the grand-stand they climbed up under the roof and sat down on one of the long bench-
25　like seats.

　There is something memorable in the experience to be had by going into a fair ground that stands at the edge of a Middle Western town on a night after the annual fair has
30　been held. The sensation is one never to be forgotten. On all sides are ghosts, not of the dead, but of living people. Here, during the day just passed, have come the people pouring in from the town and the country around.
35　Farmers with their wives and children and all the people from the hundreds of little frame houses have gathered within these board walls. Young girls have laughed and men with beards have talked of the affairs of
40　their lives. The place has been filled to overflowing with life. It has itched and squirmed with life and now it is night and the life has all gone away. The silence is almost terrifying. One conceals oneself standing silently
45　beside the trunk of a tree and what there is of a reflective tendency in his nature is intensified. One shudders at the thought of the meaninglessness of life while at the same instant, and if the people of the town are his
50　people, one loves life so intensely that tears come into the eyes.

GO ON TO THE NEXT PAGE

PRACTICE TEST—*Continued*

In the darkness under the roof of the grand-stand, George Willard sat beside Helen White and felt very keenly his own insignifi-
55 cance in the scheme of existence. Now that he had come out of town where the presence of the people stirring about, busy with a multitude of affairs, had been so irritating, the irritation was all gone. The presence of
60 Helen renewed and refreshed him. It was as though her woman's hand was assisting him to make some minute readjustment of the machinery of his life. He began to think of the people in the town where he had always
65 lived with something like reverence. He had reverence for Helen. He wanted to love and to be loved by her, but he did not want at the moment to be confused by her womanhood. In the darkness he took hold of her hand and
70 when she crept close put a hand on her shoulder. A wind began to blow and he shiv-ered. With all his strength he tried to hold and to understand the mood that had come upon him. In that high place in the darkness
75 the two oddly sensitive human atoms held each other tightly and waited. In the mind of each was the same thought. "I have come to this lonely place and here is this other," was the substance of the thing felt.

(1919)

10. Which quality in this setting brings out the "reflec-tive tendency" in a person's character?

(A) the silence and stillness
(B) the ghosts of the people who have gone home
(C) the moon lighting up the darkness
(D) the decay of the grand-stand's board seats
(E) the company of another person

11. The "two forces" that "are always fighting in people" (lines 16–17) might be identified as

(A) youth and age
(B) temptation and discipline
(C) the heart and the brain
(D) courage and fear
(E) happiness and sorrow

12. From whose point of view is this passage written?

(A) George's
(B) Helen's
(C) a first-person narrator's
(D) an omniscient narrator's
(E) a limited third-person narrator's

13. What is the effect of setting this scene at the top of the grand-stand?

(A) It physically isolates George and Helen from the town, mirroring their emotional isolation from it.
(B) It explains why George and Helen are so unhappy with each other and the town they live in.
(C) It intensifies the romance of the scene and fore-shadows what is to come.
(D) It helps the reader identify with George, Helen, and their hopes for romance.
(E) It allows the reader to understand what kind of town George and Helen come from.

14. The emotion Helen and George feel for each other in the passage is best described as

(A) romance
(B) comradeship
(C) desire
(D) wariness
(E) curiosity

15. The phrase "he did not want at the moment to be con-fused by her womanhood" (lines 67–68) implies that George

(A) does not like Helen and wants her to leave him alone
(B) would be more comfortable with Helen if she were a boy
(C) does not want to kiss Helen or talk to her of love
(D) regrets bringing Helen to the Fair Ground with him
(E) does not know what to say to Helen and hopes she will help him

16. Which major theme does the passage address?

(A) the pain of loving a person who does not respond
(B) the conformity of small-town society
(C) the reawakening of nature in spring
(D) the transition from youth to maturity
(E) the struggle between temptation and discipline

GO ON TO THE NEXT PAGE

PRACTICE TEST—*Continued*

17. Which of the following can you conclude about the narrator of the passage?

> I. He has been through experiences similar to George and Helen's.
> II. He lives in Winesburg and has often been to the Fair Ground.
> III. He is a close friend of George and Helen's.

(A) I only
(B) II only
(C) I and III only
(D) II and III only
(E) III only

Questions 18–24. Read the following poem carefully before you choose your answers.

The Wild Swans at Coole

The trees are in their autumn beauty,
The woodland paths are dry,
Under the October twilight the water
Mirrors a still sky;
5 Upon the brimming water among the stones
Are nine-and-fifty swans.

The nineteenth autumn has come upon me
Since I first made my count;
I saw, before I had well finished,
10 All suddenly mount
And scatter wheeling in great broken rings
Upon their clamorous wings.

I have looked upon those brilliant creatures,
And now my heart is sore.
15 All's changed since I, hearing at twilight,
The first time on this shore,
The bell-beat of their wings above my head,
Trod with a lighter tread.

Unwearied still, lover by lover,
20 They paddle in the cold
Companionable streams or climb the air;
Their hearts have not grown old;
Passion or conquest, wander where they will,
Attend upon them still.

25 But now they drift on the still water,
Mysterious, beautiful;
Among what rushes will they build,
By what lake's edge or pool
Delight men's eyes when I awake some day
30 To find they have flown away?

(1919)

18. The image "their clamorous wings" (line 12) appeals to which of the five senses?

(A) sight
(B) hearing
(C) taste
(D) touch
(E) smell

19. In which sense does the speaker use the phrase "attend upon" (line 24)?

(A) to pay attention to
(B) to wait for
(C) to be present at
(D) to accompany
(E) to assist; to wait on

20. For the speaker, the swans symbolize

(A) love
(B) nature
(C) grace
(D) strength
(E) serenity

21. This poem is best described as

(A) a ballad
(B) a sonnet
(C) a lyric poem
(D) a narrative poem
(E) a dramatic monologue

22. Which of the following is an example of slant rhyme?

(A) stones/swans (lines 5 and 6)
(B) creatures/twilight (lines 13 and 15)
(C) head/tread (lines 17 and 18)
(D) passion/conquest (line 23)
(E) day/away (lines 29 and 30)

23. What does the speaker mean by saying that the swans' hearts "have not grown old" (line 22)?

(A) They are not the same swans he first saw.
(B) They have made his heart sore.
(C) They are healthy and strong.
(D) They are still capable of feeling emotion.
(E) They show no physical signs of aging.

GO ON TO THE NEXT PAGE ➡

PRACTICE TEST—*Continued*

24. Which best captures the swans' effect on the speaker?

    (A) They cause his heart to ache.
    (B) They fill him with elation.
    (C) They distract him from writing.
    (D) They inspire him with awe.
    (E) They comfort him with their friendliness.

Questions 25–33. Read the following speech carefully before you choose your answers.

Friends and fellow citizens: I stand before you tonight under indictment for the alleged crime of having voted at the last presidential election, without having a lawful right to
5 vote. It shall be my work this evening to prove to you that in thus voting, I not only committed no crime, but, instead, simply exercised my citizen's rights, guaranteed to me and all United States citizens by the
10 National Constitution, beyond the power of any state to deny.

The preamble of the Federal Constitution says:

"We, the people of the United States, in order
15 to form a more perfect union, establish justice, insure domestic tranquility, provide for the common defense, promote the general welfare, and secure the blessings of liberty to ourselves and our posterity, do ordain and
20 establish this Constitution for the United States of America."

It was we, the people; not we, the white male citizens; nor yet we, the male citizens; but we, the whole people, who formed the Union.
25 And we formed it, not to give the blessings of liberty, but to secure them; not to the half of ourselves and the half of our posterity, but to the whole people—women as well as men. And it is a downright mockery to talk to
30 women of their enjoyment of the blessings of liberty while they are denied the use of the only means of securing them provided by this democratic-republican government—the ballot.

35 For any state to make sex a qualification that must ever result in the disfranchisement of one entire half of the people, is to pass a bill of attainder, or, an ex post facto law, and is therefore a violation of the supreme law of

40 the land. By it the blessings of liberty are forever withheld from women and their female posterity.

To them this government has no just powers derived from the consent of the governed. To
45 them this government is not a democracy. It is not a republic. It is an odious aristocracy; a hateful oligarchy of sex; the most hateful aristocracy ever established on the face of the globe; an oligarchy of wealth, where the
50 rich govern the poor. An oligarchy of learning, where the educated govern the ignorant, or even an oligarchy of race, where the Saxon rules the African, might be endured; but this oligarchy of sex, which makes father,
55 brothers, husband, sons, the oligarchs over the mother and sisters, the wife and daughters, of every household—which ordains all men sovereigns, all women subjects, carries dissension, discord, and rebellion into every
60 home of the nation.

Webster, Worcester, and Bouvier all define a citizen to be a person in the United States, entitled to vote and hold office.

The only question left to be settled now is:
65 Are women persons? And I hardly believe any of our opponents will have the hardihood to say they are not. Being persons, then, women are citizens; and no state has a right to make any law, or to enforce any old
70 law, that shall abridge their privileges or immunities. Hence, every discrimination against women in the constitutions and laws of the several states is today null and void, precisely as is every one against Negroes.

(1873)

 GO ON TO THE NEXT PAGE

PRACTICE TEST—*Continued*

25. Which of the following states the main idea of the speech?

    (A) "I stand before you tonight under indictment for the alleged crime of having voted at the last presidential election, without having a lawful right to vote." (lines 1–5)

    (B) "We formed it, not to give the blessings of liberty, but to secure them; not to the half of ourselves and the half of our posterity, but to the whole people—women as well as men." (lines 25–28)

    (C) "To them this government is not a democracy. It is not a republic. It is an odious aristocracy; a hateful oligarchy of sex; the most hateful aristocracy ever established on the face of the globe." (lines 43–49)

    (D) "This oligarchy of sex, which . . . ordains all men sovereigns, all women subjects, carries dissension, discord, and rebellion into every home of the nation." (lines 54–60)

    (E) "Being persons, then, women are citizens; and no state has a right to make any law, or to enforce any old law, that shall abridge their privileges or immunities." (lines 67–71)

26. What is the effect of the repetition of the word "oligarchy" throughout the fifth paragraph?

    (A) to explain why the speaker was arrested
    (B) to identify the speaker's cause with democracy and freedom
    (C) to convince the women in the audience to defy their husbands
    (D) to persuade the speaker's opponents that she is right
    (E) to support the speaker's main idea

27. Why does the speaker cite Webster, Worcester, and Bouvier (line 61)?

    (A) to show that their published writings support her argument
    (B) to suggest that everyone should go home and read their works
    (C) to explain why they accuse her of committing a crime
    (D) to demonstrate that she is an educated citizen
    (E) to emphasize that in the United States, men have more rights than women

28. Why does the speaker address her audience as "fellow citizens" (line 1)?

    I.   to draw attention to the subject and main idea of her speech
    II. to remind both male and female listeners that they are citizens
    III. to show that she is a patriotic American

    (A) I only
    (B) II only
    (C) I and III only
    (D) II and III only
    (E) I, II, and III

29. The word "posterity" (line 27) is best defined as

    (A) slaves
    (B) citizens
    (C) representatives
    (D) descendants
    (E) voters

30. Which best characterizes the speaker?

    (A) wistful, dreamy, unrealistic
    (B) emotional, upset, irrational
    (C) satirical, cynical, humorous
    (D) enraged, prejudiced, biased
    (E) stubborn, intelligent, defiant

31. What is meant by the phrase "abridge their privileges or immunities" (lines 70–71)?

    (A) curtail their rights and protections under the law
    (B) make them less able to protect themselves
    (C) allow them to read only shortened versions of important documents
    (D) abolish their right to run for state or national office
    (E) amend the Constitution to grant them the right to vote

GO ON TO THE NEXT PAGE

PRACTICE TEST—*Continued*

32. To which historical event does the speaker allude in the final sentence?

   (A) the American victory over Great Britain in the Revolutionary War
   (B) the national adoption of the Constitution by the individual states
   (C) the passage of the Reconstruction Amendments to the Constitution
   (D) the Union victory at the Battle of Gettysburg during the Civil War
   (E) the start of the Civil War at Fort Sumter, South Carolina, in 1861

33. The speech addresses all of the following universal themes EXCEPT

   (A) love
   (B) equality
   (C) freedom
   (D) progress
   (E) justice

Questions 34–40. Read the following passage carefully before you choose your answers.

And first, truly, to all them that, professing learning, inveigh against poetry, may justly be objected that they go very near to ungratefulness, to seek to deface that which, in the
5 noblest nations and languages that are known, hath been the first light-giver to ignorance, and first nurse, whose milk by little and little enabled them to feed afterwards of tougher knowledges. And will they now play
10 the hedgehog that, being received into the den, drave out his host? Or rather the vipers, that with their birth kill their parents?

Let learned Greece in any of his manifold sciences be able to show me one book before
15 Musaeus, Homer, and Hesiod, all three nothing else but poets. Nay, let any history be brought that can say any writers were there before them, if they were not men of the same skill, as Orpheus, Linus, and some
20 others are named, who, having been the first of that country that made pens deliverers of their knowledge to their posterity, may justly challenge to be called their fathers in learning; for not only in time they had this priority
25 (although in itself antiquity be venerable) but went before them, as causes to draw with their charming sweetness the wild untamed wits to an admiration of knowledge. So, as

Amphion was said to move stones with his
30 poetry to build Thebes, and Orpheus to be listened to by beasts, indeed, stony and beastly people; so among the Romans were Livius Andronicus and Ennius. So in the Italian language the first that made it aspire to
35 be a treasure-house of science were the poets Dante, Boccaccio, and Petrarch. So in our English were Gower and Chaucer, after whom, encouraged and delighted with their excellent fore-going, others have followed, to
40 beautify our mother tongue, as well in the same kind as in other arts.

(1595)

34. To "inveigh against poetry" (line 2) means

   (A) to enjoy reading it
   (B) to write it badly
   (C) to express contempt for it
   (D) to teach it in schools
   (E) to refuse to publish it

35. What is the author's main purpose in writing this passage?

   (A) to list great poets of many different nations and cultures
   (B) to praise the great poets of earlier ages
   (C) to complain about the quality of scientific and historical writing
   (D) to persuade people to read more poetry
   (E) to prove that poetry is the greatest of all the arts

36. To support his main argument, the author uses all of the following EXCEPT

   (A) specific examples
   (B) literary and historical allusions
   (C) logical reasoning
   (D) loaded language
   (E) scientific proofs

GO ON TO THE NEXT PAGE

PRACTICE TEST—*Continued*

37. When the author says that "Orpheus, Linus, and some others . . . made pens deliverers of their knowledge to their posterity" (lines 19–22), he means that

    (A) they wrote down their life stories for their descendants to read
    (B) they left their pens to their descendants in their wills
    (C) they passed on to their descendants the ability to write poetry
    (D) their descendants can find out what they knew by reading their written work
    (E) all living poets are descendants of the poets of ancient Greece

38. What claim does the author make for poetry in the statement "for not only in time they had this priority . . . but went before them, as causes to draw with their charming sweetness the wild untamed wits to an admiration of knowledge" (lines 24–28)?

    (A) It was developed later than any of the other arts.
    (B) Its beauty attracted listeners and made them want to acquire learning.
    (C) It is superior to science because it is a product of the human imagination.
    (D) It has inspired great writers in every age and culture.
    (E) It was created by the greatest and most famous of the Greek philosophers.

39. To what does the author compare poetry in the opening paragraph?

    (A) light and nourishment
    (B) nations and languages
    (C) hedgehogs and vipers
    (D) history and science
    (E) nobility and toughness

40. In what way does the author suggest that poetry is like the "first nurse" (line 7)?

    (A) It feeds the heart and soul with its beauty.
    (B) It entertains the listener or reader.
    (C) It enriches and nourishes the mind.
    (D) It provides rhymes with which nurses sing babies to sleep.
    (E) It enlightens and teaches ignorant people.

41. To what does the author compare those who criticize poetry in the opening paragraph?

    (A) ungratefulness and ignorance
    (B) first nurse and tougher knowledges
    (C) ignorance and hedgehogs
    (D) ignorance and tougher knowledges
    (E) hedgehogs and vipers

Questions 42–48. Read the following poem carefully before you choose your answers.

Bird-spirit

I am the nearest nightingale
That singeth in Eden after you;
And I am singing loud and true,
And sweet,—I do not fail.
5 I sit upon a cypress bough,
Close to the gate, and I fling my song
Over the gate and through the mail
Of the warden angels marshall'd strong,—
        Over the gate and after you!
10 And the warden angels let it pass,
Because the poor brown bird, alas,
        Sings in the garden, sweet and true.
And I build my song of high pure notes,
        Note over note, height over height,
15   Till I strike the arch of the Infinite,
And I bridge abysmal agonies
With strong, clear calms of harmonies,—
And something abides, and something floats,
In the song which I sing after you.
20   Fare ye well, farewell!
The creature-sounds, no longer audible,
        Expire at Eden's door.
        Each footstep of your treading
Treads out some cadence which ye heard before
25   Farewell! the birds of Eden
        Ye shall hear nevermore!

                                        (c. 1840)

42. For whom is the nightingale singing?

    (A) the warden angels
    (B) someone who lives in Eden
    (C) a poor brown bird
    (D) the arch of the Infinite
    (E) someone who is leaving Eden

43. What does the author mean in the use of the word "marshall'd" (line 8)?

    (A) dispersed
    (B) arranged in an orderly manner
    (C) arrayed for battle
    (D) led ceremoniously
    (E) scattered

GO ON TO THE NEXT PAGE ➡

PRACTICE TEST—*Continued*

44. Which is the best definition of "abysmal agonies" (line 16)?

    (A) profound suffering
    (B) intense physical pain
    (C) total ignorance
    (D) deep caverns
    (E) endless sorrow

45. What can you conclude about the "warden angels" (line 8)?

    (A) They do not let anyone out through the gate of Eden.
    (B) They are there to protect Eden from intruders or enemies.
    (C) They cannot hear the song of the nightingale.
    (D) They do not want the nightingale to sing.
    (E) They pass judgment on those who live in Eden.

46. The nightingale's chief characteristic is

    (A) passion
    (B) courage
    (C) loyalty
    (D) bitterness
    (E) timidity

47. The nightingale believes that her song may affect the listener by

    (A) charming him
    (B) comforting him and easing his sorrow
    (C) transforming him into another creature
    (D) making him fall in love with her
    (E) making him return to her

48. "Farewell! The birds of Eden / Ye shall hear never-more!" (lines 25–26) is an example of

    (A) a couplet
    (B) personification
    (C) enjambment
    (D) free verse
    (E) iambic pentameter

Questions 49–60. Read the following passage carefully before you choose your answers.

It was about this time I conceived the bold and arduous project of arriving at moral perfection. I wished to live without committing any fault at any time; I would conquer all
5   that either natural inclination, custom, or company might lead me into. As I knew, or thought I knew, what was right and wrong, I did not see why I might not *always* do the one and avoid the other. But I soon found I had
10 undertaken a task of more difficulty than I had imagined . . .

My list of virtues contained at first but twelve. But a Quaker friend having kindly informed me that I was generally thought
15 proud, that my pride showed itself frequently in conversation, that I was not content with being in the right when discussing any point, but was overbearing and rather insolent—of which he convinced me by mentioning several
20 instances—I determined endeavouring to cure myself if I could of this vice or folly among the rest, and I added *Humility* to my list, giving an extensive meaning to the word. I cannot boast of much success in acquiring
25 the *reality* of this virtue, but I had a good deal with regard to the *appearance* of it. I made it a rule to forbear all direct contradiction to the sentiments of others and all positive assertion of my own. I even forbid myself
30 agreeable to the old laws of our Junto,[1] the use of every word or expression in the language that imported a fixed opinion, such as *certainly, undoubtedly,* etc.; and I adopted instead of them, *I conceive, I apprehend,* or *I*
35 *imagine* a thing to be so or so, or *It so appears to me at present.* When another asserted something that I thought an error, I denied myself the pleasure of contradicting him abruptly and of showing immediately some
40 absurdity in his proposition; and in answering I began by observing that in certain cases or circumstances his opinion would be right, but in the present case there *appeared* or *seemed to me* some difference, etc. I soon
45 found the advantage of this change in my manners: The conversations I engaged in went on more pleasantly; the modest way in which I proposed my opinions procured them a readier reception and less contradic-
50 tion; I had less mortification when I was found to be in the wrong, and I more easily

[1] an informal debating and essay-writing club to which the author belonged

GO ON TO THE NEXT PAGE →

PRACTICE TEST—*Continued*

prevailed with others to give up their mistakes and join with me when I happened to be in the right. And this mode, which I at first
55 put on with some violence to natural inclination, became at length so easy and so habitual to me that perhaps for these fifty years past no one has ever heard a dogmatical expression escape me. And to this habit (after my
60 character of integrity) I think it principally owing that I had early so much weight with my fellow citizens when I proposed new institutions or alterations in the old, and so much influence in public councils when I became a
65 member. For I was but a bad speaker, never eloquent, subject to much hesitation in my choice of words, hardly correct in language, and yet I generally carried my point.

In reality there is perhaps no one of our nat-
70 ural passions so hard to subdue as *pride*; disguise it, struggle with it, beat it down, stifle it, mortify it as much as one pleases, it is still alive, and will every now and then peep out and show itself. You will see it perhaps
75 often in this history. For even if I could conceive that I had completely overcome it, I should probably be proud of my humility.

(1784)

49. In what sense is the Quaker friend "kind" to the author?

   I. in helping him see himself more accurately than before
   II. in refraining from offering any criticism of his character
   III. in helping him to identify the virtues he wants to adopt

(A) I only
(B) II only
(C) III only
(D) I and II only
(E) I and III only

50. The phrase "I had less mortification when I was found to be in the wrong" (lines 50–51) is best paraphrased as

(A) I hated to be proved mistaken, because it was so humiliating.
(B) I was so embarrassed to be proved wrong that I wanted to die.
(C) I never felt the embarrassment of being wrong, because I was always right.

(D) It was no longer so humiliating to have to admit to a mistake.
(E) Other people were more eager than before to prove that I was wrong.

51. The phrase "I should probably be proud of my humility" (line 77) is an example of

(A) a paradox
(B) a metaphor
(C) personification
(D) an allusion
(E) a play on words

52. In the third paragraph, what effect does the series of verbs beginning "disguise it" have?

(A) demonstrates how easy it is to behave humbly
(B) encourages the reader to follow the author's example
(C) supports the point made in the previous clause of the sentence
(D) proves the author's statement that he is a bad speaker
(E) explains why it is important to appear humble

53. Which best characterizes the author of the passage?

(A) self-aware and humorous
(B) haughty and arrogant
(C) mild and humble
(D) temperamental and emotional
(E) gracious and kind

54. The author uses the word "pride" to mean

(A) temperament
(B) intellect
(C) snobbery
(D) arrogance
(E) haughtiness

55. The passage is an example of

(A) an oral history
(B) a persuasive essay
(C) an autobiography
(D) a character analysis
(E) an instruction manual

GO ON TO THE NEXT PAGE

PRACTICE TEST—*Continued*

56. Why does the author find the task of "arriving at moral perfection" to be so difficult?

    (A) because he does not really know right from wrong
    (B) because he is often tempted to do something wrong
    (C) because other people make fun of his attempts to do right
    (D) because there are too many virtues on his list
    (E) because the idea of arriving at moral perfection is unrealistic

57. In which pair do the two words NOT convey the same, or approximately the same, idea?

    (A) bold and arduous (lines 1–2)
    (B) overbearing and insolent (line 18)
    (C) vice or folly (line 21)
    (D) contradiction and assertion (lines 27–29)
    (E) conceive and imagine (lines 34–35)

58. Which line from the passage best supports the writer's claim to have achieved the appearance of humility?

    (A) "I wished to live without committing any fault at any time" (lines 3–4)
    (B) "I was not content with being in the right when discussing any point" (lines 16–17)
    (C) "I soon found the advantage to this change in my manners" (lines 44–46)
    (D) "I was but a bad speaker, never eloquent . . . hardly correct in language" (lines 65–67)
    (E) "In reality there is perhaps no one of our natural passions so hard to subdue as *pride*" (lines 69–70)

59. For the author, the concept of humility encompasses all of the following EXCEPT

    (A) diplomacy
    (B) humor
    (C) modesty
    (D) politeness
    (E) tact

60. The first sentence of the last paragraph includes an example of which literary technique?

    (A) personification
    (B) alliteration
    (C) exposition
    (D) resolution
    (E) prediction

STOP

IF YOU FINISH BEFORE TIME IS CALLED, YOU MAY CHECK YOUR WORK ON THIS TEST ONLY.

DO NOT TURN TO ANY OTHER TEST IN THIS BOOK.

ANSWER KEY

1. C	21. C	41. E
2. A	22. A	42. E
3. D	23. D	43. B
4. B	24. D	44. A
5. A	25. E	45. B
6. E	26. B	46. C
7. D	27. A	47. B
8. A	28. E	48. C
9. C	29. D	49. E
10. A	30. E	50. D
11. C	31. A	51. A
12. D	32. C	52. C
13. A	33. A	53. A
14. B	34. C	54. D
15. C	35. E	55. C
16. D	36. E	56. B
17. A	37. D	57. D
18. B	38. B	58. D
19. B	39. A	59. B
20. E	40. C	60. A

ANSWERS AND EXPLANATIONS

1. **Correct Choice: C**
   Throughout the poem, the speaker associates his beloved with images of light.

2. **Correct Choice: A**
   The speaker explains that he pays no attention to what he sees during the day, when his eyes are open. The only image he cares for is that of his beloved, which he only sees at night when his eyes are closed.

3. **Correct Choice: D**
   The speaker says that he never sees his beloved except in his imagination and in his dreams. Therefore Option III must be true. Option II cannot be true because the speaker is clearly still in love. Because the two people do not meet, and the speaker never suggests that his love is returned, Option I is unlikely to be true.

4. **Correct Choice: B**
   In modern terms, *form happy show* means "make an attractive picture" or "make a lovely sight." The speaker says, in effect, "How lovely your form would appear in the clear light of day, since your image shines so brightly to my unseeing eyes at night!"

5. **Correct Choice: A**
   The poet contrasts images of darkness/light and night/day in almost every line of the sonnet.

6. **Correct Choice: E**
   Shade is used here to mean "image." The speaker cannot see the beloved clearly because she is only an image or shadow in his memory; therefore she appears *imperfect*, like an out-of-focus picture.

7. **Correct Choice: D**
   Option I is true; like all Shakespearean sonnets, this poem has three quatrains with an ABAB rhyme scheme, followed by a rhymed couplet. Option II is true because the purpose of a Shakespearean sonnet's final couplet is to sum up, resolve, and/or restate the main ideas set forth in the four quatrains. Option III is not true because lines 13 and 14 rhyme with lines 1 and 3.

8. **Correct Choice: A**
   The images are all about darkness and light and what the speaker can and cannot see.

9. **Correct Choice: C**
   The speaker's only pleasure is seeing his beloved's image, and he can only see her in his dreams at night. Therefore the days are nothing to look forward to or enjoy. Choice B is only correct in a metaphorical sense; choice C is a better description of what the speaker actually means.

10. **Correct Choice: A**
    The narrator suggests that the Fair Ground inspires reflection because it is quiet and deserted, when its normal state is to be crowded, busy, and noisy. The fact that everyone has gone home contributes to this, but it is the place itself, not the people who have gone home, that puts George and Helen in a thoughtful mood.

11. **Correct Choice: C**
    The narrator describes the two forces as animal warmth and a quality that "reflects and remembers." These can readily be identified with the brain and the emotions, or the heart.

12. **Correct Choice: D**
    Omniscient means "all-knowing." An omniscient narrator may share any or all the characters' thoughts and feelings with the reader. The narrator of this passage describes both George's and Helen's thoughts. A limited third-person narrator could only describe one character's thoughts. A first-person narrator would use the pronouns *I* and *me*.

13. **Correct Choice: A**
    The top of the grand-stand is as far as George and Helen can get from the rest of the town without leaving it. Their physical isolation up there echoes the loneliness and isolation of their mood.

14. **Correct Choice: B**
    The boy and girl achieve true mutual understanding in the passage, without having to say anything. They are united in thought and feeling. This makes them kindred spirits, comrades, or true friends. *Romance* and *desire* are inappropriate choices because George specifically does not want "to be confused by Helen's womanhood" at this moment.

15. **Correct Choice: C**
    George's feelings for Helen are intense, but they are not romantic or physical. In this scene, they respond to one another as two human beings, not as a boy and girl. For the moment, George wants to experience this deep human communication, rather than turning it into a conventional romantic or physical situation.

16. **Correct Choice: D**
    The passage describes a crucial moment in George's life (and to a lesser extent in Helen's)—the moment when he begins to leave his boyhood behind to become a mature adult.

17. **Correct Choice: A**

   The narrator never identifies himself, so there is no way to know whether he knows George and Helen or comes from the same town. He does know from his own knowledge what it is like to go to a Midwestern fair ground at night, and he describes doing much the same thing that George and Helen do; in his case, "standing silently beside the trunk of a tree" and reflecting on life and on the people in his community.

18. **Correct Choice: B**

   Clamorous means "noisy." Swans are very large birds, and when they take off in flight, their wings make a tremendous noise.

19. **Correct Choice: B**

   All five are correct definitions of *attend upon*, but the context makes it clear that the speaker uses the archaic meaning "wait for." No matter where the swans go, high adventures and strong emotions wait for them.

20. **Correct Choice: E**

   The speaker comments that the swans' "hearts have not grown old," contrasting this to his own heart, which is "sore." He characterizes them as being untroubled and "unwearied," wishing he were the same. Serenity best captures what he sees and longs for in the swans.

21. **Correct Choice: C**

   A lyric poem has a single speaker who describes his or her personal thoughts and feelings. It does not tell a story so much as it evokes an emotion in the reader.

22. **Correct Choice: A**

   Slant rhyme (or off rhyme) refers to two words that have the same consonant sounds, but different vowel sounds. *Stones/swans* is thus an example of slant rhyme. Choices C and E are exact rhymes, and choices B and D are words that do not rhyme at all.

23. **Correct Choice: D**

   In spite of the passage of years, the swans are "unwearied." "Their hearts have not grown old" means that their emotions are still those of youth—strong and passionate.

24. **Correct Choice: D**

   The speaker describes the swans as *brilliant, beautiful,* and *mysterious.* Choice D best captures the thrill that their beauty, strength, and majesty give him. Since he is unhappy, Choice B must be wrong. Choice A is wrong because, if anything, the sight of the swans' beauty seems to comfort him.

25. **Correct Choice: E**

   The speaker's main purpose is to prove to her audience that women are citizens and therefore have the right to vote.

26. **Correct Choice: B**

   By stating that her opponents support oligarchy, or government by the few, the speaker implies that those who agree with her support democracy. By repeating *oligarchy* so many times in a few sentences, she implies that her opponents and their beliefs are undemocratic, therefore un-American and wrong.

27. **Correct Choice: A**

   The speaker cites respected works of reference to prove that important writers agree with her main point.

28. **Correct Choice: E**

   Options I and II are true because the opening address emphasizes the main point; everyone born in the United States is a citizen and is thus entitled to certain rights, such as the right to vote when old enough. Option III is true because anyone who exercises the right to vote is doing his or her civic duty, taking an active part in government, and is by that very act a patriotic American.

29. **Correct Choice: D**

   The context shows that *posterity* refers to future generations of a family or society.

30. **Correct Choice: E**

   The first three choices are clearly wrong. Choice D is an overstatement; the speaker is too reasonable and logical in her argument to be labeled *biased* or *prejudiced.* Choice E fairly sums her up as someone who is so determined to fight for her rights that she is even willing to risk arrest.

31. **Correct Choice: A**

   To *abridge* means to make less, to curtail, to shorten. A *privilege,* in this context, is a legal right. An *immunity* is a legal protection.

32. **Correct Choice: C**

   The reference to "Negroes," the post–Civil War date of the passage (1873), and the fact that the topic is constitutional rights are the clues that tell you she is referring to the passage of the amendments that abolished slavery and granted African Americans the right to vote (Amendments 13–15; passed between 1865 and 1870).

33. **Correct Choice: A**

   The speech deals with *equality* of the sexes, *freedom* for women, the *progress* of society toward the ideals of democracy, and the *justice* of giving equal rights to all citizens. Only Choice A is not addressed in this speech.

34. **Correct Choice: C**

   The context makes it clear that the speaker is defending poetry against those who criticize or sneer at it.

35. **Correct Choice: E**

    Almost every sentence in the passage is written to show that poetry is the earliest and greatest of the arts. Choices A and B are secondary purposes used to support the primary purpose described in Choice E. Choice D might be an effect of reading the passage but is not part of the author's purpose.

36. **Correct Choice: E**

    The poets' names and descriptions of their activities account for choices A and B. The general tone of the passage and the specific supporting details account for choice C. The comparison to hedgehogs and vipers accounts for choice D. The only type of persuasion that does NOT appear is choice E.

37. **Correct Choice: D**

    Pens deliver knowledge by writing it down on paper, so that it can be passed on to future generations. The author is saying that Orpheus, Linus, and the others wrote down what they knew, and thus passed on their knowledge to those who came after them.

38. **Correct Choice: B**

    The author states that poetry is so charming and enticing that it made people enjoy reading and learning; because studying poetry is so delightful, people begin to seek other kinds of knowledge.

39. **Correct Choice: A**

    The author states that poetry is a "light-giver to ignorance" and humankind's "first nurse."

40. **Correct Choice: C**

    The nurse's milk feeds and nourishes the baby, making it strong enough to eat and digest solid food. In the same way, poetry enriches and nourishes the mind, stretching it and opening it up so that it can understand more difficult subjects, such as science or philosophy.

41. **Correct Choice: E**

    The author compares those who criticize poetry to hedgehogs that drive their hosts out of the den and vipers who kill their parents at birth. Ungratefulness is mentioned, but those who criticize poetry are not compared to it. Ignorance is mentioned in the context of poetry being the first light-giver. "Tougher knowledges" are the disciplines that developed from poetry.

42. **Correct Choice: E**

    The line "I fling my song / Over the gate and after you" makes it clear that the bird is in Eden, but the one for whom she sings is outside the gate. The repeated "Farewell" and the reference to "each footstep of your treading" suggest that the listener started out in Eden but is moving away.

43. **Correct Choice: B**

    The angels are the wardens of heaven and are placed in a formation as guards at the entrance. The best match is Choice B. Choices A and E are wrong because "dispersed" and "scattered" mean the opposite of orderly. These choices are also synonyms, which should indicate to you that they are wrong. Even though "marshall'd" has a military tone, choice C is wrong because the angels are not preparing for battle. Choice D is wrong because the angels are not going anywhere.

44. **Correct Choice: A**

    Abysmal means "like an abyss," therefore "profound, deep." *Agonies* in this context means "suffering."

45. **Correct Choice: B**

    The word "warden" shows that the angels are guards at the gate. It is a guard's job either to keep enemies from entering an enclosed place or to prevent prisoners from leaving. The best match to this is choice B. Because the exile is leaving Eden, choice A is wrong.

46. **Correct Choice: C**

    You can conclude that the exile from Eden must have committed a sin or crime, or he would not be sent away. The nightingale's concern for the exile, and her attempt to reach him in song, prove that she is loyal to him in spite of his transgression.

47. **Correct Choice: B**

    The line "And I bridge abysmal agonies" suggests that the nightingale sings in order to give comfort to one who is suffering.

48. **Correct Choice: C**

    A line of verse that has a punctuation mark at the end is referred to as *end-stopped*. If the line has no punctuation mark at the end, the thought continues without pause to the next line. This technique is called *enjambment*.

49. **Correct Choice: E**

    The Quaker pointed out a serious character flaw to the author, thus helping him to overcome it. Once the author sees his own flaw, he can complete his list of virtues. Option II is wrong because the Quaker did exactly the opposite of this.

50. **Correct Choice: D**

    Mortification is a somewhat more intense synonym for "humiliation" —if you are *mortified*, you literally "wish you were dead." The author explains that it was much more humiliating to be proved wrong when he was overly insistent in the first place on being right. Now that he is less insistent, he is less embarrassed when he turns out to be mistaken.

51. **Correct Choice: A**
A paradox is a statement that includes a contradiction. A truly humble person cannot be proud, because humility means the absence of pride. Yet, the possession of such a great virtue as humility is something to be proud of.

52. **Correct Choice: C**
The sentence's opening clause states that "there is . . . no one of our natural passions so hard to subdue as pride." The series of verbs supports this point by describing this as a physical effort: "struggle with it, beat it down, stifle it" all describe hard physical work.

53. **Correct Choice: A**
The author's open avowal that he is not really humble, but only appears so, shows how aware he is of his true character. The general tone of the passage is humorous, especially the final sentence.

54. **Correct Choice: D**
To the author, *pride* seems to mean an unswerving belief in the rightness of his own opinions and an insistence on proving wrong anyone who disagrees with him. *Righteousness*—a firm belief that one is always right—is the best match for this kind of pride. *Haughtiness* and *snobbery* refer to pride in one's social superiority; because the author discusses only his sense of intellectual superiority, these are not accurate definitions of *pride* as described in this passage.

55. **Correct Choice: C**
The passage describes certain experiences in the author's life. He makes some comments about his own character, but this is not the primary purpose of the passage. A reader wishing to follow the author's example might use the text as an instructional manual, but the author's primary purpose was to write the story of his life.

56. **Correct Choice: B**
The author says that speaking humbly is against his natural inclinations and that contradicting people and making them look foolish was a pleasure to him. In other words, he is accustomed to doing the wrong thing because of strong temptation. Although moral perfection sounds like an unrealistic goal, the speaker apparently did achieve it.

57. **Correct Choice: D**
A *contradiction* is a denial; an *assertion* is the opposite, a positive statement.

58. **Correct Choice: D**
This statement is the most self-deprecating, or humble, of the five choices, and thus provides the best evidence that the author has succeeded in his goal of at least appearing humble.

59. **Correct Choice: B**
The author has a sense of humor but does not suggest that humor is an essential part of being humble. He does explain and demonstrate that if a person wishes not to appear proud, he or she must master tact, modesty, diplomacy, and politeness.

60. **Correct Choice: A**
Pride is personified throughout the entire sentence as an entity that can be struggled with, beaten down, stifled and mortified.

HOW TO CALCULATE YOUR SCORE

Count the number of correct answers and enter the total below.
Count the number of wrong answers. Do NOT include any questions you did not answer.
Multiply the number of wrong answers by 0.25 and enter the total below.
Do the subtraction. The answer is your raw score. Use the scoring scale to find your scaled score.

$$\underset{\text{(number of correct answers)}}{[\text{short WOL}]} - \underset{\text{(number of wrong answers} \times 0.25)}{[\text{short WOL}]} = \underset{\text{(raw score)}}{[\text{short WOL}]}$$

Raw Score	Scaled Score	Raw Score	Scaled Score	Raw Score	Scaled Score	Raw Score	Scaled Score	Raw Score	Scaled Score
60	800	44	710	28	560	12	420	−4	260
59	800	43	700	27	550	11	410	−5	250
58	800	42	690	26	540	10	400	−6	240
57	800	41	690	25	530	9	390	−7	230
56	800	40	680	24	520	8	380	−8	220
55	800	39	670	23	510	7	370	−9	210
54	790	38	660	22	500	6	360	−10	200
53	790	37	650	21	500	5	350	−11	200
52	780	36	640	20	490	4	340	−12	200
51	770	35	630	19	490	3	330	−13	200
50	760	34	620	18	480	2	320	−14	200
49	750	33	610	17	470	1	310	−15	200
48	740	32	600	16	460	0	300		
47	740	31	590	15	450	−1	290		
46	730	30	580	14	440	−2	280		
45	720	29	570	13	430	−3	270		

Note: This is only a sample scoring scale. Scoring scales differ from exam to exam.

PRACTICE TEST 4
LITERATURE

The following practice test is designed to be just like the real SAT Literature Test. It matches the actual test in content coverage and degree of difficulty.

Once you finish the ractice test, determine your score. Carefully read the answer explanations of the questions you answered incorrectly. Identify any weaknesses in your literature skills by determining the areas in which you made the most errors. Review those sections of this book first. Then, as time permits, go back and review your strengths.

Allow one hour to take the test. Time yourself and work uninterrupted. If you run out of time, take note of where you stopped when time ran out. Remember that you lose a quarter point for each incorrect answer, but you do not lose points for questions you leave blank. Therefore, unless you can eliminate one or more of the five choices, it is best to leave a question unanswered.

Use the following formula to calculate your score:

(number of correct answers) – ¼ (number of incorrect answers)

If you treat this practice test just like the actual exam, it will accurately reflect how you are likely to perform on test day. Here are some hints on how to create test-taking conditions similar to those of the actual exam:

- Complete the test in one sitting. On test day, you will not be allowed to take a break.
- Tear out the answer sheet and fill in the ovals just as you will on the actual test day.
- Have a good eraser and more than one sharp pencil handy. On test day, you will not be able to go get a new pencil if yours breaks.
- Do not allow yourself any extra time; put down your pencil after exactly one hour, no matter how many questions are left to answer.
- Become familiar with the directions on the test. If you go in knowing what the directions say, you will not have to waste time reading and thinking about them on the actual test day.

PRACTICE TEST 4
LITERATURE

ANSWER SHEET

Tear out this answer sheet and use it to mark your answers.

1. (A) (B) (C) (D) (E)	16. (A) (B) (C) (D) (E)	31. (A) (B) (C) (D) (E)	46. (A) (B) (C) (D) (E)
2. (A) (B) (C) (D) (E)	17. (A) (B) (C) (D) (E)	32. (A) (B) (C) (D) (E)	47. (A) (B) (C) (D) (E)
3. (A) (B) (C) (D) (E)	18. (A) (B) (C) (D) (E)	33. (A) (B) (C) (D) (E)	48. (A) (B) (C) (D) (E)
4. (A) (B) (C) (D) (E)	19. (A) (B) (C) (D) (E)	34. (A) (B) (C) (D) (E)	49. (A) (B) (C) (D) (E)
5. (A) (B) (C) (D) (E)	20. (A) (B) (C) (D) (E)	35. (A) (B) (C) (D) (E)	50. (A) (B) (C) (D) (E)
6. (A) (B) (C) (D) (E)	21. (A) (B) (C) (D) (E)	36. (A) (B) (C) (D) (E)	51. (A) (B) (C) (D) (E)
7. (A) (B) (C) (D) (E)	22. (A) (B) (C) (D) (E)	37. (A) (B) (C) (D) (E)	52. (A) (B) (C) (D) (E)
8. (A) (B) (C) (D) (E)	23. (A) (B) (C) (D) (E)	38. (A) (B) (C) (D) (E)	53. (A) (B) (C) (D) (E)
9. (A) (B) (C) (D) (E)	24. (A) (B) (C) (D) (E)	39. (A) (B) (C) (D) (E)	54. (A) (B) (C) (D) (E)
10. (A) (B) (C) (D) (E)	25. (A) (B) (C) (D) (E)	40. (A) (B) (C) (D) (E)	55. (A) (B) (C) (D) (E)
11. (A) (B) (C) (D) (E)	26. (A) (B) (C) (D) (E)	41. (A) (B) (C) (D) (E)	56. (A) (B) (C) (D) (E)
12. (A) (B) (C) (D) (E)	27. (A) (B) (C) (D) (E)	42. (A) (B) (C) (D) (E)	57. (A) (B) (C) (D) (E)
13. (A) (B) (C) (D) (E)	28. (A) (B) (C) (D) (E)	43. (A) (B) (C) (D) (E)	58. (A) (B) (C) (D) (E)
14. (A) (B) (C) (D) (E)	29. (A) (B) (C) (D) (E)	44. (A) (B) (C) (D) (E)	59. (A) (B) (C) (D) (E)
15. (A) (B) (C) (D) (E)	30. (A) (B) (C) (D) (E)	45. (A) (B) (C) (D) (E)	60. (A) (B) (C) (D) (E)

PRACTICE TEST 4
Time: 60 minutes

Directions: This test consists of selections from literary works and questions on their content, form, and style. After reading each passage or poem, choose the best answer to each question and then fill in the corresponding oval on the answer sheet.

Note: Pay particular attention to the requirements of questions that contain the words NOT or EXCEPT.

Questions 1–9. Read the following dramatic excerpt carefully before you choose your answers.

ACT I SCENE 2
A room in Sir Peter Teazle's house.
(Enter Sir Peter.)

SIR PETER. When an old bachelor marries a young wife, what is he to expect? 'Tis now six months since Lady Teazle made me the happiest of men—and I have been the most miserable dog ever since! We
5　tiffed a little going to church, and fairly quarreled before the bells had done ringing. I was more than once nearly choked with gall during the honeymoon, and had lost all comfort in life before my friends had done wishing me joy. Yet I chose with caution—a girl
10　bred wholly in the country, who never knew luxury beyond one silk gown, nor dissipation above the annual gala of a race ball. Yet she now plays her part in all the extravagant fopperies of fashion and the town, with as ready a grace as if she never had seen a
15　bush or a grass-plot out of Grosvenor Square! I am sneered at by all my acquaintance, and paragraphed in the newspapers. She dissipates my fortune, and contradicts all my humors; yet the worst of it is, I doubt I love her, or I should never bear all this. However, I'll
20　never be weak enough to own it.

(Enter Rowley.)

ROWLEY. Oh! Sir Peter, your servant: how is it with you, sir?

SIR PETER. Very bad, Master Rowley, very bad. I meet with nothing but crosses and vexations.

25　ROWLEY. What can have happened since yesterday?

SIR PETER. A good question to a married man!

ROWLEY. Nay, I'm sure, Sir Peter, your lady can't be the cause of your uneasiness.

SIR PETER. Why, has anybody told you she was dead?

30　ROWLEY. Come, come, Sir Peter, you love her, notwithstanding your tempers don't exactly agree.

SIR PETER. But the fault is entirely hers, Master Rowley. I am, myself, the sweetest-tempered man alive, and hate a teasing temper; and so I tell her a hundred
35　times a day.

ROWLEY. Indeed!

SIR PETER. Ay; and what is very extraordinary, in all our disputes she is always in the wrong!

(1777)

1. When Sir Peter says he was "nearly choked with gall" (line 7), he means he felt

(A) angry
(B) bitter
(C) foolish
(D) upset
(E) jealous

2. Which of the following is closest in meaning to "tiffed" (line 5)?

(A) argued
(B) kissed
(C) ate
(D) prayed
(E) delayed

3. Why is Sir Peter surprised that Lady Teazle enjoys "the extravagant fopperies of fashion and the town"?

(A) When he met her, she was living simply, quietly, and modestly.
(B) He thought she was too much in love with him to want to go out all the time.
(C) He knows that she is a quarrelsome person who does not enjoy society.
(D) Before their marriage, she had promised to be a thrifty and frugal wife.
(E) She married him in order to have children as soon as possible.

4. In which sense does Sir Peter use the word "doubt" (line 18)?

(A) state
(B) wish
(C) hate
(D) question
(E) believe

GO ON TO THE NEXT PAGE

PRACTICE TEST—*Continued*

5. This play is best described as

   (A) a tragedy
   (B) a comedy
   (C) a morality play
   (D) theater of the absurd
   (E) a romance

6. "She dissipates my fortune" (line 17) means

   (A) It is my bad luck that she likes to spend money.
   (B) She has brought me bad luck.
   (C) She spends my money too freely.
   (D) She takes money from me to send home to her parents.
   (E) I always argue with her about money.

7. The frequent use of hyperbole in Sir Peter's long opening speech allows the reader to conclude that he

   (A) wishes he had married an older woman
   (B) gets irritated and annoyed over every little thing
   (C) has an optimistic view of his situation
   (D) enjoys feeling sorry for himself
   (E) has a poetic streak in his nature

8. From the comment "I'll never be weak enough to own it" (line 20), you can conclude that

   (A) Sir Peter is not a strong or forceful man
   (B) Sir Peter sees marriage as a battle that he is determined to win
   (C) Lady Teazle has no power over Sir Peter
   (D) Lady Teazle knows how much Sir Peter loves her
   (E) Sir Peter is a generous husband

9. Which best describes Rowley's main function in this excerpt?

   (A) to set up funny lines spoken by Sir Peter
   (B) to win the audience's sympathy and interest
   (C) to defend Lady Teazle from Sir Peter's attacks
   (D) to act as a go-between for Sir Peter and Lady Teazle
   (E) to show the audience that Sir Peter is a wealthy man

Questions 10–18. Read the following poem carefully before you choose your answers.

Dover Beach

The sea is calm to-night,
The tide is full, the moon lies fair
Upon the Straits;—on the French coast, the light
Gleams, and is gone; the cliffs of England stand,

5 Glimmering and vast, out in the tranquil bay.
Come to the window, sweet is the night air!
Only, from the long line of spray
Where the ebb meets the moon-blanch'd sand,
Listen! you hear the grating roar
10 Of pebbles which the waves suck back, and fling,
At their return, up the high strand,
Begin, and cease, and then again begin,
With tremulous cadence slow, and bring
The eternal note of sadness in.

15   Sophocles long ago
Heard it on the Aegean, and it brought
Into his mind the turbid ebb and flow
Of human misery; we
Find also in the sound a thought,
20 Hearing it by this distant northern sea.

The sea of faith
Was once, too, at the full, and round earth's shore
Lay like the folds of a bright girdle furl'd;
But now I only hear
25 Its melancholy, long, withdrawing roar,
Retreating to the breath
Of the night-wind down the vast edges drear
And naked shingles of the world.

Ah, love, let us be true
30 To one another! for the world, which seems
To lie before us like a land of dreams,
So various, so beautiful, so new,
Hath really neither joy, nor love, nor light,
Nor certitude, nor peace, nor help for pain;
35 And we here as on a darkling plain
Swept with confused alarms of struggle and flight,
Where ignorant armies clash by night.

(1867)

10. "Certitude" (line 34) is best defined as

    (A) facts and statistics
    (B) insanity or lack of reason
    (C) equality under the law
    (D) sense of right and wrong
    (E) unarguable belief or faith

GO ON TO THE NEXT PAGE

PRACTICE TEST—*Continued*

11. "The moon-blanch'd sand" (line 8) appears to be which color?

    (A) black
    (B) white
    (C) gold
    (D) tan
    (E) red

12. Which experience does the speaker share with Sophocles?

    (A) hearing the sea waves wash pebbles up on the shore
    (B) having a serious talk with a lover late one night
    (C) realizing that the world is a place without hope or faith
    (D) looking at the Aegean Sea by the light of the moon
    (E) viewing the French coast and the English cliffs by night

13. What is the source of the speaker's perception of the world as a joyless and dark place?

    (A) the prevalence of wars between nations
    (B) the decline of religious faith
    (C) the extent of human misery
    (D) his memories of Sophocles
    (E) the tone of his lover's remarks

14. In the lines "And we here as on a darkling plain / Swept with confused alarms of struggle and flight, / Where ignorant armies clash by night" (lines 35–37), the speaker compares himself and his lover to

    (A) soldiers
    (B) prisoners of war
    (C) criminals
    (D) refugees
    (E) survivors

15. To the speaker, the sound of the "grating roar / Of pebbles which the waves suck back" (lines 9–10) seems

    (A) eerie
    (B) calming
    (C) ominous
    (D) terrifying
    (E) painful

16. During the course of the poem, the speaker's mood changes from

    (A) pensive to alert
    (B) serene to apprehensive
    (C) anxious to calm
    (D) romantic to sensible
    (E) amused to outraged

17. How does the speaker contradict his own statement that the world "Hath really neither joy, nor love, nor light / Nor certitude, nor peace, nor help for pain (lines 33–34)?

    (A) by perceiving the "eternal note of sadness" in the sound of the sea
    (B) by recalling Sophocles' meditations on human misery
    (C) by appealing to his lover to remain true
    (D) by comparing the "sea of faith" to "a bright girdle"
    (E) by comparing the faithless to "ignorant armies"

18. The word "turbid" (line 17) means

    (A) evil, wicked
    (B) raucous, noisy
    (C) nonstop, endless
    (D) spinning, dizzy
    (E) muddy, unclear

Questions 19–24. Read the following poem carefully before you choose your answers.

E'en like two little bank-dividing brooks,
    That wash the pebbles with their wanton streams,
And having ranged and search'd a thousand nooks,
    Meet both at length in silver-breasted Thames,
5   Where in a greater current they conjoin:
So I my Best-belovèd's am; so He is mine.

E'en so we met; and after long pursuit,
    E'en so we joined; we both became entire;
No need for either to renew a suit,
10   For I was flax, and He was flames of fire:
       Our firm-united souls did more than twine;
So I my Best-belovèd's am; so He is mine.

If all those glittering Monarchs, that command
    The servile quarters of this earthly ball,
15 Should tender in exchange their shares of land,
    I would not change my fortunes for them all:
       Their wealth is but a counter to my coin:
       The world's but theirs; but my Belovèd's mine.

(1635)

GO ON TO THE NEXT PAGE

PRACTICE TEST—*Continued*

19. In what sense does the poet use the word "counter" (line 17)?

    (A) one who adds up items to find a total

    (B) a chip or token used in place of actual money

    (C) a weight used to balance a scale

    (D) a response that disagrees with a statement

    (E) a long, hard, table-like surface

20. The poet uses the extended comparison to "two little bank-dividing brooks" (line 1) to show the speaker's

    (A) appreciation of the beauties of nature

    (B) understanding of natural science

    (C) sense of profound unity with the Beloved

    (D) dwelling-place by the riverbank

    (E) passionate desire for the Beloved

21. In the third stanza, the speaker will not "change my fortunes" for which of the following?

    (A) a gala ball given in the speaker's honor

    (B) the riches of all the local merchants

    (C) a promise of eternal life in heaven

    (D) the kingdoms of the earth

    (E) a beautiful new house with rich furnishings

22. The Beloved might be identified with which of the following?

    I. God

    II. the speaker's spouse or lover

    III. the speaker's favorite child

    (A) I and II only

    (B) II only

    (C) II and III only

    (D) III only

    (E) I, II, and III

23. The repetition of the line "So I my Best-belovèd's am; so He is mine"

    (A) stresses the speaker's belief that the union with the Beloved is eternal

    (B) explains why the speaker is attached to the Beloved

    (C) emphasizes the strength of the speaker's attachment to the Beloved

    (D) clarifies that the Beloved dominates the speaker in their relationship

    (E) reveals the meaning of the figurative language in lines 10 and 17

24. The phrase "their wanton streams" (line 2) means

    (A) the speaker and the Beloved desire one another

    (B) the water in the brooks tumbles playfully over the pebbles

    (C) the speaker treats the Beloved with willful cruelty

    (D) the stream is a popular meeting-place for lovers

    (E) the speaker and the Beloved feel merry when they see the water

Questions 25–32. Read the following passage carefully before you choose your answers.

Into the First National Bank of San Rosario the newcomer walked, never slowing his brisk step until he stood at the cashier's window. The bank opened for business at nine,
5 and the working force was already assembled, each member preparing his department for the day's business. The cashier was examining the mail when he noticed the stranger standing at his window.

10 "Bank doesn't open 'til nine," he remarked, curtly, but without feeling. He had had to make that statement so often to early birds since San Rosario adopted city banking hours.

15 "I am well aware of that," said the other man, in cool, brittle tones. "Will you kindly receive my card?"

J. F. C. NETTLEWICK

National Bank Examiner

"Oh—er—will you walk around inside, Mr.—er—Nettlewick. Your first visit—didn't
20 know your business, of course. Walk right around, please."

GO ON TO THE NEXT PAGE →

PRACTICE TEST—*Continued*

The examiner was quickly inside the sacred precincts of the bank, where he was ponderously introduced to each employee in turn by
25 Mr. Edlinger, the cashier—a middle-aged gentleman of deliberation, discretion, and method.

"I was kind of expecting Sam Turner round again, pretty soon," said Mr. Edlinger. "Sam's been examining us now for about four years.
30 I guess you'll find us all right, though, considering the tightness in business. Not overly much money on hand, but able to stand the storms, sir, stand the storms."

"Mr. Turner and I have been ordered by the
35 Comptroller to exchange districts," said the examiner, in his decisive, formal tones. "He is covering my old territory in southern Illinois and Indiana. I will take the cash first, please."

Perry Dorsey, the teller, was already arrang-
40 ing his cash on the counter for the examiner's inspection. He knew it was right to a cent, and he had nothing to fear, but he was nervous and flustered. So was every man in the bank. There was something so icy and swift,
45 so impersonal and uncompromising about this man that his very presence seemed an accusation. He looked to be a man who would never make nor overlook an error.

Mr. Nettlewick first seized the currency, and
50 with a rapid, almost juggling motion, counted it by packages. Then he spun the sponge cup toward him and verified the count by bills. His thin, white fingers flew like some expert musician's upon the keys of a piano. He dumped
55 the gold upon the counter with a crash, and the coins whined and sang as they skimmed across the marble slab from the tips of his nimble digits. The air was full of fractional currency when he came to the halves and
60 quarters. He counted the last nickel and dime. He had the scales brought, and he weighed every sack of silver in the vault. He questioned Dorsey concerning each of the cash memoranda—certain checks, charge slips, etc., car-
65 ried over from the previous day's work—with unimpeachable courtesy, yet with something so mysteriously momentous in his frigid manner, that the teller was reduced to pink cheeks and a stammering tongue.

70 This newly imported examiner was so different from Sam Turner. It had been Sam's way to enter the bank with a shout, pass the cigars, and tell the latest stories he had picked up on his rounds. His customary
75 greeting to Dorsey had been, "Hello, Perry! Haven't skipped out with the boodle yet, I see." Turner's way of counting the cash had been different, too. He would finger the packages of bills in a tired kind of way, and
80 then go into the vault and kick over a few sacks of silver, and the thing was done. Halves and quarters and dimes? Not for Sam Turner. "No chicken feed for me," he would say when they were set before him. "I'm not
85 in the agricultural department." But then, Turner was a Texan, an old friend of the bank's president, and had known Dorsey since he was a baby.

(c. 1905)

25. Which detail suggests the cause for the Comptroller's order that Nettlewick and Turner exchange districts?

(A) "Into the First National Bank of San Rosario the newcomer walked, never slowing his brisk step until he stood at the cashier's window." (lines 1–4)

(B) "He knew it was right to a cent, and he had nothing to fear, but he was nervous and flustered. So was every man in the bank." (lines 41–44)

(C) "There was something so icy and swift, so impersonal and uncompromising about this man that his very presence seemed an accusation." (lines 44–47)

(D) "He dumped the gold upon the counter with a crash, and the coins whined and sang as they skimmed across the marble slab from the tips of his nimble digits." (lines 54–58)

(E) "He would finger the packages of bills in a tired kind of way, and then go into the vault and kick over a few sacks of silver, and the thing was done." (lines 78–81)

26. The author uses all of the following to characterize Mr. Nettlewick EXCEPT

(A) his manner of speaking
(B) his effect on the other characters
(C) his approach to his job
(D) his physical appearance
(E) his differences from Sam Turner

GO ON TO THE NEXT PAGE

PRACTICE TEST—*Continued*

27. "His thin, white fingers flew like some expert musician's upon the keys of a piano" (lines 52–54) shows that Mr. Nettlewick

    (A) is a fine musician
    (B) enjoys listening to music
    (C) is highly skilled at his job
    (D) likes to do magic tricks with money
    (E) is eager to impress the staff of the bank

28. Why is Sam Turner's approach to examining the bank's assets so different from Mr. Nettlewick's?

    (A) Turner is less competent at the job.
    (B) Turner prefers to avoid his friends during business hours.
    (C) Turner is older and slower than Nettlewick.
    (D) Turner knows and trusts the bank's employees.
    (E) Turner hopes to be transferred to another district.

29. What about Mr. Nettlewick makes the bank's staff feel "nervous and flustered"?

    (A) his early-morning arrival
    (B) the courtesy in his manner
    (C) his high degree of efficiency
    (D) the fact that he has come to examine the bank
    (E) the fact that he is a stranger to them

30. Mr. Nettlewick treats the bank employees formally and without warmth for which of the following reasons?

    I. He has never met any of them before.
    II. He must maintain objectivity in order to do his job properly.
    III. His is formal, precise, and cool by nature.

    (A) I only
    (B) I and II only
    (C) II only
    (D) III only
    (E) I, II, and III

31. By saying that Mr. Edlinger is a "gentleman of deliberation" (lines 25–26), the author means that

    (A) he is slow and unhurried in his actions
    (B) he means exactly what he says at all times
    (C) he has a habit of debating issues with others
    (D) he can be trusted to keep a secret
    (E) he is prone to using colorful figures of speech

32. The word "ponderously" (lines 23–24) is best defined as

    (A) cautiously
    (B) weightily
    (C) cordially
    (D) quickly
    (E) nervously

Questions 33–40. Read the following poem carefully before you choose your answers.

The Poetess' Hasty Resolution

Reading my verses, I liked them so well,
Self-love did make my judgment to rebel.
Thinking them so good, I thought more to write;
Considering not how others would them like.
5 I writ so fast, I thought, if I lived long,
A pyramid of fame to build thereon.
Reason observing which way I was bent,
Did stay my hand, and asked me what I meant;
Will you, said she, thus waste your time in vain,
10 On that which in the world small praise shall gain?
For shame leave off, said she, the Printer spare,
He'll lose by your ill poetry, I fear.
Besides the world hath already such a weight
Of useless books, as it is over fraught.
15 Then pity take, do the world a good turn,
And all you write cast in the fire, and burn.
Angry I was, and Reason struck away,
When I did hear, what she to me did say.
Then all in haste I to the press it sent,
20 Fearing persuasion might my book prevent:
But now 'tis done, with grief repent do I,
Hang down my head with shame, blush, sigh, and cry.
Take pity, and my drooping spirits raise,
Wipe off my tears with handkerchiefs of praise.

(1653)

33. Who is the "she" who speaks in lines 9–16?

    (A) the poetess
    (B) Reason
    (C) Self-love
    (D) the Printer
    (E) persuasion

GO ON TO THE NEXT PAGE

PRACTICE TEST—*Continued*

34. Whom does the speaker address in the last two lines?

    (A) her readers
    (B) her friends
    (C) her parents
    (D) her husband
    (E) her doctor

35. "Angry I was, and Reason struck away" (line 17) is best paraphrased as

    (A) Listening to Reason always made me angry.
    (B) It struck me that Reason was getting angry with me.
    (C) Reason knocked my poems off the desk, which made me angry.
    (D) When Reason saw she had made me angry, she went away.
    (E) I was angry at Reason, so I pushed her away.

36. Which two forces are in conflict in this poem?

    (A) the printer and the speaker
    (B) the poet and the speaker
    (C) the speaker and the critics
    (D) the speaker's heart and brain
    (E) the speaker and the readers

37. Which of the following best characterizes the speaker?

    (A) emotional and impulsive
    (B) tough and determined
    (C) cheerful and easygoing
    (D) deliberate and cautious
    (E) violent and fierce

38. Why does the speaker repent having sent her poems to the press?

    (A) She is afraid that people will not like her poems.
    (B) She knows in her heart that her poems are not good.
    (C) She knows she cannot afford to pay for the poems to be printed.
    (D) She hopes that her poems will please the critics.
    (E) She realizes that it is too late to stop publication.

39. The speaker gets angry at Reason because

    (A) Reason is responsible for the speaker's failure
    (B) Reason has right on her side
    (C) Reason is unsympathetic and critical
    (D) Reason refuses to print the speaker's poems
    (E) Reason does not like to read poetry

40. Which of the following motivates the speaker to write poetry?

    I. She wants to become a famous author.
    II. She is pleased with the evidence of her own talent.
    III. She needs to write in order to earn money.

    (A) I only
    (B) I and II only
    (C) III only
    (D) II and III only
    (E) I, II, and III

Questions 41–50. Read the following passage carefully before you choose your answers.

None of them knew the color of the sky. Their eyes glanced level, and were fastened upon the waves that swept toward them. These waves were of the hue of slate, save for the tops,
5 which were of foaming white, and all of the men knew the colors of the sea. The horizon narrowed and widened, and dipped and rose, and at all times its edge was jagged with waves that seemed thrust up in points like rocks.

10 Many a man ought to have a bathtub larger than the boat which here rode upon the sea. These waves were most wrongfully and barbarously abrupt and tall, and each froth-top was a problem in small boat navigation.

15 The cook squatted in the bottom and looked with both eyes at the six inches of gunwale which separated him from the ocean. His sleeves were rolled over his fat forearms, and the two flaps of his unbuttoned vest dangled
20 as he bent to bail out the boat. Often he said: "Gawd! That was a narrow clip." As he remarked it, he invariably gazed eastward over the broken sea.

The oiler, steering with one of the two oars in
25 the boat, sometimes raised himself suddenly to keep clear of water that swirled in over the stern. It was a thin little oar, and it seemed often ready to snap.

The correspondent, pulling at the other oar,
30 watched the waves and wondered why he was there.

GO ON TO THE NEXT PAGE

PRACTICE TEST—*Continued*

The injured captain, lying in the bow, was at this time buried in that profound dejection and indifference which comes, temporarily
35 at least, to even the bravest and most enduring when, willy-nilly, the firm fails, the army loses, the ship goes down. The mind of the master of a vessel is rooted deep in the timbers of her, though he command for a day or
40 a decade; and this captain had on him the stern impression of a scene in the grays of dawn of seven turned faces, and later a stump of a topmast with a white ball on it, that slashed to and fro at the waves, went low
45 and lower, and down. Thereafter there was something strange in his voice. Although steady, it was deep with mourning, and of a quality beyond oration or tears.

"Keep 'er a little more south, Billie," said he.

50 "A little more south, sir," said the oiler in the stern.

A seat in this boat was not unlike a seat upon a bucking bronco, and, by the same token, a bronco is not much smaller. The craft
55 pranced and reared and plunged like an animal. As each wave came, and she rose for it, she seemed like a horse making at a fence outrageously high. The manner of her scramble over these walls of water is a mystic
60 thing, and, moreover, at the top of them were ordinarily these problems in white water, the foam racing down from the summit of each wave requiring a new leap, and a leap from the air. Then, after scornfully bumping a
65 crest, she would slide and race and splash down a long incline, and arrive bobbing and nodding in front of the next menace.

A singular disadvantage of the sea lies in the fact that after successfully surmounting one
70 wave, you discover that there is another behind it just as important and just as nervously anxious to do something effective in the way of swamping boats. In a ten-foot dinghy one can get an idea of the resources
75 of the sea in the line of waves that is not probable to the average experience which is never at sea in a dinghy. As each slaty wall of water approached, it shut all else from the view of the men in the boat, and it was not
80 difficult to imagine that this particular wave was the final outburst of the ocean, the last effort of the grim water. There was a terrible

grace in the move of the waves, and they came in silence, save for the snarling of the
85 crests.

(1897)

41. Why does none of the men know the color of the sky?

(A) They are too busy maintaining their boat to look up.
(B) It is too dark to see the color of the sky.
(C) Their eyes are dazzled by the light of the sun.
(D) The sky is the same color as the sea.
(E) The bulk of the boat hides the sky from their view.

42. Why are the four men in the dinghy?

(A) Their ship had an accident and sank.
(B) They are traveling for business.
(C) They are escaping from a mutiny.
(D) They are going for help to save the ship.
(E) They are trying to get the captain to a doctor.

43. The statement "Many a man ought to have a bathtub larger than the boat which here rode upon the sea" (lines 10–11) exaggerates

(A) the danger the men are in
(B) the small size of the dinghy
(C) the safety of being in a bathtub
(D) the amount of water washing into the boat
(E) the sailing skills of the four men

44. The four men perceive the ocean as all of the following EXCEPT

(A) tireless
(B) endless
(C) threatening
(D) powerful
(E) magical

45. Which is NOT a reasonable conclusion to draw about the captain?

(A) He feels responsible for the loss of his ship.
(B) He was injured during the shipwreck.
(C) He is an experienced sailor.
(D) He is too proud to row or bail water.
(E) He is not in the habit of showing much emotion.

GO ON TO THE NEXT PAGE

PRACTICE TEST—*Continued*

46. What is the effect of the extended comparison of the boat to a bucking bronco?

    (A) It shows that the dinghy has a mind of its own.
    (B) It demonstrates that the captain is a poor navigator.
    (C) It helps the reader feel the unsteady motion of the boat.
    (D) It proves that the men can easily control the dinghy.
    (E) It shows that the characters know more about horses than boats.

47. Why do the characters have so little to say to each other?

    (A) They blame one another for the shipwreck.
    (B) They do not all speak the same language.
    (C) They are all strangers to each other.
    (D) They put all their energy into keeping the dinghy afloat.
    (E) They feel no interest in or sympathy with one another.

48. The tone of the passage is best described as

    (A) mournful
    (B) suspenseful
    (C) melancholy
    (D) serene
    (E) satirical

49. Which major theme(s) does the passage address?

    I. the struggle between man and nature
    II. the unpredictability of existence
    III. the importance of courage in the face of impossible odds

    (A) I only
    (B) II only
    (C) I and II only
    (D) II and III only
    (E) I, II, and III

50. From whose perspective or point of view does the reader experience the events in the passage?

    (A) the captain's
    (B) the cook's
    (C) the correspondent's
    (D) the oiler's
    (E) the author's or narrator's

Questions 51–60. Read the following passage carefully before you choose your answers.

She conceived a true estimate of Drouet. To her, and indeed to all the world, he was a nice, good-hearted man. There was nothing evil in the fellow. He gave her the money out
5 of a good heart—out of a realization of her want. He would not have given the same amount to a poor young man, but we must not forget that a poor young man could not, in the nature of things, have appealed to him
10 like a poor young girl. Femininity affected his feelings. He was the creature of an inborn desire. Yet no beggar could have caught his eye and said, "My God, mister, I'm starving," but he would gladly have handed out what
15 was considered the proper portion to give beggars and thought no more about it. There would have been no speculation, no philosophising. He had no mental process in him worthy the dignity of either of those
20 terms. In his good clothes and fine health, he was a merry, unthinking moth of the lamp. Deprived of his position, and struck by a few of the involved and baffling forces which sometimes play upon man, he would have
25 been as helpless as Carrie—as helpless, as non-understanding, as pitiable, if you will, as she.

Now, in regard to his pursuit of women, he meant them no harm, because he did not
30 conceive of the relation which he hoped to hold with them as being harmful. He loved to make advances to women, to have them succumb to his charms, not because he was a cold-blooded, dark, scheming villain, but
35 because his inborn desire urged him to that as a chief delight. He was vain, he was boastful, he was as deluded by fine clothes as any silly-headed girl. A truly deep-dyed villain could have hornswaggled him as readily as
40 he could have flattered a pretty shop-girl. His fine success as a salesman lay in his geniality and the thoroughly reputable standing of his house. He bobbed about among men, a veritable bundle of enthusiasm—no power wor-
45 thy the name of intellect, no thoughts worthy the adjective noble, no feelings long continued

GO ON TO THE NEXT PAGE ➤

PRACTICE TEST—*Continued*

in one strain. A Madame Sappho would have called him a pig; a Shakespeare would have said "my merry child"; old, drinking Caryoe[1]
50 thought him a clever, successful business-man. In short, he was as good as his intellect conceived.

The best proof that there was something open and commendable about the man was the fact
55 that Carrie took the money. No deep, sinister soul with ulterior motives could have given her fifteen cents under the guise of friendship. The unintellectual are not so helpless. Nature has taught the beasts of the field to fly when
60 some unheralded danger threatens. She has put into the small, unwise head of the chipmunk the untutored fear of poisons. "He keepeth His creatures whole," was not written of beasts alone. Carrie was unwise, and, there-
65 fore, like the sheep in its unwisdom, strong in feeling. The instinct of self-protection, strong in all such natures, was roused but feebly, if at all, by the overtures of Drouet.

(1900)

[1]co-owner of the firm, or "house," for which Drouet works

51. The word "hornswaggled" (line 39) is best defined as

   (A) befriended
   (B) insulted
   (C) conned
   (D) hired
   (E) fought

52. Which of the following does NOT characterize Drouet?

   (A) generosity
   (B) kindness
   (C) subtlety
   (D) honesty
   (E) friendliness

53. The metaphor "he was a merry, unthinking moth of the lamp" (lines 20–21) implies which of the following about Drouet?

   (A) He does what he likes without thinking about possible consequences.
   (B) His ready interest in other people often gets him into trouble.
   (C) He impresses Carrie with his warmth of personality and enthusiasm.

   (D) He is so successful at his job that he can afford to enjoy himself in his free time.
   (E) He is especially cheerful in the bright lights of a restaurant or theater at night.

54. Which best describes the author's attitude toward Drouet?

   (A) condescending
   (B) respectful
   (C) compassionate
   (D) wary
   (E) affectionate

55. The author suggests that the difference between Drouet and "a cold-blooded, dark, scheming villain" (lines 33–34) is that

   (A) Drouet is an unrefined man of the world.
   (B) Drouet does not intend or wish to harm or injure anyone.
   (C) Drouet's behavior is guided largely by selfishness.
   (D) Drouet chases after women and often tells them lies.
   (E) Drouet has no sensitivity toward other people.

56. The author suggests that Carrie trusts Drouet because

   (A) his offer of money is a generous one
   (B) his boss has assured her that he is a good man
   (C) she has no experience of evil men
   (D) her instincts tell her that he can be trusted
   (E) she finds him handsome and attractive

57. Drouet hopes that Carrie will eventually become his

   (A) friend
   (B) wife
   (C) lover
   (D) colleague
   (E) employee

58. What is the author's main purpose in this passage?

   (A) to examine the relationship between Drouet and Carrie
   (B) to analyze Drouet's personality for the reader
   (C) to explain why Carrie finds Drouet attractive
   (D) to show the reader how Carrie and Drouet are alike
   (E) to portray a successful salesman of the period

GO ON TO THE NEXT PAGE

PRACTICE TEST—*Continued*

59. Which of the following supports the author's suggestion that Carrie will come to no harm by trusting Drouet?

    (A) ". . . to all the world, he was a nice, good-hearted man" (lines 2–3)
    (B) "He would not have given the same amount to a poor young man" (lines 6–7)
    (C) "He was the creature of an inborn desire" (lines 11–12)
    (D) "He loved to make advances to women, to have them succumb to his charms" (lines 31–32)
    (E) "He bobbed about among men, a veritable bundle of enthusiasm" (lines 43–44)

60. The author suggests that Drouet's main motive for helping Carrie is

    (A) his concern for her plight
    (B) his understanding of her character
    (C) his desire to think well of himself
    (D) his true nobility of character
    (E) his physical desire for her

STOP

IF YOU FINISH BEFORE TIME IS CALLED, YOU MAY CHECK YOUR WORK ON THIS TEST ONLY.

DO NOT TURN TO ANY OTHER TEST IN THIS BOOK.

ANSWER KEY

1. B	21. D	41. A
2. A	22. A	42. A
3. A	23. C	43. B
4. E	24. B	44. E
5. B	25. E	45. D
6. C	26. D	46. C
7. D	27. C	47. D
8. B	28. D	48. B
9. A	29. C	49. E
10. E	30. E	50. E
11. B	31. A	51. C
12. A	32. B	52. C
13. B	33. B	53. A
14. D	34. A	54. E
15. C	35. E	55. B
16. B	36. D	56. D
17. D	37. A	57. C
18. E	38. B	58. B
19. B	39. C	59. A
20. C	40. B	60. E

ANSWERS AND EXPLANATIONS

1. **Correct Choice: B**
   Gall, also called *bile*, is a fluid secreted by the liver. *Gall* has been a literary synonym for bitterness of spirit since the Middle Ages.

2. **Correct Choice: A**
   The context makes it clear that Sir Peter and his lady had a spat followed by a more serious quarrel.

3. **Correct Choice: A**
   Sir Peter is surprised at his wife's behavior because he thought she would want to continue living in the modest style she was accustomed to.

4. **Correct Choice: E**
   Today, to *doubt* means to question or disbelieve. However, in the late eighteenth century, English people used the word in ordinary conversation to mean just the opposite. As the context shows, "I doubt I love her" means "I believe I love her."

5. **Correct Choice: B**
   The tried-and-true comic staple of a marriage between an old bachelor and a young girl, the wordplay, and the funny lines make it clear that this play is a comedy.

6. **Correct Choice: C**
   Dissipates means "scatters." *Fortune*, in this context, refers to wealth rather than luck. Lady Teazle is spending money far more freely than Sir Peter had anticipated she would.

7. **Correct Choice: D**
   Sir Peter would not express his discontent with so much wit and style if he were not enjoying wallowing in self-pity. He is perfectly well aware that things are not as bad as he suggests; the point of humorous exaggeration is that you know you are exaggerating for effect. Choice A is wrong because he confesses that he loves his wife; choice B is wrong because he is complaining about a major difference of views between himself and his wife, not a series of little things.

8. **Correct Choice: B**
   If a person is worried about showing weakness, that implies he considers the other person to be his enemy. Sir Peter sees his marriage as a power struggle in which Lady Teazle will gain more power if he admits that he loves her.

9. **Correct Choice: A**
   Rowley acts as a "straight man"; four of his five lines set up laugh lines spoken by Sir Peter.

10. **Correct Choice: E**
    Certitude means much the same as "certainty." It implies an unshakable belief or faith in something, not so much because there is factual proof of it, but because one is completely convinced of its existence or rightness.

11. **Correct Choice: B**
    Blanch'd is derived from the Latin for "white." The strong, bright light of the moon makes the sand appear white.

12. **Correct Choice: A**
    The speaker comments that "Sophocles long ago / Heard it on the Aegean." *It* refers to the same sound he hears himself—the waves breaking on the shore.

13. **Correct Choice: B**
    The sound of the sea retreating from the shore inspires the speaker to think about the widespread loss of religious faith.

14. **Correct Choice: D**
    The speaker suggests that he and his love will be caught up in the middle of a war, not as participants on either side, but rather trapped between armies. "Refugees" most closely matches this comparison.

15. **Correct Choice: C**
    When the speaker hears this sound, it directs his thoughts toward the future and suggests that the world is a terrible place. *Ominous*, which means "portending or predicting evil," is the best match to the sound's effect on him.

16. **Correct Choice: B**
    In the first six lines of the poem, the words *calm, full, fair, light, tranquil,* and *sweet* convey the speaker's serene mood. The word *Only* (line 7) begins the transition to a mood of apprehension, as he meditates on the terrors that lie ahead in a faithless and hopeless society.

17. **Correct Choice: D**
    Since the speaker has a lover, and he says "Let us be true / To one another," there *is* still love and hope in the world, even though he asserts there is not.

18. **Correct Choice: E**
    Turbid waters have been stirred up, disturbing the sediment on the bottom and making the water cloudy and dark. *Turbid* and *disturbed* come from the same root.

19. **Correct Choice: B**
    All five are accurate definitions of *counter*. In this context, the speaker contrasts *counter* with *coin*, showing that choice B is correct. The speaker has the true wealth—love—while the "glittering Monarchs" can offer only a counter—fake money—in exchange.

20. **Correct Choice: C**
    The comparison shows that the two brooks become one, inseparable and indivisible, when

they meet in the river. In the same way, the speaker considers herself so close to the beloved that they form one entity.

21. **Correct Choice: D**

"Those glittering Monarchs, that command / The servile quarters of this earthly ball" can be paraphrased "The kings who rule the nations of the earth." The speaker would not exchange the Beloved even for this.

22. **Correct Choice: A**

The Beloved is male, and the nouns and pronouns which refer to him are capitalized; this supports Option I. The central importance of the love in the speaker's life, its intensity, and the metaphors of indivisible union support Option II. Parents do not normally express love for their children in terms like those used in this poem, so Option III is unlikely.

23. **Correct Choice: C**

Writers often use repetition for emphasis. In this case, line 12's exact repetition of line 6 (and the partial repetition again in line 18) underscores the speaker's profound sense of union with the Beloved and the enormous importance of the relationship.

24. **Correct Choice: B**

The phrase describes the brooks, not the speaker and the Beloved. The word *wanton* can mean "playful and lively," which fits the context of water rushing over pebbles.

25. **Correct Choice: E**

Nettlewick's actions in the bank show that Turner has not been doing the job thoroughly or properly. The Comptroller probably reasons that Turner will be more thorough and less friendly and trusting with people who are strangers to him.

26. **Correct Choice: D**

The passage does not describe Nettlewick's appearance except to say that he has thin fingers, which does not reveal anything about his character.

27. **Correct Choice: C**

The statement is an imaginative comparison; Nettlewick is not himself a musician. The word *expert* and the description of his quick, accurate, and thorough actions show that choice C is correct.

28. **Correct Choice: D**

The author states that Turner has known Dorsey "since he was a baby" and is an old friend of the bank's president. Knowing and trusting the staff for many years, Turner feels no need to check up on every small detail.

29. **Correct Choice: C**

The men are nervous because Nettlewick is so efficient that they think he "would neither make nor overlook an error." His efficiency shows both in the way he does his job and in his refusal to waste any words.

30. **Correct Choice: E**

All three options are reasonable possibilities. Many people are stiff and formal with strangers, especially in professional situations. Nettlewick's whole manner is in keeping with his formal and precise diction, so it may be that he is always this way. And if the bank employees are the examiner's friends, he might find it awkward to check up on them in detail, as the job requires. Nettlewick probably finds that his job is easier if he keeps his distance.

31. **Correct Choice: A**

A *deliberate* person does not like to be rushed. The author indicates that Mr. Erdlinger is the opposite of an *impulsive* person. He moves at his own slow pace, not letting anyone hurry him.

32. **Correct Choice: B**

Ponderously is derived from the Latin word for "weight." The author means that Mr. Erdlinger carried out the introductions in a slow, heavy, plodding way, without haste.

33. **Correct Choice: B**

Lines 7–8 show that Reason is the speaker of lines 9–16.

34. **Correct Choice: A**

The speaker pleads with her readers to be kinder than Reason. She hopes they will like her poems so much that she can stop repenting having sent them to the printer.

35. **Correct Choice: E**

The speaker is made angry by Reason's criticism of her verse. "Reason struck away" means literally that she "put these thoughts out of my mind."

36. **Correct Choice: D**

The conflict is between the speaker and "Reason": in other words, between what her brain tells her (don't try to publish your work) and what her heart tells her (I want to publish my work).

37. **Correct Choice: A**

The speaker's refusal to listen to Reason and her rush to deliver her poems before she thinks better of it, plus the anger she feels toward Reason, show that she is emotional and impulsive.

38. **Correct Choice: B**

The speaker behaves as though she thinks Reason was right after all and that she feels certain her work will not be well received. The title "The Poetess' Hasty Resolution" also supports the idea that sending the manuscript out was not a wise decision, because the work is not really very good.

39. **Correct Choice: C**
Reason refers to the speaker's "ill poetry" and tells her that it will make a "useless" book. Reason is both critical and unkind.

40. **Correct Choice: B**
The speaker says she likes her verses so well that she wants to write more and that she hopes, if she writes enough, to become famous. She does not say anything about needing to earn money.

41. **Correct Choice: A**
The author says that the men's "eyes glanced level, and were fastened upon the waves."

42. **Correct Choice: A**
The sixth paragraph describes the sinking of the ship. The men are in the lifeboat trying to reach the shore.

43. **Correct Choice: B**
The dingy is ten feet long, so it is quite a bit larger than a bathtub. The author exaggerates to contrast the tiny boat with the huge ocean and to emphasize how little shelter it gives the men.

44. **Correct Choice: E**
Tireless: There is always another wave coming along and washing over the boat. Endless: They can see nothing but the ocean in every direction. Threatening: The waves are trying to swamp the boat. Powerful: The waves are strong and they toss the boat about without mercy.

45. **Correct Choice: D**
The captain's failure to take an oar or bail is not due to pride but necessity. He is injured, and he is the only man in the boat with enough skill and experience to navigate. The other four choices are supported by various details in the passage.

46. **Correct Choice: C**
Phrases like "pranced and reared and plunged" and "scramble over these walls of water" draws the reader in with a vivid description of the way the waves toss the little boat about.

47. **Correct Choice: D**
The men are so busy rowing, bailing, and watching the sea that they do not even take time to look up at the sky; clearly, then, they have no energy or attention to waste on unnecessary conversation.

48. **Correct Choice: B**
The author puts his characters in a life-threatening situation that they may or may not survive. The reader keeps reading in order to find out whether they will reach the shore or be rescued.

49. **Correct Choice: E**
The passage addresses all three themes. Option I: The characters are in a life-and-death struggle against the sea. Option II: None of the men ever dreamed he would find himself fighting for his life in a leaky ten-foot boat. Option III: The men greatly improve their chances of survival by following the captain's orders and not giving in to panic or fear.

50. **Correct Choice: E**
The passage allows the reader to know the thoughts of two characters: the correspondent, who "wondered why he was there," and the captain, who still has the impression of the sinking ship before his eyes. Only an outside narrator, or the author, can see into the thoughts of more than one character.

51. **Correct Choice: C**
The author describes Drouet as unsuspicious—someone who would be helpless if faced with a schemer who wanted to harm him. *Hornswaggled* is an American dialect word that means "deliberately made a fool of" or "took advantage of"—that is, conned.

52. **Correct Choice: C**
Drouet is described as someone who is exactly what he appears to be on the surface; someone who has no secrets and no hidden depths.

53. **Correct Choice: A**
A moth flies into a lamp because the lamplight is an irresistible lure. Similarly, Drouet finds women irresistible. Whenever he meets an attractive woman, he succumbs to the attraction just as the moth succumbs to the glow of the light.

54. **Correct Choice: E**
The author emphasizes Drouet's good qualities—generosity, warmth, friendliness—and points out that he is harmless. The tone is affectionate.

55. **Correct Choice: B**
A scheming villain would have offered Carrie money in order to get her into his power, most probably to seduce and then abandon her. Drouet has no such harmful intentions toward Carrie; he is genuinely attracted to her and behaves accordingly.

56. **Correct Choice: D**
The author compares Carrie to animals who rely on their instincts to protect them from predators. She knows nothing about Drouet except what she can perceive for herself; her trust is not based on information, but on what her instincts tell her about him.

57. **Correct Choice: C**
Drouet wants Carrie "to succumb to his charms" and he feels an "inborn desire" for her. The passage is dated 1900; at that time, it was highly improper for a young woman to accept money from a man. It was understood that he expected to become her lover in return for it.

58. **Correct Choice: B**

    Almost every line of the passage describes Drouet's unique personality. The author drops only a few hints and statements about Drouet's relationship with Carrie, so this is not his main purpose. Choice E is wrong because the author is interested in Drouet as an individual, not a representative type.

59. **Correct Choice: A**

    Carrie is not likely to come to great harm with a "nice, good-hearted man" whose intentions are generous and kind, if partly selfish.

60. **Correct Choice: E**

    Drouet's main motive is his own appetite. His concern for Carrie's plight is only a secondary motive; as the author notes, he would not have felt the same concern if Carrie had been a boy instead of a pretty girl.

▬▬ HOW TO CALCULATE YOUR SCORE

Count the number of correct answers and enter the total below.
Count the number of wrong answers. Do NOT include any questions you did not answer.
Multiply the number of wrong answers by 0.25 and enter the total below.
Do the subtraction. The answer is your raw score. Use the scoring scale to find your scaled score.

$$\underset{\text{(number of correct answers)}}{\text{[short WOL]}} - \underset{\text{(number of wrong answers} \times 0.25)}{\text{[short WOL]}} = \underset{\text{(raw score)}}{\text{[short WOL]}}$$

Raw Score	Scaled Score	Raw Score	Scaled Score	Raw Score	Scaled Score	Raw Score	Scaled Score	Raw Score	Scaled Score
60	800	44	710	28	560	12	420	−4	260
59	800	43	700	27	550	11	410	−5	250
58	800	42	690	26	540	10	400	−6	240
57	800	41	690	25	530	9	390	−7	230
56	800	40	680	24	520	8	380	−8	220
55	800	39	670	23	510	7	370	−9	210
54	790	38	660	22	500	6	360	−10	200
53	790	37	650	21	500	5	350	−11	200
52	780	36	640	20	490	4	340	−12	200
51	770	35	630	19	490	3	330	−13	200
50	760	34	620	18	480	2	320	−14	200
49	750	33	610	17	470	1	310	−15	200
48	740	32	600	16	460	0	300		
47	740	31	590	15	450	−1	290		
46	730	30	580	14	440	−2	280		
45	720	29	570	13	430	−3	270		

Note: This is only a sample scoring scale. Scoring scales differ from exam to exam.

PRACTICE TEST 5

LITERATURE

The following practice test is designed to be just like the real SAT Literature Test. It matches the actual test in content coverage and degree of difficulty.

Once you finish the practice test, determine your score. Carefully read the answer explanations of the questions you answered incorrectly. Identify any weaknesses in your literature skills by determining the areas in which you made the most errors. Review those sections of this book first. Then, as time permits, go back and review your strengths.

Allow one hour to take the test. Time yourself and work uninterrupted. If you run out of time, take note of where you stopped when time ran out. Remember that you lose a quarter point for each incorrect answer, but you do not lose points for questions you leave blank. Therefore, unless you can eliminate one or more of the five choices, it is best to leave a question unanswered.

Use the following formula to calculate your score:

(number of correct answers) – ¼ (number of incorrect answers)

If you treat this practice test just like the actual exam, it will accurately reflect how you are likely to perform on test day. Here are some hints on how to create test-taking conditions similar to those of the actual exam:

- Complete the test in one sitting. On test day, you will not be allowed to take a break.
- Tear out the answer sheet and fill in the ovals just as you will on the actual test day.
- Have a good eraser and more than one sharp pencil handy. On test day, you will not be able to go get a new pencil if yours breaks.
- Do not allow yourself any extra time; put down your pencil after exactly one hour, no matter how many questions are left to answer.
- Become familiar with the directions on the test. If you go in knowing what the directions say, you will not have to waste time reading and thinking about them on the actual test day.

PRACTICE TEST 5

LITERATURE

ANSWER SHEET

Tear out this answer sheet and use it to mark your answers.

1. Ⓐ Ⓑ Ⓒ Ⓓ Ⓔ	16. Ⓐ Ⓑ Ⓒ Ⓓ Ⓔ	31. Ⓐ Ⓑ Ⓒ Ⓓ Ⓔ	46. Ⓐ Ⓑ Ⓒ Ⓓ Ⓔ
2. Ⓐ Ⓑ Ⓒ Ⓓ Ⓔ	17. Ⓐ Ⓑ Ⓒ Ⓓ Ⓔ	32. Ⓐ Ⓑ Ⓒ Ⓓ Ⓔ	47. Ⓐ Ⓑ Ⓒ Ⓓ Ⓔ
3. Ⓐ Ⓑ Ⓒ Ⓓ Ⓔ	18. Ⓐ Ⓑ Ⓒ Ⓓ Ⓔ	33. Ⓐ Ⓑ Ⓒ Ⓓ Ⓔ	48. Ⓐ Ⓑ Ⓒ Ⓓ Ⓔ
4. Ⓐ Ⓑ Ⓒ Ⓓ Ⓔ	19. Ⓐ Ⓑ Ⓒ Ⓓ Ⓔ	34. Ⓐ Ⓑ Ⓒ Ⓓ Ⓔ	49. Ⓐ Ⓑ Ⓒ Ⓓ Ⓔ
5. Ⓐ Ⓑ Ⓒ Ⓓ Ⓔ	20. Ⓐ Ⓑ Ⓒ Ⓓ Ⓔ	35. Ⓐ Ⓑ Ⓒ Ⓓ Ⓔ	50. Ⓐ Ⓑ Ⓒ Ⓓ Ⓔ
6. Ⓐ Ⓑ Ⓒ Ⓓ Ⓔ	21. Ⓐ Ⓑ Ⓒ Ⓓ Ⓔ	36. Ⓐ Ⓑ Ⓒ Ⓓ Ⓔ	51. Ⓐ Ⓑ Ⓒ Ⓓ Ⓔ
7. Ⓐ Ⓑ Ⓒ Ⓓ Ⓔ	22. Ⓐ Ⓑ Ⓒ Ⓓ Ⓔ	37. Ⓐ Ⓑ Ⓒ Ⓓ Ⓔ	52. Ⓐ Ⓑ Ⓒ Ⓓ Ⓔ
8. Ⓐ Ⓑ Ⓒ Ⓓ Ⓔ	23. Ⓐ Ⓑ Ⓒ Ⓓ Ⓔ	38. Ⓐ Ⓑ Ⓒ Ⓓ Ⓔ	53. Ⓐ Ⓑ Ⓒ Ⓓ Ⓔ
9. Ⓐ Ⓑ Ⓒ Ⓓ Ⓔ	24. Ⓐ Ⓑ Ⓒ Ⓓ Ⓔ	39. Ⓐ Ⓑ Ⓒ Ⓓ Ⓔ	54. Ⓐ Ⓑ Ⓒ Ⓓ Ⓔ
10. Ⓐ Ⓑ Ⓒ Ⓓ Ⓔ	25. Ⓐ Ⓑ Ⓒ Ⓓ Ⓔ	40. Ⓐ Ⓑ Ⓒ Ⓓ Ⓔ	55. Ⓐ Ⓑ Ⓒ Ⓓ Ⓔ
11. Ⓐ Ⓑ Ⓒ Ⓓ Ⓔ	26. Ⓐ Ⓑ Ⓒ Ⓓ Ⓔ	41. Ⓐ Ⓑ Ⓒ Ⓓ Ⓔ	56. Ⓐ Ⓑ Ⓒ Ⓓ Ⓔ
12. Ⓐ Ⓑ Ⓒ Ⓓ Ⓔ	27. Ⓐ Ⓑ Ⓒ Ⓓ Ⓔ	42. Ⓐ Ⓑ Ⓒ Ⓓ Ⓔ	57. Ⓐ Ⓑ Ⓒ Ⓓ Ⓔ
13. Ⓐ Ⓑ Ⓒ Ⓓ Ⓔ	28. Ⓐ Ⓑ Ⓒ Ⓓ Ⓔ	43. Ⓐ Ⓑ Ⓒ Ⓓ Ⓔ	58. Ⓐ Ⓑ Ⓒ Ⓓ Ⓔ
14. Ⓐ Ⓑ Ⓒ Ⓓ Ⓔ	29. Ⓐ Ⓑ Ⓒ Ⓓ Ⓔ	44. Ⓐ Ⓑ Ⓒ Ⓓ Ⓔ	59. Ⓐ Ⓑ Ⓒ Ⓓ Ⓔ
15. Ⓐ Ⓑ Ⓒ Ⓓ Ⓔ	30. Ⓐ Ⓑ Ⓒ Ⓓ Ⓔ	45. Ⓐ Ⓑ Ⓒ Ⓓ Ⓔ	60. Ⓐ Ⓑ Ⓒ Ⓓ Ⓔ

PRACTICE TEST 5
Time: 60 minutes

Directions: This test consists of selections from literary works and questions on their content, form, and style. After reading each passage or poem, choose the best answer to each question and then fill in the corresponding oval on the answer sheet.

Note: Pay particular attention to the requirements of questions that contain the words NOT or EXCEPT.

Questions 1–9. Read the following passage carefully before you choose your answers.

The slaves selected to go to the Great House Farm, for the monthly allowance for themselves and their fellow-slaves, were peculiarly enthusiastic. While on their way, they would
5 make the dense old woods, for miles around, reverberate with their wild songs, revealing at once the highest joy and the deepest sadness. They would compose and sing as they went along, consulting neither time nor tune. The
10 thought that came up, came out—if not in the word, in the sound;—and as frequently in the one as in the other. They would sometimes sing the most pathetic sentiment in the most rapturous tone, and the most rapturous senti-
15 ment in the most pathetic tone. Into all of their songs they would manage to weave something of the Great House Farm. Especially would they do this, when leaving home. They would then sing most exultingly the following words:

20 *I am going away to the Great House Farm!*
O, yea! O, yea! O!

This they would sing, as a chorus, to words which to many would seem unmeaning jargon, but which, nevertheless, were full of
25 meaning to themselves. I have sometimes thought that the mere hearing of those songs would do more to impress some minds with the horrible character of slavery, than the reading of whole volumes of philosophy on
30 the subject could do.

I did not, when a slave, understand the deep meaning of those rude and apparently incoherent songs. I was myself within the circle; so that I neither saw nor heard as those with-
35 out might see and hear. They told a tale of woe which was then altogether beyond my feeble comprehension; they were tones loud, long, and deep; they breathed the prayer and complaint of souls boiling over with the bit-
40 terest anguish. Every tone was a testimony against slavery, and a prayer to God for deliverance from chains. The hearing of those wild notes always depressed my spirit, and filled me with ineffable sadness. I have frequently
45 found myself in tears while hearing them. The mere recurrence to those songs, even now, afflicts me; and while I am writing these lines, an expression of feeling has already found its way down my cheek. To those songs
50 I trace my first glimmering conception of the dehumanizing character of slavery. I can never get rid of that conception. Those songs still follow me, to deepen my hatred of slavery, and quicken my sympathies for my
55 brethren in bonds. If anyone wishes to be impressed with the soul-killing effects of slavery, let him go to Colonel Lloyd's plantation, and, on allowance-day, place himself in the deep pine woods, and there let him, in
60 silence, analyze the sounds that shall pass through the chambers of his soul,—and if he is not thus impressed, it will only be because "there is no flesh in his obdurate heart."

I have often been utterly astonished, since I
65 came to the north, to find persons who could speak of the singing, among slaves, as evidence of their contentment and happiness. It is impossible to conceive of a greater mistake. Slaves sing most when they are most
70 unhappy. The songs of the slave represent the sorrows of his heart; and he is relieved by them, only as an aching heart is relieved by its tears. At least, such is my experience. I have often sung to drown my sorrow, but seldom
75 to express my happiness. Crying for joy, and singing for joy, were alike uncommon to me while in the jaws of slavery. The singing of a man cast away upon a desolate island might be as appropriately considered as evidence
80 of contentment and happiness, as the singing of a slave; the songs of the one and of the other are prompted by the same emotion.

(1845)

GO ON TO THE NEXT PAGE

PRACTICE TEST—*Continued*

1. "An expression of feeling has already found its way down my cheek" (lines 48–49) is the author's way of saying that

   (A) his reflection in the mirror reminds him of his days as a slave
   (B) thinking about the past affects his emotions
   (C) he does not like to write about unpleasant topics
   (D) a tear is running down his face
   (E) his story will upset many readers

2. The author uses the phrase "his obdurate heart" (line 63) to show that those who are not moved by the slaves' songs are

   (A) brutal and cruel
   (B) ignorant and stupid
   (C) selfish and greedy
   (D) unfeeling and harsh
   (E) just and upright

3. In what sense does the author use the word "rude" (line 32)?

   (A) ill-mannered
   (B) incomplete
   (C) rough and unrefined
   (D) rugged and strong
   (E) violent and savage

4. According to the author, slaves sing in order to

   (A) release their pent-up emotions
   (B) communicate with each other
   (C) celebrate joyous occasions
   (D) make their working hours seem shorter
   (E) persuade people that slavery is a cruel system

5. The slaves are "peculiarly enthusiastic" (lines 3–4) about the trip to the Great House Farm because

   I. it provides a brief holiday from their usual labors
   II. they receive food and supplies at the end of the journey
   III. taking a journey gives them the sense of being free

   (A) I and II only
   (B) II and III only
   (C) I and III only
   (D) III only
   (E) I, II, and III

6. The author uses the words "wild" (line 6), "rapturous" (line 14), and "exultingly" (line 19) to show that the slaves' songs are characterized by

   (A) beautiful melodies and harmonies
   (B) strong passions and emotions
   (C) catchy tunes and clever lyrics
   (D) a loud volume of sound
   (E) primitive and exotic rhythms

7. Phrases such as "the dehumanizing character of slavery" (line 51), "my hatred of slavery" (lines 53–54), and "the soul-killing effects of slavery" (lines 56–57) suggest that the author's main purpose is to

   (A) describe his feelings and emotions
   (B) show readers what it is like to live as a slave
   (C) persuade readers to oppose and abolish slavery
   (D) place the details of his past life on record
   (E) reminisce about important events in his early youth

8. Why does the author believe that hearing slaves sing "would do more to impress some minds with the horrible character of slavery, than the reading of whole volumes of philosophy on the subject" (lines 27–30)?

   (A) Music has a more immediate and direct emotional impact than words.
   (B) Songs come from the slaves themselves, while books are written by outside observers.
   (C) The same piece of music can mean different things to different listeners.
   (D) It is easier to learn by listening than it is to learn by reading.
   (E) Music is a universal language that can be understood by any listener.

9. The author uses the word "glimmering" (line 50) to explain

   (A) how abominable he finds the system of human slavery
   (B) how fragmentary his original grasp of the evils of slavery was
   (C) how slowly and gradually he comprehended the evils of slavery
   (D) how bitter he felt when he first realized he was a slave
   (E) how eager he is to make others understand his views on slavery

GO ON TO THE NEXT PAGE →

PRACTICE TEST—*Continued*

Questions 10–18. Read the following poem carefully before you choose your answers.

If by dull rhymes our English must be chained,
And, like Andromeda, the Sonnet sweet
Fettered, in spite of pained loveliness;
Let us find out, if we must be constrained,
5 Sandals more interwoven and complete
To fit the naked foot of poesy;
Let us inspect the lyre, and weigh the stress
Of every chord, and see what may be gained
By ear industrous, and attention meet;
10 Misers of sound and syllable, no less
Than Midas of his coinage, let us be
Jealous of dead leaves in the bay wreath crown;
So, if we may not let the Muse be free,
She will be bound with garlands of her own.

(1819)

10. When the poet writes, "Misers of sound and syllable, no less / Than Midas of his coinage" (lines 10–11), he means that

   (A) his fellow poets are misers with words because they fail to adhere to the traditional rhyme schemes
   (B) his fellow poets should be restrictive with their words the way Midas was with his gold
   (C) his fellow poets are restrictive with their words the way Midas was with his gold because of their insistence to adhering to traditional rhyme schemes
   (D) his fellow poets fail to be misers with words because they love elaborate language the way that Midas loved large quantities of gold
   (E) his fellow poets should not be misers just because writing poetry does not pay well

11. This poem meets all the usual standards for a sonnet EXCEPT in which category?

   (A) meter
   (B) line length
   (C) rhyme scheme
   (D) number of lines
   (E) rhythm

12. Which best sums up the argument of the poem?

   (A) We must find more truly poetic and meaningful ways to use rhyme in poetry.
   (B) We must stop allowing the Muse to force us to use rhymes in poetry.
   (C) We must do away with rhyme altogether if poetry is to survive as a form.
   (D) We must recite our poems aloud to be sure of their quality before we publish.
   (E) We will destroy poetry as a form of writing if we continue to write in the old ways.

13. By "Sandals more interwoven and complete / To fit the naked foot of poesy" (lines 5–6), the poet means

   (A) end rhymes that will make every new poem complete
   (B) new schemes of internal rhyme that will improve the art of writing poetry
   (C) metric feet that suit the content of each individual poem
   (D) shoes and clothing that fit properly for greater ease in writing
   (E) rhyme schemes that relate more closely to the meaning of a poem

14. Which best describes the relationship between the content and structure of the poem?

   (A) The content describes the poet's inability to write, and the irregular structure proves his point.
   (B) The content alludes to ancient tales, and the structure is borrowed from ancient forms of poetry.
   (C) The content laments the scarcity of great love poetry, and the structure echoes that of great love poems of the past.
   (D) The content argues for new poetic forms and demonstrates their worth by employing an irregular structure.
   (E) The content suggests that rhyme should be eliminated from poetry, and the structure is unrhymed.

GO ON TO THE NEXT PAGE

PRACTICE TEST—*Continued*

15. The phrase "Jealous of dead leaves in the bay wreath crown" (line 12) is best paraphrased as

   (A) envious of the works of ancient, long-dead poets
   (B) distrustful of old, outworn rules for writing poetry
   (C) suspicious of time-honored poetic forms
   (D) competitive with other poets for high honors
   (E) strictly observant of ancient methods of artistic creation

16. Which best describes the poet's attitude toward rhyme in poetry?

   (A) He believes that poems should not have to rhyme.
   (B) He enjoys the challenge of making his ideas fit the accepted rhyme schemes.
   (C) He feels that a poet should adapt a rhyme scheme to fit the content of the poem.
   (D) He respects and honors the rhymes schemes that poets have always used.
   (E) He finds it very difficult to rhyme English words.

17. The poet uses the word "meet" (line 9) to mean

   (A) encounter
   (B) assemble
   (C) fulfill
   (D) confront
   (E) appropriate

18. "Let us inspect the lyre, and weigh the stress / Of every chord, and see what may be gained, / By ear industrous, and attention meet" (lines 7–9) means that poets should

   (A) take great care to choose words that sound exactly right
   (B) spend more time listening to music
   (C) read their work aloud as they write and revise
   (D) take care that their poems are neither too long nor too short
   (E) pay more attention to the structure of their poems

Questions 19–25. Read the following poem carefully before you choose your answers.

The Lake

In youth's spring, it was my lot
To haunt of the wide earth a spot
The which I could not love the less;
So lovely was the loneliness
5 Of a wild lake, with black rock bound.
And the tall pines that tower'd around.
But when the night had thrown her pall
Upon that spot—as upon all,
And the wind would pass me by
10 In its stilly melody,
My infant spirit would awake
To the terror of the lone lake.
Yet that terror was not fright—
But a tremulous delight,
15 And a feeling undefin'd,
Springing from a darken'd mind.
Death was in that poison'd wave
And in its gulf a fitting grave
For him who thence could solace bring
20 To his dark imagining;
Whose wild'ring thought could even make
An Eden of that dim lake.

(1827)

19. Which quality most strongly attracts the speaker to the lake?

   (A) its isolated setting
   (B) its border of black rocks
   (C) its appearance at night
   (D) the taste of its water
   (E) the nearby graves

GO ON TO THE NEXT PAGE

PRACTICE TEST—*Continued*

20. Which best explains the speaker's meaning when he says "Yet that terror was not fright" (line 13)?

    (A) Terror and fear are similar emotions.
    (B) Terror attracts me rather than making me want to run away.
    (C) I concealed my terror so that no one would know I was frightened.
    (D) Something terrible happened to me at the lake.
    (E) The lake made me feel both terror and fear.

21. Why does the speaker describe his mind as "darken'd" (line 16)?

    (A) He is enthralled by images of death and terror.
    (B) He likes wandering in the woods at night.
    (C) He would rather be alone than with other people.
    (D) He is attracted by water even though he cannot swim.
    (E) He likes the nighttime better than the day.

22. The "feeling undefin'd" (line 15) in the speaker's mind can best be described as

    (A) idle curiosity
    (B) painful anxiety
    (C) wondering awe
    (D) morbid fascination
    (E) ignorant bliss

23. The word "Eden" (line 22) is particularly effective because it shows that the speaker

    (A) is worried by the attraction he feels for the lake
    (B) is determined to make the lake a more beautiful place
    (C) is a person of profound gloom who takes pleasure in desolation
    (D) is imaginative enough to pretend that the lake is beautiful
    (E) is a deeply religious person who prefers to worship in isolation

24. The word "haunt" (line 2) contributes to the poem's mood of

    (A) mysteriousness
    (B) suspense
    (C) horror
    (D) decay
    (E) ominousness

25. The rhythmic irregularities in the poem contribute which of the following to the overall effect?

    I. They mirror the disturbed state of the speaker's mind.
    II. They help to portray the lake as a strange and eerie place.
    III. They create an unsettled feeling in the reader.

    (A) I and II only
    (B) I and III only
    (C) II only
    (D) II and III only
    (E) I, II, and III

Questions 26–35. Read the following passage carefully before you choose your answers.

"What a splendid night it is!"

"You like this weather?"

"It suits my purpose. Watson, I mean to burgle Milverton's house tonight."

5 I had a catching of the breath, and my skin went cold at the words, which were slowly uttered in a tone of concentrated resolution. As a flash of lightning in the night shows up in an instant every detail of a wide land-
10 scape, so at one glance I seemed to see every possible result of such an action—the detection, the capture, the honored career ending in irreparable failure and disgrace, my friend himself lying at the mercy of the odious
15 Milverton.

"For Heaven's sake, Holmes, think what you are doing," I cried.

"My dear fellow, I have given it every consideration. I am never precipitate in my
20 actions, nor would I adopt so energetic and indeed dangerous a course if any other were possible. Let us look at the matter clearly and fairly. I suppose that you will admit that the action is morally justifiable, though
25 technically criminal. To burgle his house is no more than to forcibly take his pocket-book—an action in which you were prepared to aid me."

GO ON TO THE NEXT PAGE

PRACTICE TEST—*Continued*

I turned it over in my mind.

30 "Yes," I said; "it is morally justifiable so long as our object is to take no articles save those which are used for an illegal purpose."

"Exactly. Since it is morally justifiable I have only to consider the question of personal
35 risk. Surely a gentleman should not lay much stress upon this when a lady is in most desperate need of his help?"

"You will be in such a false position."

"Well, that is part of the risk. There is no
40 other possible way of regaining these letters. The unfortunate lady has not the money, and there are none of her people in whom she could confide. Tomorrow is the last day of grace, and unless we can get the letters
45 tonight this villain will be as good as his word and will bring about her ruin. I must, therefore, abandon my client to her fate or I must play this last card. Between ourselves, Watson, it's a sporting duel between this
50 fellow Milverton and me. He had, as you saw, the best of the first exchanges; but my self-respect and my reputation are concerned to fight it to a finish."

"Well, I don't like it; but I suppose it must
55 be," said I. "When do we start?"

"You are not coming."

"Then you are not going," said I. "I give you my word of honor—and I never broke it in my life—that I will take a cab straight to the
60 police station and give you away unless you let me share this adventure with you."

"You can't help me."

"How do you know that? You can't tell what may happen. Anyway, my resolution is taken.
65 Other people besides you have self-respect and even reputations."

Holmes had looked annoyed, but his brow cleared, and he clapped me on the shoulder.

"Well, well, my dear fellow, be it so. We have
70 shared the same room for some years, and it would be amusing if we ended up sharing the same cell . . . We shall have some cold supper before we start. It is now nine-thirty. At eleven we shall drive as far as Church
75 Row. It is a quarter of an hour's walk from there to Appledore Towers. We shall be at work

before midnight. Milverton is a heavy sleeper and retires punctually at ten-thirty. With any luck we should be back here by two, with the
80 Lady Eva's letters in my pocket."

(c. 1904)

26. The author uses the phrase "my skin went cold at the words" (lines 5–6) to show that Watson

    (A) is shocked to learn that Holmes is a criminal
    (B) knows that Holmes is walking into a trap
    (C) has a strict sense of right and wrong
    (D) is cautious and prudent by nature
    (E) is dismayed by the consequences Holmes may suffer

27. Why does Watson threaten to give Holmes up to the police "unless you let me share this adventure with you" (lines 60–61)?

    (A) He wants to be on the spot to protect and defend Holmes if necessary.
    (B) He believes that what Holmes is doing is wrong and foolish.
    (C) He knows that Holmes's plan has no chance of succeeding.
    (D) He does not trust Holmes to carry out his plan unassisted.
    (E) He does not want to miss out on the excitement of the adventure.

28. The word "precipitate" (line 19) means

    (A) damp and rainy
    (B) hasty and rash
    (C) visible or audible
    (D) honest and open
    (E) brave or daring

29. Holmes believes that breaking into Milverton's house is "morally justifiable" (line 24) because

    (A) he has made a bet with Milverton that he does not want to lose
    (B) he and Milverton do not like one another
    (C) Milverton made him lose face in an earlier encounter
    (D) he wants to prevent Milverton from committing a crime
    (E) Watson once offered to help him take Milverton's pocket-book

GO ON TO THE NEXT PAGE →

PRACTICE TEST—*Continued*

30. From the facts in the passage, you can conclude that Milverton is

    (A) a thief
    (B) a murderer
    (C) a blackmailer
    (D) a burglar
    (E) an arsonist

31. Watson is characterized by all of the following EXCEPT

    (A) courage
    (B) loyalty
    (C) honesty
    (D) morality
    (E) impulsiveness

32. Holmes is annoyed at Watson's insistence on joining him because

    I.   he does not want to involve Watson in any risks
    II. he prefers to get the better of Milverton on his own
    III. he is not interested in Watson's self-respect or reputation

    (A) I and II only
    (B) II only
    (C) I and III only
    (D) III only
    (E) I, II, and III

33. The fact that Holmes speaks with "concentrated resolution" (line 7) shows that he

    (A) is unlikely to change his mind now that it is made up
    (B) has carefully thought through every detail of his plans
    (C) will insist on carrying out his intentions by himself
    (D) is well aware that he is going into danger
    (E) dislikes the idea of committing a crime

34. Which of the following does NOT describe Holmes's state of mind as he prepares to burgle Milverton's house?

    (A) determined
    (B) confident
    (C) cautious
    (D) enthusiastic
    (E) reluctant

35. The word "false" (line 38) means

    (A) contrary to truth
    (B) imprudent
    (C) arising from mistaken ideas
    (D) not keeping faith
    (E) not genuine or real

Questions 36–45. Read the following poem carefully before you choose your answers.

The Second Coming

Turning and turning in the widening gyre
The falcon cannot hear the falconer;
Things fall apart; the center cannot hold;
Mere anarchy is loosed upon the world,
5 The blood-dimmed tide is loosed, and everywhere
The ceremony of innocence is drowned;
The best lack all conviction, and the worst
Are full of passionate intensity.

Surely some revelation is at hand;
10 Surely the Second Coming is at hand.
The Second Coming! Hardly are those words out
When a vast image out of *Spiritus Mundi* [1]
Troubles my sight; somewhere in the sands of the desert
15 A shape with lion body and the head of a man,
A gaze blank and pitiless as the sun,
Is moving its slow thighs, while all about it
Reel shadows of the indignant desert birds.
The darkness drops again; but now I know
20 That twenty centuries of stony sleep
Were vexed to nightmare by a rocking cradle,
And what rough beast, its hour come round at last,
Slouches towards Bethlehem to be born?

(1921)

[1] literally, "Spirit of the World"; defined by the poet as a collection of universally understood symbols and images

GO ON TO THE NEXT PAGE ➤

PRACTICE TEST—*Continued*

36. The speaker describes anarchy as "mere" (line 4) in order to show that it

    (A) is insignificant and unimportant
    (B) is total and absolute
    (C) is happening in a foreign country
    (D) cannot be reversed or halted
    (E) is a temporary condition

37. Which is the best explanation of the statement "The best lack all conviction, and the worst / Are full of passionate intensity" (lines 7–8)?

    (A) Good people have few followers because they lack enthusiasm; evil people sway crowds by speaking with strong feeling.
    (B) Those who seem good are actually evil; those who seem evil are actually good.
    (C) The best that can be said of people is that they have strong feelings; the worst that can be said is that they believe in nothing.
    (D) It is better to be without strong beliefs and ideals than to have strong and intense emotions.
    (E) People pay more attention to a good person who lacks conviction than they pay to an evil person who speaks with passion.

38. Which best describes the tone of the poem?

    (A) disgusted
    (B) angry
    (C) somber
    (D) desperate
    (E) disappointed

39. The passage "A gaze blank and pitiless as the sun, / Is moving its slow thighs, while all about it / Reel shadows of the indignant desert birds / The darkness drops again;" (lines 15–18) contains examples of all of the following EXCEPT

    (A) alliteration
    (B) simile
    (C) personification
    (D) imagery
    (E) rhyme

40. Why does the speaker believe that "some revelation is at hand" (line 9)?

    (A) He has seen a vision of a terrifying future.
    (B) He has heard news of a strange event in the desert.
    (C) He knows that the current state of unrest cannot continue.

(D) He sees that the world has awakened to a new awareness of danger.
(E) He feels an inexplicable dread of what is to come.

41. The poem's thematic content is echoed and reflected by which of the following elements?

        I. its lack of rhyme
        II. the rhythmic and metric irregularities in the second stanza
        III. its use of figurative language

    (A) I only
    (B) I, II and III
    (C) II only
    (D) II and III only
    (E) III only

42. The falcon and falconer in line 1 symbolize

    (A) slave and master
    (B) child and parent
    (C) follower and leader
    (D) lover and beloved
    (E) poet and muse

43. Which best describes the nature of the event the speaker anticipates?

    (A) An evil force will be let loose upon the world.
    (B) All living creatures on earth will die.
    (C) A mysterious lion-man creature will be born in Bethlehem.
    (D) A war between nations will destroy the world.
    (E) People and animals will lose their ability to communicate.

44. When the speaker says "The darkness drops again" (line 18), he means

    (A) chaos and disorder have cast the world into darkness
    (B) the image of the lion-man and birds is frightening and ominous
    (C) the "shadows of the indignant desert birds" create patches of darkness on the sands
    (D) night falls on the lion-man and the birds of the desert
    (E) his momentary vision vanishes from sight

GO ON TO THE NEXT PAGE

PRACTICE TEST—*Continued*

45. The "rocking cradle" (line 20) is a metaphor for which of the following?

    (A) the restless and chaotic state of society
    (B) the manger in which the baby Jesus slept
    (C) the assassination of a major head of state
    (D) the first shot fired in an international war
    (E) the earthquake that awoke the sleeping beast in the desert

Questions 46–52. Read the following passage carefully before you choose your answers.

And so at last we may ask what are the joys of Ignorance. Are they to enjoy what one has, to be molested by no one, to be superior to all cares and annoyance, to live a secure and
5 quiet life in so far as possible? Truly, this is the life of any wild beast or bird that has its little nest in the deepest and most distant forests, as near as possible to the sky, and there rears its nestlings, flies around in
10 search of food with no fear of being hunted, and warbles in its sweet songs at dawn and sunset. Why crave for the heavenly power of the mind in addition to these pleasures? Ergo, let Ignorance throw off her humanity,
15 let her have Circe's cup and betake herself on all fours to the beasts.

To the beasts, indeed? But they refuse to receive such a foul guest, if they have any share in an inferior kind of reason—as many
20 observers have thought that they do—or have an intelligence that is due to some strong instinct, or make use of the arts or of anything resembling the arts among themselves. For, according to Plutarch, dogs in pursuit of
25 game are said to have some sense of logic and to make obvious use of the disjunctive syllogism when they happen to come to a fork in the road. Aristotle notes that the nightingale is in the habit of giving some
30 kind of musical instruction to her young. Almost every beast is its own doctor, and many of them have taught notable medical lessons to mankind. The Egyptian ibis has shown us the value of purges, and the hip-
35 popotamus of phlebotomy. Who can deny a knowledge of astronomy to those from whom come so many warnings of winds, rain, floods, and calm weather? With what prudent and stern discipline the geese check
40 their dangerous garrulity with pebbles in their bills when they are flung over Mt. Taurus! Our domestic science owes much to the ants, and our political science to the bees. Military art thanks the cranes for the principle of
45 posting sentinels and forming the triangular phalanx. The beasts are too intelligent to admit Ignorance to their company and fellowship; they put her lower down.

So what then? Must she go to the trees and
50 the stones. The very trees and shrubs, and the entire forest tore away from their roots to run after the elegant music of Orpheus. Often they have had mysterious powers and have given divine oracles, as the oaks at Dodona did.
55 Rocks also respond with some docility to the sacred voice of the poets. And will not even the rocks spurn Ignorance away? And so, since she is lower than every kind of brute, lower than the trees and rocks, lower than
60 every order known to Nature, will it be granted to Ignorance to find rest in the not-being of the Epicureans? No, not there, since it is necessary, that what is worse, what is viler, what is more wretched, what is lower, should
65 be Ignorance.

(1632)

46. The author uses the word "docility" (line 55) to show that the rocks

    (A) are made to soften and crumble by the poets' voices
    (B) are open and obedient to the poets' teaching
    (C) cannot hear or understand what the poets say
    (D) refuse to allow Ignorance to come near them
    (E) provide the poets with a place to sit and sing their verses

47. According to the author, geese demonstrate "prudent and stern discipline" (line 39) by

    (A) always flying along the same safe route
    (B) being silent when honking would endanger them
    (C) collecting pebbles with which to build shelters
    (D) calling to warn each other of nearby predators
    (E) avoiding areas where they know they may be hunted

GO ON TO THE NEXT PAGE

PRACTICE TEST—*Continued*

48. The phrase "Let her have Circe's cup" (line 15) is best interpreted as

    (A) let her be fatally poisoned
    (B) let her fall in love with the first person she sees
    (C) let her forget everything she ever knew
    (D) let her be transformed into a pig
    (E) let her sleep for a hundred years

49. When the author says that dogs can "make obvious use of the disjunctive syllogism" (lines 26–27), he means that

    (A) they are easily confused and misled
    (B) their minds can grasp complicated instructions
    (C) they are highly skilled at tracking their prey
    (D) they can find their way home without help
    (E) they are capable of choosing the better of two alternatives

50. The third paragraph of the argument might be considered weak because it

    (A) relies on evidence from works of imaginative literature
    (B) discusses trees and stones
    (C) asks several questions of the reader
    (D) defines Ignorance as the lowest and most vile element
    (E) repeats an earlier statement that Ignorance is lower than the beasts

51. The author proves that animals are not ignorant of any of the following EXCEPT

    (A) music
    (B) medicine
    (C) art
    (D) astronomy
    (E) logic

52. The speaker implies throughout the passage that "the joys of Ignorance" (lines 26–27) are

    (A) contentment
    (B) peace
    (C) safety
    (D) intelligence
    (E) nonexistent

Questions 53–60. Read the following poem carefully before you choose your answers.

Another II

As loving hind that (hartless) wants her deer,
Scuds through the woods and fern with hark'ning ear,
Perplext, in every bush and nook doth pry,
Her dearest deer, might answer ear or eye;
5 So doth my anxious soul, which now doth miss
A dearer dear (far dearer heart) than this.
Still wait with doubts, and hopes, and failing eye,
His voice to hear or person to descry.
Or as the pensive dove doth all alone
10 (On withered bough) most uncouthly bemoan
The absence of her love and loving mate,
Whose loss hath made her so unfortunate,
Ev'n thus do I, with many a deep sad groan,
Bewail my turtle true, who now is gone,
15 His presence and his safe return still woos,
With thousand doleful sighs and mournful coos.
Or as the loving mullet, that true fish,
Her fellow lost, nor joy nor life do wish,
But launches on that shore, there for to die,
20 Where she her captive husband doth espy.
Mine being gone, I lead a joyless life,
I have a loving peer, yet seem no wife;
But worst of all, to him can't steer my course,
I here, he there, alas, both kept by force.
25 Return my dear, my joy, my only love,
Unto thy hind, thy mullet, and thy dove,
Who neither joys in pasture, house, nor streams,
The substance gone, O me, these are but dreams.
Together at one tree, oh let us browse,
30 And like two turtles roost within one house,
And like the mullets in one river glide,
Let's still remain but one, till death divide.
Thy loving love and dearest dear,
At home, abroad, and everywhere.

(c. 1650)

GO ON TO THE NEXT PAGE →

PRACTICE TEST—*Continued*

53. Which line of the poem best sums up the speaker's message to her husband?

   (A) "[I] Bewail my turtle true, who now is gone" (line 14)
   (B) "I have a loving peer, yet seem no wife" (line 22)
   (C) "I here, he there, alas, both kept by force" (line 24)
   (D) "The substance gone, O me, these are but dreams" (line 28)
   (E) "Let's still remain but one, till death divide" (line 32)

54. The first six lines of the poem are characterized by which of the following?

   (A) extended metaphor
   (B) enjambment
   (C) wordplay
   (D) paradox
   (E) literary allusions

55. The author uses the hind, mullet, and turtledove to symbolize all of the following EXCEPT

   (A) longing
   (B) loyalty
   (C) love
   (D) sorrow
   (E) fidelity

56. Which best describes the speaker's situation?

   (A) She and her husband are temporarily apart.
   (B) Her husband has recently died and left her alone.
   (C) She has lost her husband's love to another woman.
   (D) She has permanently abandoned her husband.
   (E) She no longer loves her husband.

57. The change in meter at line 33 alerts the reader to which of the following?

   (A) a new rhyme scheme
   (B) a shift in tone or mood
   (C) the conclusion of the poem
   (D) a change in speakers
   (E) the introduction of a new subject

58. The author uses words like "anxious" (line 5), "doubts" (line 7), "bemoan" (line 10), and "doleful" (line 16) to contribute to a mood of

   (A) despair
   (B) mourning
   (C) passion
   (D) grief
   (E) hope

59. The author uses the phrase "failing eye" (line 7) to show that the speaker

   (A) is searching for her mate in a dark forest
   (B) is unable to hear any trace of her mate
   (C) cannot see what she is looking for
   (D) is weeping with unhappiness over her loss
   (E) does not know where to look for her mate

60. The speaker's sorrow is best characterized as

   (A) shocking and traumatic
   (B) momentary and trivial
   (C) absolute and total
   (D) wistful and loving
   (E) bitter and resentful

S T O P

IF YOU FINISH BEFORE TIME IS CALLED, YOU MAY CHECK YOUR WORK ON THIS TEST ONLY.

DO NOT TURN TO ANY OTHER TEST IN THIS BOOK.

■ ANSWER KEY

1. D	21. A	41. B
2. D	22. D	42. C
3. C	23. C	43. A
4. A	24. E	44. E
5. E	25. E	45. A
6. B	26. E	46. B
7. C	27. A	47. B
8. A	28. B	48. D
9. B	29. D	49. E
10. C	30. C	50. A
11. C	31. E	51. C
12. A	32. A	52. E
13. E	33. A	53. E
14. D	34. E	54. C
15. B	35. B	55. D
16. C	36. B	56. A
17. E	37. A	57. C
18. A	38. D	58. D
19. C	39. E	59. C
20. B	40. C	60. D

ANSWERS AND EXPLANATIONS

1. **Correct Choice: D**
   The author says he frequently wept while listening to slaves singing and that even thinking about the music makes him sad. This context makes it clear that the "expression of feeling" he refers to is another tear trickling down his cheek.

2. **Correct Choice: D**
   Obdurate is derived from a Latin word meaning "hard." If a person has an *obdurate* heart, he is "hardhearted" or unfeeling.

3. **Correct Choice: C**
   In this sense, *rude* means "crude, rough, unrefined." The slaves' songs are not finished compositions by trained musicians; they are made up on the spot.

4. **Correct Choice: A**
   The author says that slaves sing in order to relieve the sorrows of the heart.

5. **Correct Choice: E**
   All three options are reasonable causes for the slaves to feel happy and excited about going to the Great House Farm.

6. **Correct Choice: B**
   The three words in the question all refer to the emotions felt by the singers.

7. **Correct Choice: C**
   The author repeatedly expresses his hatred of slavery as an institution. Because this appears to be his major focus, the inference follows that he wants to persuade others to hate slavery as much as he does.

8. **Correct Choice: A**
   Most of the author's references to the songs are to their emotional impact on himself as well as on others. He is so strongly affected by the memory of the songs that he believes the effect will be equally strong on other listeners. He believes that this appeal to emotion is stronger than a book's appeal to reason.

9. **Correct Choice: B**
   A *glimmering* conception is one that is only faintly comprehended.

10. **Correct Choice: C**
    The author calls his fellow poets misers because they are stingy with their words to make them fit into traditional rhyme schemes. Because the argument of the poem is that poets should attempt new rhyme schemes or else poetry will die as an art, choice A must be wrong, because "fail to adhere" indicates that not following traditional rhyme schemes is a negative characteristic. The author argues that poets expand their uses of words, and choice B is the exact opposite of this argument. Choice D

is wrong because the author *does* call his fellow poets misers. Choice E is wrong because there is nothing in the poem about how well poetry pays as a profession.

11. **Correct Choice: C**
    Most sonnets follow one of two set rhyme schemes—Italian or Shakespearean. This sonnet has an irregular rhyme scheme all its own.

12. **Correct Choice: A**
    The speaker says that if we *must* use rhymes in poetry, then we need to find ways to make rhyme contribute more to the artistic effect of the whole poem.

13. **Correct Choice: E**
    The speaker is comparing rhyme schemes to sandals. Just as a sandal should perfectly and comfortably fit a person's bare foot, a rhyme scheme should be a perfect and comfortable fit for the language and meaning of a poem. *Poesy* refers to the art and practice of writing poetry.

14. **Correct Choice: D**
    The sonnet argues that new and better rhyme schemes are needed to replace the old patterns. It proves its point by employing an irregular rhyme scheme.

15. **Correct Choice: B**
    In this context, *jealous* means "distrustful, suspicious." "Dead leaves" is a metaphorical reference to long-established poetic forms and techniques, which the poet believes have outworn their welcome. He says, in effect, that poets should distrust old ways of writing poetry rather than using them unthinkingly or automatically.

16. **Correct Choice: C**
    The poet's main argument is not that rhyme should be eliminated but that it should always be adapted to serve the poem's content. He believes that poets should adapt a rhyme scheme to fit the ideas they want to express, rather than making their ideas fit into a set rhyme scheme.

17. **Correct Choice: E**
    The context shows that this archaic definition of *meet* is the correct one.

18. **Correct Choice: A**
    The poem's overall message is that poets must pay close attention to both the meaning and the sound of their words. The lyre is a musical instrument; the words *lyre*, *chord*, and *ear* all suggest that in these lines, the poet is primarily concerned with urging his colleagues to think about sound.

19. **Correct Choice: C**
The speaker is first drawn to the lake by its loneliness, but it does not exert a true fascination for him until he sees it at night. In the darkness, it terrifies him, and he exults in the feeling of terror.

20. **Correct Choice: B**
The phrase "tremulous delight" (line 14) implies that the speaker defines fear as an emotion that would drive him away and terror as an emotion that attracts and thrills him.

21. **Correct Choice: A**
The speaker says that terror delights him and that he finds *solace*, or comfort, in the thoughts of his own death by drowning in the lake.

22. **Correct Choice: D**
The speaker is fascinated by thoughts of his own death. *Morbid* comes from a Latin root meaning "death."

23. **Correct Choice: C**
In the Book of Genesis, the Garden of Eden is an earthly paradise where people and animals enjoy untroubled happiness. Only a gloomy and morbid person could compare an isolated lake, with its towering pines and black rocks, to this biblical pleasure garden.

24. **Correct Choice: E**
Ominousness is the best choice because an air of foreboding, of approaching disaster, hangs over the poem. The speaker appears to be emotionally unstable, to be attracted to dark and lonely places, and to feel a thrill at the thought of his own death.

25. **Correct Choice: E**
All three are true statements. The speaker's unstable mind has produced a poem with an unstable rhythmic structure. The jerky rhythm of many of the lines affects the reader's impression of everything the speaker describes, including the lake. The irregularities of the rhythm upset the reader's natural expectation that the rhymed couplets will proceed in a smooth and regular rhythm.

26. **Correct Choice: E**
Choices C and D are true statements, but these facts about Watson would not cause a strong emotional reaction, such as the author describes. Watson reacts strongly because he is afraid for Holmes—afraid for the consequences to his career and reputation if he is caught.

27. **Correct Choice: A**
The greatest fear Watson expresses about the burglary is that Holmes may get caught. Therefore, his most probable reason for going along is his friendship for Holmes—he wants to help and protect his friend.

28. **Correct Choice: B**
Holmes explains that his action is not hasty and rash, but rather that he has thought carefully before making his decision.

29. **Correct Choice: D**
Details in the passage show that Milverton intends to commit a crime against Holmes's client, Lady Eva. Holmes intends to prevent a crime by committing one of his own. Because he is stealing nothing except items "which are used for an illegal purpose," he feels that his act is justifiable.

30. **Correct Choice: C**
The references to money, "the letters," and Lady Eva's "ruin" imply that Milverton is blackmailing her—that her letters contain secrets that can destroy her reputation, and that he will publish these letters unless she pays him not to.

31. **Correct Choice: E**
Courage: Watson insists on sharing what he knows to be a serious risk. Loyalty: To help and protect his friend, Watson is willing to set aside his strong sense of right and wrong. Honesty: Watson is open with Holmes about his objections to the plan and clearly disapproves of the crime as a dishonest act, despite the "moral justification." Morality: Watson shows moral disapproval of the planned burglary but also the moral sense to admit that Milverton plans an even worse crime. The caution Watson exhibits in the passage shows that choice E must be the correct answer.

32. **Correct Choice: A**
Holmes's remark, "it's a sporting duel between this fellow Milverton and me," suggests that he wants to defeat Milverton all by himself (the word *duel*, by definition, is a contest between two people). Holmes is well aware that he is about to commit a crime, and naturally he hesitates to involve Watson. Therefore, Options I and II are reasonable. Option III cannot be supported, because Holmes's annoyed expression disappears when Watson reminds him that he too has a reputation to consider.

33. **Correct Choice: A**
A *resolute* person is one who is determined—one whose mind is made up and who will not easily be persuaded to change it. Choice C is wrong because this particular phrase involves only the determination to carry out the act; it does not relate to Holmes's original intention of carrying it out alone.

34. **Correct Choice: E**
Determined: Holmes is clearly resolved on his course of action and will change his mind. Confident: He states that Milverton will be asleep

and that he expects to "be back here by two," having carried out his plan. Cautious: Holmes has thought the matter through and laid his plans very carefully so as to take no unnecessary risk. Enthusiastic: The phrases "a sporting duel" and "fight it to a finish" show that Holmes is eager to defeat Milverton. This leaves choice E.

35. **Correct Choice: B**
There is nothing untruthful about Holmes's intention to burgle Milverton's house. *Imprudent* means unwise, or ill-advised. In this context, this is the correct answer. Choice C does not make sense because Holmes does not have any mistaken ideas about the risks he is taking. Choice D is wrong because Holmes does not have a trusting relationship with Milverton to betray. Choice E is incorrect because Holmes is not pretending to be something or someone else.

36. **Correct Choice: B**
The context shows that this archaic sense of *mere* must be correct. The line means "Total anarchy is loosed upon the world."

37. **Correct Choice: A**
The first six lines describe a society in chaos. "The best" and "the worst" refers to the political and/or religious leaders who influence and control society for good or evil ends. The speaker observes that the good leaders lose followers because they show no conviction, or belief in their own cause. The evil forces, on the other hand, attract followers by speaking forcefully and with passion.

38. **Correct Choice: D**
The poem is about the author's despair over the decline of Western civilization. Various words and phrases in the poem convey this feeling: "Mere anarchy is loosed upon the world" (line 4) and "The blood-dimmed tide is loosed" (line 6).

39. **Correct Choice: E**
Alliteration: "Darkness drops again" uses a repeating *d* sound to create the effect of a dull thud. Simile: "blank and pitiless *as* the sun." Personification: "indignant desert birds." Imagery: The lines contain vivid visual images. None of the lines rhymes with any of the others, so choice E is correct.

40. **Correct Choice: C**
The speaker believes that the world around him is coming to an end; that the Apocalypse—the end of one world and the beginning of a new one—is near. The speaker compares his own world with that described in the Bible and believes that the biblical prophecy is about to come true and that the world will begin again, in some new fashion.

41. **Correct Choice: B**
The major theme of the poem is the destruction of order in the world. This is mirrored by the poem's lack of structural order—its unrhymed lines and the frequent shift away from the basic meter of iambic pentameter. Option III is wrong because the presence of figurative language in a poem is normal; The figurative language in the poem supports a theme of everything being wrong, chaotic, or out of order.

42. **Correct Choice: C**
The poem describes chaos in two realms: one of faith (the references to the second coming of Jesus) and one of government (the reference to anarchy and "the blood-dimmed tide" of war). Political and religious leaders (falconers) can no longer make their followers (the falcons) hear them, because they "lack all conviction" (line 7) and they have lost control.

43. **Correct Choice: A**
The speaker describes a "rough beast" that "slouches towards Bethlehem to be born." This is a metaphor for some new force that will appear in the world, which the speaker believes will have as much influence as Jesus once had. The language "troubles my sight," "its gaze blank and pitiless," "rough beast," and "slouches" all suggest that the new force will be evil rather than good.

44. **Correct Choice: E**
The vision described in lines 13–17 is an image or picture brightly visible in the speaker's imagination. When it disappears, "the darkness drops again." The mind's eye is once more a blank surface waiting for new impressions.

45. **Correct Choice: A**
The speaker believes that an evil force has been awakened by the "rocking cradle" of a society that is no longer peaceful, ordered, or controlled.

46. **Correct Choice: B**
A *docile* person is teachable, tractable, or obedient.

47. **Correct Choice: B**
Garrulity means "talkativeness." The geese carry pebbles in their beaks to stop themselves from honking or calling, when making that noise would endanger them.

48. **Correct Choice: D**
The phrase "betake herself on all fours" is a reference to being turned into an animal. (This allusion refers to Circe, a character in the *Odyssey* who transforms Odysseus' crew into swine, or pigs.)

49. **Correct Choice: E**
The phrase "a fork in the road" is the context clue that tells you the author is referring to a dog's ability to choose the better alternative when confronted with two options. *Disjunctive* refers to two mutually exclusive alternatives, and a *syllogism* is a rule of logic.

50. **Correct Choice: A**

The evidence in the second paragraph is all based on direct observations of animals that can be scientifically proved. The evidence about the intelligence and higher instincts of trees and rocks, however, is drawn from mythology, a form of imaginative literature. The fact that a phenomenon appears in a work of fiction is not solid proof that it exists in reality.

51. **Correct Choice: C**

The author gives specific examples of animal knowledge of the other four choices. He does not suggest that animals are able to create pictures, statues, or other works of visual art.

52. **Correct Choice: E**

In the first paragraph, the author lists several possible "joys of Ignorance," including those described in choices A–C. He then shows that animals are able to live in peace, security, and contentment precisely because they are *not* ignorant. The entire passage implies that Ignorance is a joyless state.

53. **Correct Choice: E**

The speaker addresses her husband directly only in the final ten lines, which eliminates choices A, B, and C. Choice E sums up the main idea toward which the entire poem has been building.

54. **Correct Choice: C**

The poet plays with *hart/heart* and *dear/deer*—words that sound alike but mean different things.

55. **Correct Choice: D**

The author is sorrowful because her husband is away, but the three animals do not symbolize sorrow. They symbolize her feelings of love, loyalty, fidelity, and longing for her absent mate.

56. **Correct Choice: A**

"Let's still remain but one, till death divide" (line 32) implies that the husband is still alive. Nothing in the poem suggests that she and her husband do not love one another. Because the speaker describes herself and her husband as "kept [apart] by force" (line 24), it appears that he has gone away on some necessary business and will return.

57. **Correct Choice: C**

It is a standard poetic technique to signal the end of a poem, or a scene in a verse play, with a rhymed couplet. Because this entire poem is in rhymed couplets, the author has changed the meter instead of the rhyme scheme; the final two lines are one metric foot shorter than the rest of the verse.

58. **Correct Choice: D**

The speaker feels deep grief over the absence of her husband. Despair is too strong a word, because she still feels hope that he will return; mourning is too strong a word because he is still alive.

59. **Correct Choice: C**

"Failing eye" means that her eyes fail to *descry*, or see, his *person*, or physical presence. She cannot see him because he is absent.

60. **Correct Choice: D**

Every line of the poem tells of the speaker's love and her wish that her husband should return soon. The fact that she indulges in wordplay and metaphoric conceits shows that her sorrow cannot be so "absolute and total" that she has lost her wit and sense of fun.

▰ HOW TO CALCULATE YOUR SCORE

Count the number of correct answers and enter the total below.
Count the number of wrong answers. Do NOT include any questions you did not answer.
Multiply the number of wrong answers by 0.25 and enter the total below.
Do the subtraction. The answer is your raw score. Use the scoring scale to find your scaled score.

$$\underset{\text{(number of correct answers)}}{[\text{short WOL}]} - \underset{\text{(number of wrong answers} \times 0.25)}{[\text{short WOL}]} = \underset{\text{(raw score)}}{[\text{short WOL}]}$$

Raw Score	Scaled Score	Raw Score	Scaled Score	Raw Score	Scaled Score	Raw Score	Scaled Score	Raw Score	Scaled Score
60	800	44	710	28	560	12	420	−4	260
59	800	43	700	27	550	11	410	−5	250
58	800	42	690	26	540	10	400	−6	240
57	800	41	690	25	530	9	390	−7	230
56	800	40	680	24	520	8	380	−8	220
55	800	39	670	23	510	7	370	−9	210
54	790	38	660	22	500	6	360	−10	200
53	790	37	650	21	500	5	350	−11	200
52	780	36	640	20	490	4	340	−12	200
51	770	35	630	19	490	3	330	−13	200
50	760	34	620	18	480	2	320	−14	200
49	750	33	610	17	470	1	310	−15	200
48	740	32	600	16	460	0	300		
47	740	31	590	15	450	−1	290		
46	730	30	580	14	440	−2	280		
45	720	29	570	13	430	−3	270		

Note: This is only a sample scoring scale. Scoring scales differ from exam to exam.

PRACTICE TEST 6
LITERATURE

The following practice test is designed to be just like the real SAT Literature Test. It matches the actual test in content coverage and degree of difficulty.

Once you finish the practice test, determine your score. Carefully read the answer explanations of the questions you answered incorrectly. Identify any weaknesses in your literature skills by determining the areas in which you made the most errors. Review those sections of this book first. Then, as time permits, go back and review your strengths.

Allow one hour to take the test. Time yourself and work uninterrupted. If you run out of time, take note of where you stopped when time ran out. Remember that you lose a quarter point for each incorrect answer, but you do not lose points for questions you leave blank. Therefore, unless you can eliminate one or more of the five choices, it is best to leave a question unanswered.

Use the following formula to calculate your score:

(number of correct answers) – ¼ (number of incorrect answers)

If you treat this practice test just like the actual exam, it will accurately reflect how you are likely to perform on test day. Here are some hints on how to create test-taking conditions similar to those of the actual exam:

- Complete the test in one sitting. On test day, you will not be allowed to take a break.
- Do not allow yourself any extra time; put down your pencil after exactly one hour, no matter how many questions are left to answer.
- Tear out the answer sheet and fill in the ovals just as you will on the actual test day.
- Have a good eraser and more than one sharp pencil handy. On test day, you will not be able to go get a new pencil if yours breaks.
- Become familiar with the directions on the test. If you go in knowing what the directions say, you will not have to waste time reading and thinking about them on the actual test day.

PRACTICE TEST 6
LITERATURE

ANSWER SHEET

Tear out this answer sheet and use it to mark your answers.

1. Ⓐ Ⓑ Ⓒ Ⓓ Ⓔ	16. Ⓐ Ⓑ Ⓒ Ⓓ Ⓔ	31. Ⓐ Ⓑ Ⓒ Ⓓ Ⓔ	46. Ⓐ Ⓑ Ⓒ Ⓓ Ⓔ
2. Ⓐ Ⓑ Ⓒ Ⓓ Ⓔ	17. Ⓐ Ⓑ Ⓒ Ⓓ Ⓔ	32. Ⓐ Ⓑ Ⓒ Ⓓ Ⓔ	47. Ⓐ Ⓑ Ⓒ Ⓓ Ⓔ
3. Ⓐ Ⓑ Ⓒ Ⓓ Ⓔ	18. Ⓐ Ⓑ Ⓒ Ⓓ Ⓔ	33. Ⓐ Ⓑ Ⓒ Ⓓ Ⓔ	48. Ⓐ Ⓑ Ⓒ Ⓓ Ⓔ
4. Ⓐ Ⓑ Ⓒ Ⓓ Ⓔ	19. Ⓐ Ⓑ Ⓒ Ⓓ Ⓔ	34. Ⓐ Ⓑ Ⓒ Ⓓ Ⓔ	49. Ⓐ Ⓑ Ⓒ Ⓓ Ⓔ
5. Ⓐ Ⓑ Ⓒ Ⓓ Ⓔ	20. Ⓐ Ⓑ Ⓒ Ⓓ Ⓔ	35. Ⓐ Ⓑ Ⓒ Ⓓ Ⓔ	50. Ⓐ Ⓑ Ⓒ Ⓓ Ⓔ
6. Ⓐ Ⓑ Ⓒ Ⓓ Ⓔ	21. Ⓐ Ⓑ Ⓒ Ⓓ Ⓔ	36. Ⓐ Ⓑ Ⓒ Ⓓ Ⓔ	51. Ⓐ Ⓑ Ⓒ Ⓓ Ⓔ
7. Ⓐ Ⓑ Ⓒ Ⓓ Ⓔ	22. Ⓐ Ⓑ Ⓒ Ⓓ Ⓔ	37. Ⓐ Ⓑ Ⓒ Ⓓ Ⓔ	52. Ⓐ Ⓑ Ⓒ Ⓓ Ⓔ
8. Ⓐ Ⓑ Ⓒ Ⓓ Ⓔ	23. Ⓐ Ⓑ Ⓒ Ⓓ Ⓔ	38. Ⓐ Ⓑ Ⓒ Ⓓ Ⓔ	53. Ⓐ Ⓑ Ⓒ Ⓓ Ⓔ
9. Ⓐ Ⓑ Ⓒ Ⓓ Ⓔ	24. Ⓐ Ⓑ Ⓒ Ⓓ Ⓔ	39. Ⓐ Ⓑ Ⓒ Ⓓ Ⓔ	54. Ⓐ Ⓑ Ⓒ Ⓓ Ⓔ
10. Ⓐ Ⓑ Ⓒ Ⓓ Ⓔ	25. Ⓐ Ⓑ Ⓒ Ⓓ Ⓔ	40. Ⓐ Ⓑ Ⓒ Ⓓ Ⓔ	55. Ⓐ Ⓑ Ⓒ Ⓓ Ⓔ
11. Ⓐ Ⓑ Ⓒ Ⓓ Ⓔ	26. Ⓐ Ⓑ Ⓒ Ⓓ Ⓔ	41. Ⓐ Ⓑ Ⓒ Ⓓ Ⓔ	56. Ⓐ Ⓑ Ⓒ Ⓓ Ⓔ
12. Ⓐ Ⓑ Ⓒ Ⓓ Ⓔ	27. Ⓐ Ⓑ Ⓒ Ⓓ Ⓔ	42. Ⓐ Ⓑ Ⓒ Ⓓ Ⓔ	57. Ⓐ Ⓑ Ⓒ Ⓓ Ⓔ
13. Ⓐ Ⓑ Ⓒ Ⓓ Ⓔ	28. Ⓐ Ⓑ Ⓒ Ⓓ Ⓔ	43. Ⓐ Ⓑ Ⓒ Ⓓ Ⓔ	58. Ⓐ Ⓑ Ⓒ Ⓓ Ⓔ
14. Ⓐ Ⓑ Ⓒ Ⓓ Ⓔ	29. Ⓐ Ⓑ Ⓒ Ⓓ Ⓔ	44. Ⓐ Ⓑ Ⓒ Ⓓ Ⓔ	59. Ⓐ Ⓑ Ⓒ Ⓓ Ⓔ
15. Ⓐ Ⓑ Ⓒ Ⓓ Ⓔ	30. Ⓐ Ⓑ Ⓒ Ⓓ Ⓔ	45. Ⓐ Ⓑ Ⓒ Ⓓ Ⓔ	60. Ⓐ Ⓑ Ⓒ Ⓓ Ⓔ

PRACTICE TEST 6
Time: 60 minutes

Directions: This test consists of selections from literary works and questions on their content, form, and style. After reading each passage or poem, choose the best answer to each question and then fill in the corresponding oval on the answer sheet.

Note: Pay particular attention to the requirements of questions that contain the words NOT or EXCEPT.

Questions 1–9. Read the following passage carefully before you choose your answers.

"My dear Mr. Bennet," said his lady to him one day, "have you heard that Netherfield Park is let at last?"

Mr. Bennet replied that he had not.

5 "But it is," returned she; "for Mrs. Long has just been here, and she told me all about it."

Mr. Bennet made no answer.

"Do not you want to know who has taken it?" cried his wife impatiently.

10 "*You* want to tell me, and I have no objection to hearing it."

This was invitation enough.

"Why, my dear, you must know, Mrs. Long says that Netherfield is taken by a young
15 man of large fortune from the north of England; that he came down on Monday in a chaise-and-four to see the place, and was so much delighted with it that he agreed with Mr. Morris immediately; that he is to
20 take possession before Michaelmas, and some of his servants are to be in the house by the end of next week."

"What is his name?"

"Bingley."

25 "Is he married or single?"

"Oh! single, my dear, to be sure! A single man of large fortune; four or five thousand a year. What a fine thing for our girls!"

"How so? how can it affect them?"

30 "My dear Mr. Bennet," replied his wife, "how can you be so tiresome! you must know that I am thinking of his marrying one of them."

"Is that his design in settling here?"

"Design! nonsense, how can you talk so! But
35 it is very likely that he *may* fall in love with one of them, and therefore you must visit him as soon as he comes."

"I see no occasion for that. You and the girls may go, or you may send them by them-
40 selves, which perhaps will be still better, for as you are as handsome as any of them, Mr. Bingley might like you the best of the party."

"My dear, you flatter me. I certainly *have* had my share of beauty, but I do not pretend
45 to be anything extraordinary now. When a woman has five grown-up daughters, she ought to give over thinking of her own beauty."

"In such cases, a woman has not often much
50 beauty to think of."

"But, my dear, you must indeed go and see Mr. Bingley when he comes into the neighborhood."

"It is more than I engage for, I assure you."

55 "But consider your daughters. Only think what an establishment it would be for one of them. Sir William and Lady Lucas are determined to go, merely on that account, for in general, you know, they visit no newcomers.
60 Indeed you must go, for it will be impossible for *us* to visit him, if you do not."

"You are over-scrupulous, surely. I dare say Mr. Bingley will be very glad to see you; and I will send a few lines by you to assure him of
65 my hearty consent to his marrying whichever he chooses of the girls; though I must throw in a good word for my little Lizzy."

"I desire you will do no such thing. Lizzy is not a bit better than the others; and I am sure
70 she is not half so handsome as Jane, nor half so good-humored as Lydia. But you are always giving *her* the preference."

GO ON TO THE NEXT PAGE ▶

PRACTICE TEST—*Continued*

"They have none of them much to recommend them," replied he; "they are all silly and
75 ignorant like other girls; but Lizzy has something more of quickness than her sisters."

"Mr. Bennet, how can you abuse your own children in such a way? You take delight in vexing me. You have no compassion on my
80 poor nerves."

"You mistake me, my dear. I have a high respect for your nerves. They are my old friends. I have heard you mention them with consideration these twenty years at least."

85 "Ah! you do not know what I suffer."

"But I hope you will get over it, and live to see many young men of four thousand a year come into the neighborhood."

"It will be no use to us if twenty such should
90 come, since you will not visit them."

"Depend upon it, my dear, that when there are twenty, I will visit them all."

(1813)

1. From the fact that Lizzy is his favorite daughter, you can conclude that Mr. Bennet

    (A) likes talking to people with a sense of humor
    (B) values intelligence more than any other quality
    (C) enjoys seeing pretty faces around him
    (D) avoids argument and conflict within the family
    (E) appreciates having good-natured and pretty children

2. The statement "*You* want to tell me, and I have no objection to hearing it" (lines 10–11) implies which of the following?

    (A) Mr. Bennet is not much interested in hearing his wife's news.
    (B) Mrs. Bennet is disappointed by her husband's objections.
    (C) Mr. Bennet already knows what his wife is about to tell him.
    (D) Mr. and Mrs. Bennet understand each other without having to say anything.
    (E) Mrs. Bennet hesitates to speak without being coaxed and encouraged.

3. Mrs. Bennet uses the word "let" (line 3) to mean that Netherfield Park has been

    (A) allowed, permitted
    (B) abandoned, left behind
    (C) leased, rented
    (D) prevented, hindered
    (E) assigned, appointed

4. Mrs. Bennet's repeated insistence that Mr. Bennet visit Mr. Bingley reveals all of the following EXCEPT

    (A) she is not a subtle person
    (B) she focuses all her attention on what is most important to her
    (C) she will make every effort to see that her daughters marry well
    (D) she does not understand her husband's character
    (E) she is not practical or realistic by nature

5. Why does Mr. Bennet promise that "when there are twenty, I will visit them all" (line 92)?

    (A) He does not wish to make any effort on his daughters' behalf.
    (B) He enjoys teasing and provoking his wife.
    (C) He will only bestir himself on an extraordinary occasion.
    (D) He sees no point in visiting only one newcomer to the neighborhood.
    (E) He knows one young man cannot marry all five of his daughters.

6. All of the following statements help to reveal Mr. Bennet's sense of humor EXCEPT

    (A) ". . . you may send them by themselves, which perhaps will be still better, for as you are as handsome as any of them, Mr. Bingley might like you the best of the party." (lines 39–42)
    (B) "I will send a few lines by you to assure him of my hearty consent to his marrying whichever he chooses of the girls." (lines 64–66)
    (C) ". . . they are all silly and ignorant, like other girls; but Lizzy has something more of quickness than her sisters." (lines 74–76)
    (D) "I have a high respect for your nerves. They are my old friends. I have heard you mention them with consideration these twenty years at least." (lines 81–84)
    (E) "But I hope you will get over it, and live to see many young men of four thousand a year come into the neighborhood." (lines 86–88)

GO ON TO THE NEXT PAGE

PRACTICE TEST—*Continued*

7. Which of the following suggests that Mr. Bennet shares his wife's concern for their daughters' future?

   (A) his wish that his daughters were not silly and ignorant
   (B) his promise to visit twenty young men when they move to the neighborhood
   (C) his suggestion that his wife and daughters should visit Mr. Bingley
   (D) his immediate question as to whether Bingley is married or single
   (E) his promise to consent to Bingley's marrying one of his daughters

8. What accounts for Mrs. Bennet's reaction when Mr. Bennet says "I must throw in a good word for my little Lizzy" (lines 66–67)?

   I. She does not regard Lizzy's quickness as an attractive quality.
   II. She is a little jealous of Mr. Bennet's affection for Lizzy.
   III. She is fonder of Jane and Lydia than she is of Lizzy.

   (A) I and II only
   (B) I and III only
   (C) II and III only
   (D) III only
   (E) I, II, and III

9. Mr. Bennet's attitude toward Mrs. Bennet is best described as

   (A) loving and affectionate
   (B) detached and ironic
   (C) irritated and contemptuous
   (D) suspicious and jealous
   (E) cold and indifferent

Questions 10–16. Read the following poem carefully before you choose your answers.

Fear no more the heat o' th' sun,
    Nor the furious winter's rages;
Thou thy worldly task hast done,
    Home art gone, and ta'en thy wages.
5   Golden lads and girls all must,
    As chimney-sweepers, come to dust.

Fear no more the frown o' th' great;
    Thou art past the tyrant's stroke.
Care no more to clothe and eat;
10   To thee the reed is as the oak.
The scepter, learning, physic, must
All follow this, and come to dust.

Fear no more the lightning flash,
    Nor th' all-dreaded thunder-stone.
15 Fear not slander, censure rash;
    Thou hast finish'd joy and moan.
All lovers young, all lovers must
Consign to thee, and come to dust.

No exorciser harm thee!
20 Nor no witchcraft charm thee!
Ghost unlaid forbear thee!
Nothing ill come near thee!
Quiet consummation have,
And renownéd be thy grave!

(c. 1609)

10. "Golden lads and girls all must / As chimney-sweepers, come to dust" (lines 5–6) is an example of

   (A) a play on words
   (B) a metaphor
   (C) verbal irony
   (D) personification
   (E) a tragedy

11. "The scepter" (line 11) symbolizes which of the following?

   (A) a doctor
   (B) a ghost
   (C) a monarch
   (D) a poet
   (E) a lover

12. The metaphor "Home art gone, and ta'en thy wages" (line 4) implies that the person addressed has

   (A) gone home
   (B) quit her job
   (C) left town
   (D) died
   (E) abandoned the speaker

13. Which best explains the meaning of "Ghost unlaid forbear thee!" (line 21)?

   (A) Let nothing haunt you.
   (B) Let ghosts fear you.
   (C) Let ghosts help carry your burdens.
   (D) Let us always remember you.
   (E) Let your spirit rest.

GO ON TO THE NEXT PAGE

PRACTICE TEST—*Continued*

14. The phrase "Quiet consummation have" (line 23) is best paraphrased as

    (A) May you find true love and fulfillment.
    (B) May you find happiness in marriage.
    (C) May you be blessed with peace and happiness.
    (D) May you die with courage.
    (E) May your dead body lie quietly in the earth.

15. Which best describes the wish the speaker expresses for the person addressed as "thee" in lines 19–24?

    (A) that she will sleep peacefully and well
    (B) that she will lie quiet and undisturbed in her grave
    (C) that she will learn not to fear so many things
    (D) that she will forget the haunting memories of the past
    (E) that she will return to him one day in the future

16. "To thee the reed is as the oak" (line 10) is the speaker's way of saying that

    (A) neither weakness nor strength mean anything to you now
    (B) you once seemed weak, but you now show great strength
    (C) you can no longer tell the difference between a reed and an oak tree
    (D) it does not matter to you where we shelter you from the weather
    (E) you are just as happy to be poor as to be rich

Questions 17–25. Read the following dramatic excerpt carefully before you choose your answers.

(By learning to speak like a lady, flower-seller Liza Doolittle hopes to make a better life for herself. Speech professor Henry Higgins agrees to house her at his expense during her training. Liza's father, hearing of her good fortune, comes to Higgins and his colleague Pickering to ask them for money.)

DOOLITTLE. What am I, Governors both? I ask you, what am I? I'm one of the undeserving poor: that's what I am. Think of what that means to a man. It means that he's up agen middle-class morality all the
5 time. If there's anything going, and I put in for a bit of it, it's always the same story: "You're undeserving; so you can't have it." But my needs is as great as the most deserving widow's that ever got money out of six different charities in one week for the death of the same
10 husband. I don't need less than a deserving man: I need more. I don't eat less hearty than him; and I drink a lot more. I want a bit of amusement, 'cause I'm a

thinking man. I want cheerfulness and a song and a band when I feel low. Well, they charge me just the
15 same for everything as they charge the deserving. What is middle-class morality? Just an excuse for never giving me anything. Therefore, I ask you, as two gentlemen, not to play that game on me. I'm playing straight with you. I ain't pretending to be deserving. I'm undeserving;
20 and I mean to go on being undeserving. I like it; and that's the truth. Will you take advantage of a man's nature to do him out of the price of his own daughter what he's brought up and fed and clothed by the sweat of his brow until she's growed big enough to be inter-
25 esting to you two gentlemen? Is five pounds unreasonable? I put it to you; and I leave it to you.

HIGGINS *[rising, and going over to Pickering].* Pickering: if we were to take this man in hand for three months, he could choose between a seat in the Cabinet and a
30 popular pulpit in Wales.

PICKERING. What do you say to that, Doolittle?

DOOLITTLE. Not me, Governor, thank you kindly. I've heard all the preachers and all the prime ministers—for I'm a thinking man and game for politics or religion or
35 social reform same as all the other amusements—and I tell you it's a dog's life any way you look at it. Undeserving poverty is my line. Taking one station in society with another, it's—it's—well, it's the only one that has any ginger in it, to my taste.

40 HIGGINS. I suppose we must give him a fiver.

PICKERING. He'll make a bad use of it, I'm afraid.

DOOLITTLE. Not me, Governor, so help me I won't. Don't you be afraid that I'll save it and spare it and live idle on it. There won't be a penny of it left by Monday:
45 I'll have to go to work same as if I'd never had it. It won't pauperize me, you bet. Just one good spree for myself and the missus, giving pleasure to ourselves and employment to others, and satisfaction to you to think it's not been throwed away. You couldn't spend it better.

50 HIGGINS *[taking out his pocket book and coming between Doolittle and the piano].* This is irresistible. Let's give him ten. *[He offers two notes to the dustman[1]].*

DOOLITTLE. No, Governor. She wouldn't have the
55 heart to spend ten; and perhaps I shouldn't neither. Ten pounds is a lot of money: it makes a man feel prudent like; and then goodbye to happiness. You give me what I ask you, Governor: not a penny more, and not a penny less.

(1916)

---

[1] British term for "garbage collector," Doolittle's occupation

 GO ON TO THE NEXT PAGE

PRACTICE TEST—*Continued*

17. When Higgins says that Doolittle "could choose between a seat in the Cabinet and a popular pulpit in Wales" (lines 29–30), he acknowledges that Doolittle

    I.   is a charming and entertaining speaker
    II. has a natural ability to express himself clearly and well
    III. has strong political convictions and deep religious faith

    (A) I only
    (B) II only
    (C) III only
    (D) I and II only
    (E) II and III only

18. Why does Doolittle believe that feeling "prudent like" means "goodbye to happiness" (line 57)?

    (A) Prudent people save money and thus deprive themselves of the enjoyment it can buy.
    (B) People who are prudent disapprove of many ordinary amusements.
    (C) A prudent person would need more than five pounds for "one good spree."
    (D) Prudent people let their spouses dictate what they will do with their income.
    (E) A prudent person feels that he has no responsibilities to others.

19. In what sense is Doolittle "undeserving" as used in the passage according to the standards of "middle-class morality"?

    (A) He has a job and can thus afford to pay his own way.
    (B) He drinks heavily, relies on his charm, and spends his money freely.
    (C) He does not support his daughter's effort to improve her situation.
    (D) He has never succeeded in borrowing money from a charity.
    (E) He does not want to rise to a higher social rank.

20. Why does Doolittle believe that "undeserving poverty" is the only station in life "that has any ginger in it" (lines 36–39)?

    (A) It qualifies him for assistance from various charities.
    (B) It allows him to talk to those of higher rank as if they were his equals.
    (C) It offers him the chance to rise to a better position in society.

(D) It lets him depend on others for his support.
(E) It gives him the freedom to be irresponsible and enjoy himself as he likes.

21. Higgins's use of the word "irresistible" (line 51) shows that he

    (A) is charmed by Doolittle's personality
    (B) is convinced by Doolittle's logic
    (C) feels compassion for Doolittle's poverty
    (D) is angered by Doolittle's request for money
    (E) feels guilty at having to refuse Doolittle's request

22. Doolittle's example of "the most deserving widow that ever got money out of six different charities in one week for the death of the same husband" (lines 8–10) demonstrates his belief that

    (A) widows who apply to charities are not really deserving of help
    (B) charities will not help someone like himself who has a job
    (C) he would have to die before his "missus" could get help from a charity
    (D) middle-class moralists are hypocritical
    (E) the "deserving" poor will always find someone to give them a helping hand

23. Which of the following best supports Doolittle's statement "I'm a thinking man" (line 34)?

    (A) "What am I, Governors both? I ask you, what am I? I'm one of the undeserving poor: that's what I am." (lines 1–3)
    (B) "Well, they charge me just the same for everything as they charge the deserving. What is middle-class morality? Just an excuse for never giving me anything." (lines 14–17)
    (C) "Taking one station in society with another, it's—it's—well, it's the only one that has any ginger in it, to my taste." (lines 37–39)
    (D) "Don't you be afraid that I'll save it and spare it and live idle on it. There won't be a penny of it left by Monday." (lines 43–44)
    (E) "No, Governor. She wouldn't have the heart to spend ten; and perhaps I shouldn't neither." (lines 54–55)

GO ON TO THE NEXT PAGE

PRACTICE TEST—*Continued*

24. What does Doolittle mean by asking, "Will you take advantage of a man's nature to do him out of the price of his own daughter what he's brought up and fed and clothed by the sweat of his brow until she's growed big enough to be interesting to you two gentlemen?" (lines 21–25)

   (A) Higgins and Pickering have deprived him of his daughter through their educational experiment, but have failed to compensate him.
   (B) Higgins and Pickering are training Eliza for free, so members of her family would also benefit from their generosity.
   (C) His poverty makes him unable to provide for his daughter.
   (D) Now that Higgins and Pickering are financially supporting Eliza, they can also support him.
   (E) He has always struggled to support Liza, and now he needs help to continue to do so.

25. Doolittle's long speech beginning "What am I, Governors both" (line 1) represents or includes all of the following EXCEPT

   (A) monologue
   (B) dialect
   (C) repetition
   (D) parallel structure
   (E) irony

Questions 26–35. Read the following poem carefully before you choose your answers.

Beat! Beat! Drums!

Beat! beat! drums!—blow! bugles! blow!
Through the windows—through doors—burst like a ruthless
force,
Into the solemn church, and scatter the congregation,
Into the school where the scholar is studying;
5 Leave not the bridegroom quiet—no happiness must he
have now with his bride,
Nor the peaceful farmer any peace, ploughing his field or
gathering his grain,
So fierce you whirr and pound you drums—so shrill you
bugles blow.

Beat! beat! drums!—blow! bugles! blow!
Over the traffic of cities—over the rumble of wheels in the
streets;
10 Are beds prepared for sleepers at night in the houses? no
sleepers must sleep in those beds,
No bargainers' bargains by day—no brokers or speculators—
would they continue?
Would the talkers be talking? would the singer attempt to
sing?

Would the lawyer rise in the court to state his case before
the judge?
Then rattle quicker, heavier drums—you bugles wilder blow.

15 Beat! beat! drums!—blow! bugles! blow!
Make no parley—stop for no expostulation,
Mind not the timid—mind not the weeper or prayer,
Mind not the old man beseeching the young man,
Let not the child's voice be heard, nor the mother's
entreaties,
20 Make even the trestles to shake the dead where they lie
awaiting the hearses,
So strong you thump O terrible drums—so loud you bugles
blow.

(1861)

26. The poet begins each stanza with the same line in order to

   (A) seize and hold the reader's attention
   (B) interrupt the people as they go about their everyday business
   (C) emphasize the insistence and urgency of the call to arms
   (D) show that everyone must obey the bugles and drums
   (E) echo the excitement young men feel as they go off to war

27. What is the effect of the regular iambic rhythm that characterizes the final line of each stanza?

   I. It reminds the reader of English poetic tradition.
   II. It disturbs the reader's expectations of irregular rhythms.
   III. It echoes the rhythm of the drumbeats that call soldiers to arms.

   (A) I only
   (B) II only
   (C) I and II only
   (D) III only
   (E) I and III only

GO ON TO THE NEXT PAGE

PRACTICE TEST—*Continued*

28. Which best conveys the meaning of the word "expostulation" (line 16)?

    (A) shouting
    (B) protest
    (C) mourning
    (D) pleading
    (E) questions

29. What are the old man, child, and mother (lines 18–19) pleading for?

    (A) a speedy conclusion to the war
    (B) their loved ones not to go into the dangers of battle
    (C) their side of the conflict to be victorious in the end
    (D) peace to be declared before any fighting begins
    (E) the terrible noise of bugles and drums to stop frightening them

30. The personification of the bugles and drums in the opening and closing lines of each stanza

    (A) makes the call to war seem unswerving and pitiless
    (B) shows that the bugles and drums play all by themselves
    (C) demonstrates the seriousness of the call to arms
    (D) underscores the strength and power of the enemy army
    (E) appeals to the reader's sense of sight

31. In the second stanza, why must the drums "rattle quicker, heavier" and the bugles "wilder blow" (line 21)?

    (A) to persuade potential recruits that war is a gallant adventure
    (B) to frighten the soldiers in the enemy army
    (C) to calm the prayers and entreaties of anxious family members
    (D) to make themselves heard over the everyday tasks at which people work
    (E) to drown out arguments made by those who do not want to join up

32. The word "parley" (line 16) is especially appropriate in this poem because of its association with

    (A) musical notation
    (B) literary theory
    (C) poetic form and structure
    (D) American history
    (E) military procedure

33. Which best characterizes the speaker's attitude toward war?

    (A) He feels frightened and uneasy about it.
    (B) He regrets it as a necessary evil.
    (C) He wishes he were young enough to join up.
    (D) He regards it as a destructive force.
    (E) He enthusiastically welcomes and supports it.

34. The imagery throughout the poem appeals most strongly to the sense of

    (A) sight
    (B) hearing
    (C) touch
    (D) taste
    (E) smell

35. In what way does the poem's structure reflect its content?

    (A) The content states that the call to arms insists on obedience, and the lines describing the drums and bugles impose their own regularity on an otherwise free-verse poem.
    (B) The content describes a variety of people who will be affected by the coming war, and the lines show a variety of rhymes and rhythms.
    (C) The structure has three stanzas with the same number of lines, and the content describes three different kinds of people.
    (D) The structure is free-verse, and the content describes people's free responses to the call to arms.
    (E) The content is about war, and the structure conforms to military regularity.

Questions 36–42. Read the following poem carefully before you choose your answers.

Fair Cynthia, all the homage that I may
Unto a creature, unto thee I pay;
In lonesome woods to meet so kind a guide,
To me's more worth than all the world beside.
5 Some joy I felt just now, when sage got o'er
Yon surly river to this rugged shore,
Deeming rough welcomes from these clownish trees
Better than lodgings with Nereides.
Yet swelling fears surprise; all dark appears—
10 Nothing but light can dissipate those fears.

GO ON TO THE NEXT PAGE

PRACTICE TEST—*Continued*

My fainting vitals can't lend strength to say,
But softly whisper, O I wish 'twere day.
The murmur hardly warmed the ambient air,
Ere thy bright aspect rescues from despair:
15 Makes the old hag her sable mantle loose,
And a bright joy does through my soul diffuse.
The boisterous trees now lend a passage free,
And pleasant prospects thou giv'st light to see.

(1704)

36. Which of the following does the author address as "fair Cynthia" (line 1)?

(A) the sun
(B) the moon
(C) the river
(D) the night
(E) the clouds

37. The words "clownish" (line 7) and "boisterous" (line 17) suggest that the trees

(A) offer safety and shelter from the weather
(B) appear dark and forbidding
(C) are tossing about in the wind
(D) provide welcome shade from the sun
(E) amuse the speaker with their unusual shapes

38. Which of the following best defines "prospects" (line 18)?

(A) plans and intentions
(B) expectations for the future
(C) views of the countryside
(D) people who mine for precious metals
(E) outlines of what is to come

39. Which of the following is responsible for the "swelling fears" (line 9) the speaker feels?

(A) the surly river (line 6)
(B) the rugged shore (line 6)
(C) the clownish trees (line 7)
(D) the ambient air (line 13)
(E) the sable mantle (line 15)

40. Which of the following is NOT an example of personification?

(A) "yon surly river" (line 6)
(B) "these clownish trees" (line 7)
(C) "my fainting vitals" (line 11)
(D) "the ambient air" (line 13)
(E) "the old hag" (line 15)

41. The speaker uses the word "sage" (line 5) to mean

(A) wise from experience
(B) well-behaved
(C) prudent and cautious
(D) spicy and sweet
(E) solemn and grave

42. "Swelling fears surprise" (line 9) is best paraphrased as

(A) I suddenly realize that I feel a growing fear.
(B) I'm surprised to discover that I'm scared.
(C) I'm frightened by the mysterious swelling of the ground.
(D) It surprises me that I'm not at all afraid.
(E) The best way to conquer fear is to surprise it.

Questions 43–51. Read the following passage carefully before you choose your answers.

Amory decided to sit for a while on the front steps, so he bade them good night.

The great tapestries of trees had darkened to ghosts back at the last edge of twilight. The
5 early moon had drenched the arches with pale blue, and, weaving over the night, in and out of the gossamer rifts of moon, swept a song, a song with more than a hint of sadness, infinitely transient, infinitely regretful.

10 He remembered that an alumnus of the nineties had told him of one of Booth Tarkington's[1] amusements: standing in mid-campus in the small hours and singing tenor songs to the stars, arousing mingled emotions in the
15 couched undergraduates according to the sentiment of their moods.

Now, far down the shadowy line of University Place a white-clad phalanx broke the gloom, and marching figures, white-shirted, white-
20 trousered, swung rhythmically up the street, with linked arms and heads thrown back:

[1] Princeton alumnus and Pulitzer Prize–winning novelist

GO ON TO THE NEXT PAGE →

PRACTICE TEST—*Continued*

"Going back—going back,
Going—back—to—Nas-sau—Hall,
Going back—going back—
25 *To the—Best—Old—Place—of—All.*
Going back—going back,
From all—this—earth-ly—ball,
We'll—clear—the—track—as—we—go—back—
Going—back—to—Nas-sau—Hall!"

30 Amory closed his eyes as the ghostly procession drew near. The song soared so high that
all dropped out except the tenors, who bore
the melody triumphantly past the danger-
point and relinquished it to the fantastic
35 chorus. Then Amory opened his eyes, half
afraid that sight would spoil the rich illusion
of harmony.

He sighed eagerly. There at the head of the
white platoon marched Allenby, the football
40 captain, slim and defiant, as if aware that
this year the hopes of the college rested on
him, that his hundred-and-sixty pounds were
expected to dodge to victory through the
heavy blue and crimson lines.

45 Fascinated, Amory watched each rank of
linked arms as it came abreast, the faces
indistinct above the polo shirts, the voices
blent in a pæan of triumph—and then the
procession passed through shadowy Camp-
50 bell Arch, and the voices grew fainter as it
wound eastward over the campus.

The minutes passed and Amory sat there
very quietly. He regretted the rule that
would forbid freshmen to be outdoors after
55 curfew, for he wanted to ramble through
the shadowy scented lanes, where Witherspoon brooded like a dark mother over
Whig and Clio, her Attic children, where the
black Gothic snake of Little curled down to
60 Cuyler and Patton,[2] these in turn flinging
the mystery out over the placid slope rolling
to the lake.

(1920)

[2] Witherspoon, Whig, Clio, Little, Cuyler, and Patton
Halls—buildings on the Princeton campus

43. Amory thinks of the group of singing students as a "ghostly procession" (lines 30–31) and a "fantastic chorus" (lines 34–35) because

(A) none of them is a close friend of his
(B) they are upperclassmen and he is a freshman
(C) he is eager for the day when he can join their group
(D) he is captivated by the sound of their singing
(E) they are indistinct white shapes in the dusk

44. The author uses the words "phalanx" (line 18) and "platoon" (line 39) to compare the students to

(A) football players
(B) soldiers
(C) fraternity brothers
(D) ghosts
(E) kings

45. The phrases "gossamer rifts of moon" (line 17), "a hint of sadness" (lines 8–9), "the rich illusion" (line 36), and "he sighed eagerly" (line 38) contribute to the passage's mood of

(A) nostalgia
(B) romance
(C) innocence
(D) regret
(E) anxiety

46. Which phrase might be described as a contradiction in terms?

(A) "infinitely transient" (line 9)
(B) "mingled emotions" (line 14)
(C) "ghostly procession" (lines 30–31)
(D) "rich illusion" (line 36)
(E) "slim and defiant" (line 40)

47. The author personifies the college buildings in the last paragraph in order to

(A) clarify why Amory wants to explore the campus after curfew
(B) provide the reader with visual details of the setting
(C) emphasize the history and traditions of the university
(D) contribute to the sense of enchantment Amory feels
(E) explain why the upperclassmen are so glad to be back on campus

GO ON TO THE NEXT PAGE

PRACTICE TEST—*Continued*

48. "The heavy blue and crimson lines" (line 44) is an allusion to

   (A) bruises the players will acquire during the games

   (B) the colors of rival universities' football teams

   (C) a professor's marks on a highly graded essay or exam

   (D) the valedictory speech that Allenby will make at graduation

   (E) the uniform worn by the Princeton football squad

49. The author's use of the word "mystery" (line 61) contributes to the sense that

   (A) everything on the campus is new and strange to Amory

   (B) Amory has no friends among the upperclassmen

   (C) Amory is afraid he will not do well at Princeton

   (D) the singing students are all unknown to Amory

   (E) Princeton is making Amory homesick and unhappy

50. The author recounts the anecdote about Booth Tarkington in order to

     I. emphasize the sense of tradition and continuity embodied in the university

     II. draw the reader into Amory's emotions as he listens to the upperclassmen singing

     III. poke sly fun at Amory's excitement when he hears the singing

   (A) I only

   (B) II only

   (C) I and II only

   (D) III only

   (E) I, II, and III

51. All of the following details are examples of metaphorical language EXCEPT

   (A) "The great tapestries of trees had darkened to ghosts" (lines 3–4)

   (B) "The early moon had drenched the arches with pale blue" (lines 5–6)

   (C) "weaving over the night . . . swept a song" (lines 6–8)

   (D) "singing tenor songs to the stars" (lines 13–14)

   (E) "the black Gothic snake of Little curled down to Cuyler and Patton" (lines 59–60)

Questions 52–60. Read the following poem carefully before you choose your answers.

Strange Meeting

It seemed that out of battle I escaped
Down some profound dull tunnel, long since scooped
Through granites which titanic wars had groined.
Yet also there encumbered sleepers groaned,
5 Too fast in thought or death to be bestirred.
Then, as I probed them, one sprang up, and stared
With piteous recognition in fixed eyes,
Lifting distressful hands, as if to bless.
And by his smile, I knew that sullen hall—
10 By his dead smile I knew we stood in Hell.
With a thousand pains that vision's face was grained;
Yet no blood reached there from the upper ground,
And no guns thumped, or down the flues made moan.
"Strange friend," I said, "here is no cause to mourn."
15 "None," said that other, "save the undone years,
The hopelessness. Whatever hope is yours,
Was my life also; I went hunting wild
After the wildest beauty in the world,
Which lies not calm in eyes, or braided hair,
20 But mocks the steady running of the hour,
And if it grieves, grieves richlier than here.
For by my glee might many men have laughed,
And of my weeping something had been left,
Which must die now. I mean the truth untold,
25 The pity of war, the pity war distilled.
Now men will go content with what we spoiled,
Or, discontent, boil bloody, and be spilled.
They will be swift with swiftness of the tigress.
None will break ranks, though nations trek from progress.
30 Courage was mine, and I had mystery,
Wisdom was mine, and I had mastery:
To miss the march of this retreating world
Into vain citadels that are not walled.
Then, when much blood had clogged their chariot-wheels,
35 I would go up and wash them from sweet wells
Even with truths that lie too deep for taint.
I would have poured my spirit without stint
But not through wounds; not on the cess of war.
Foreheads of men have bled where no wounds were.
40 I am the enemy you killed, my friend.
I knew you in this dark: for so you frowned
Yesterday through me as you jabbed and killed.
I parried; but my hands were loath and cold.
Let us sleep now . . ."

                            (1917)

GO ON TO THE NEXT PAGE ▶

PRACTICE TEST—*Continued*

52. The structure of "Strange Meeting" relies on which of the following literary devices?

    (A) exact rhyme
    (B) free verse
    (C) hyperbole
    (D) colloquialisms
    (E) heroic couplets

53. The speaker believes that "here is no cause to mourn" (line 14) because

    I. he and the stranger are meeting in Hell
    II. they are safe from the weapons and blood-shed of battle
    III. the soldiers around them are peacefully asleep in death

    (A) I only
    (B) II only
    (C) III only
    (D) II and III only
    (E) I, II, and III

54. What does the stranger mean by saying that beauty "mocks the steady running of the hour" (line 20)?

    (A) It prefers to be independent of others.
    (B) It laughs at everything that surrounds it.
    (C) It refuses to be careful or prudent.
    (D) It does not fear the passage of time.
    (E) It looks forward eagerly to the future.

55. Which line best expresses the major theme of the poem?

    (A) "By his dead smile I knew we stood in Hell." (line 10)
    (B) "'Strange friend,' I said, 'here is no cause to mourn.'" (line 14)
    (C) "The pity of war, the pity war distilled." (line 25)
    (D) "I would go up and wash them from sweet wells" (line 35)
    (E) "I am the enemy you killed, my friend." (line 40)

56. When the stranger says "Now men will go content . . . Into vain citadels that are not walled" (lines 26–33), he predicts that

    (A) men will continue to make war on each other
    (B) his country will be defeated in the war

    (C) leaders will come together to make peace
    (D) one nation will force the other to retreat
    (E) he and the speaker will kill one another

57. When the stranger says that his hands were "loath" (line 43), he means they were

    (A) unskilled
    (B) unwilling
    (C) ugly
    (D) wounded
    (E) frozen

58. All of the following lines contain opposing or contradictory elements or ideas EXCEPT

    (A) "For by my glee might many men have laughed" (line 22)
    (B) "None will break ranks, though nations trek from progress" (line 29)
    (C) "Into vain citadels that are not walled" (line 33)
    (D) "Foreheads of men have bled where no wounds were" (line 39)
    (E) "I am the enemy you killed, my friend" (line 40)

59. The stranger's desire to share "the truth untold" (line 24) and "truths that lie too deep for taint" (line 36) implies that if he had lived, he would have been

    (A) a politician
    (B) a general
    (C) a clergyman
    (D) a writer
    (E) a doctor

60. Which best expresses the meaning of the word "taint" (line 36)?

    (A) perception, awareness
    (B) expression, utterance
    (C) removing, erasing
    (D) falsehoods, lies
    (E) contamination, corruption

STOP

IF YOU FINISH BEFORE TIME IS CALLED, YOU MAY CHECK YOUR WORK ON THIS TEST ONLY.

DO NOT TURN TO ANY OTHER TEST IN THIS BOOK.

ANSWER KEY

1. B	21. A	41. A
2. A	22. D	42. A
3. C	23. B	43. E
4. E	24. A	44. B
5. B	25. E	45. B
6. C	26. C	46. A
7. D	27. D	47. D
8. E	28. B	48. B
9. B	29. B	49. A
10. A	30. A	50. A
11. C	31. D	51. D
12. D	32. E	52. E
13. A	33. D	53. B
14. E	34. B	54. D
15. B	35. A	55. C
16. A	36. B	56. A
17. D	37. C	57. B
18. A	38. C	58. A
19. B	39. E	59. D
20. E	40. D	60. E

ANSWERS AND EXPLANATIONS

1. **Correct Choice: B**
   Mr. Bennet says that "Lizzy has something more of quickness than her sisters." *Quickness* refers to intelligence and wit.

2. **Correct Choice: A**
   "I have no objection to hearing it" indicates that Mr. Bennet feels only the mildest interest in hearing Mrs. Bennet's news.

3. **Correct Choice: C**
   All five are accurate definitions of the word *let*, but the context makes it clear that Mr. Bingley has just leased the house and will soon "take possession," or move in.

4. **Correct Choice: E**
   Mrs. Bennet shows her lack of subtlety by asking straight out for what she wants. The repetition of her demand shows her ability to focus on what she thinks is important—introducing her daughters to a potential husband. If she understood Mr. Bennet better, she would approach the question in a way that would make him respond in a more satisfactory manner. However, she is clearly practical; getting acquainted with Bingley is a necessary first step toward the good marriage she hopes one of her daughters will make.

5. **Correct Choice: B**
   Both of the Bennets know quite well that 20 rich young men will not arrive in the neighborhood. Mrs. Bennet exaggerates out of disappointment, and Mr. Bennet's tone throughout the passage shows that he finds amusement in baiting his wife.

6. **Correct Choice: C**
   Mr. Bennet appears to mean this remark literally, but the other four comments are made to indulge his mildly sarcastic sense of humor and to tease his wife. Her comment "You take delight in vexing me" is truer than she realizes.

7. **Correct Choice: D**
   Because "Is he married or single" is almost the first thing Mr. Bennet asks after hearing his wife say that the newcomer is "a young man of large fortune," it appears he shares her desire to see her daughters well-provided for in marriage.

8. **Correct Choice: E**
   Mrs. Bennet is irritated by her husband's quick wits and intelligence, so she most likely finds the same qualities equally irritating in her daughter. Mr. Bennet teases his wife rather than showing affection for her, so she is probably a little jealous of his affection for Lizzy. She praises Jane and Lydia in comparison to Lizzy, suggesting that she prefers them.

9. **Correct Choice: B**
   Mr. Bennet speaks to his wife with courtesy, irony, and a complete lack of emotional involvement. Most of his statements poke fun at her, gently but sarcastically; as she says, he "takes delight" in teasing her. "Detached" is the best description of this attitude.

10. **Correct Choice: A**
    The author puns on two different definitions of *dust*. Chimney-sweepers find literal dust and ashes in the process of doing their jobs; young people "come to dust" when they die and their bones gradually crumble.

11. **Correct Choice: C**
    A *scepter* is a rod or staff carried by a monarch on ceremonial occasions.

12. **Correct Choice: D**
    The line is a metaphor for death. Several other lines in the poem, such as "And renowned be thy grave," support this. (In the play from which this song is taken, two young men sing it over the body of a beloved friend.)

13. **Correct Choice: A**
    The idiom "to lay one's ghosts" means to come to terms with unresolved issues in one's past. An "unlaid ghost" is one that still haunts or bothers a person. The speaker hopes that all such "ghosts" from the past will *forbear* his friend, or leave her in peace.

14. **Correct Choice: E**
    In this context, *consummation* refers to the completion of a task. The person addressed has completed her life; the speaker hopes that her body will lie quiet and undisturbed in her grave.

15. **Correct Choice: B**
    A careful reading of the poem shows beyond any question that the person addressed is dead. Therefore, only choice B is possible.

16. **Correct Choice: A**
    The person addressed is dead. In almost every line of the poem, the speaker tells her that she has nothing further to worry about. In this line, he says that to the dead, reeds (a symbol of weakness and fragility) and oaks (a symbol of strength and might) are exactly alike; the dead cannot perceive any difference between them.

17. **Correct Choice: D**
    Higgins is impressed on two levels by Doolittle's skill as a speaker. First, Doolittle is amusing and entertaining, as Higgins acknowledges by calling him "irresistible." Second, Doolittle has interesting ideas about life in a rigid class-based society and is able to express those ideas clearly and well.

18. **Correct Choice: A**
Doolittle finds happiness in enjoying life in the present moment, without thought for the future. A *prudent* person would sacrifice today's pleasure in order to provide for tomorrow's needs.

19. **Correct Choice: B**
"Middle-class morality" expects people to attend church, behave soberly, support their families, and obey the authorities. Doolittle mentions that he is a heavy drinker and that he is not "prudent" but prefers to spend his money freely; and it is reasonable to conclude that his approach to Higgins is not the first time he has charmed someone out of a small sum of money. This irresponsible, pleasure-loving attitude to life makes him "undeserving."

20. **Correct Choice: E**
Doolittle thinks that being a prime minister or preacher would be "a dog's life," because these are positions that mean care and responsibility. As a working man, he is free to do what he likes, when he likes.

21. **Correct Choice: A**
Charm is a quality of personality that wins other people over, as Doolittle's frank discussion of his beliefs wins Higgins.

22. **Correct Choice: D**
Doolittle points out that the middle-class moralists overlook the widow's dishonesty in repeatedly cashing in on her husband's death. He rightly regards this as evidence of hypocrisy.

23. **Correct Choice: B**
The structure of society and one's own place in that structure are abstract intellectual issues. Choice B shows that Doolittle is "a thinking man" because he has pondered those issues and come to definite conclusions about them.

24. **Correct Choice: A**
The phrase "do him out of the price of his own daughter" means that Higgins and Pickering are cheating Doolittle of the money his daughter is worth. Choices B and D are wrong because Doolittle does not claim to deserve the same consideration as Liza. Remember that because these answer choices essentially say the same thing, they must be wrong. Choice C is incorrect because Doolittle argues that he has spent his entire life providing for Liza. He claims no desire to continue to support Liza, so choice E is wrong.

25. **Correct Choice: E**
The speech is a monologue—a long speech made by one actor. Dialect: Doolittle's grammar and vocabulary do not strictly conform to Standard English usage (for example, he says *agen* for *against*). Repetition: "What am I? I ask you, what am I?" Parallel structure: "I put it to you; and I leave it to you." The speech lacks irony; Doolittle is entirely in earnest in what he says.

26. **Correct Choice: C**
The repetition echoes the relentlessness of the authorities' insistence that all young men who hear the call join up and fight. The entire poem insists that no considerations can excuse anyone from answering the call, and the repeated first line underscores this insistence.

27. **Correct Choice: D**
Option I is wrong because nothing in the poem's subject matter relates to literary history or the writing of poetry. Option II is wrong because readers are conditioned to expect regularity in poetry; irregularities are what cause surprise. Option III is correct; it's impossible not to hear the drumbeats when reading the lines aloud.

28. **Correct Choice: B**
To *expostulate* means to protest or argue.

29. **Correct Choice: B**
The phrase "the old man beseeching the young man" and the earlier references to weeping and praying support the idea that fathers, children, wives, and mothers are pleading with young men to stay home where it is safe, not to join up and get killed.

30. **Correct Choice: A**
Even though the bugles and drums are personified, the reader is still aware that they are inanimate objects. It is frightening to think that mechanical objects—objects that cannot feel or think—nonetheless have the power to start a war.

31. **Correct Choice: D**
The second stanza describes ordinary people working at their jobs and ignoring the drums and bugles. The speaker urges them to play more loudly to get the attention of those who are carrying on with their lives.

32. **Correct Choice: E**
When leaders of opposing armies meet to discuss an issue such as a truce or an exchange of prisoners, this is referred to as a *parley*. A military term like this is perfect for a poem about war.

33. **Correct Choice: D**
Words such as *fierce, shrill, terrible,* and *loud* and the portrayal of the call to arms as a force that destroys families and puts an end to peaceful occupations—all show the speaker's negative view of war.

34. **Correct Choice: B**
The drums, bugles, entreaties, prayers, references to conversation, talking, singing, parley, and more are all sound effects, appealing to readers' sense of hearing.

35. **Correct Choice: A**
The content states that the call to arms imposes its inflexible will on everyone. In the same way, in the first and last lines of each stanza, the drums and bugles impose their own regular rhythmic structure on an otherwise free-verse poem.

36. **Correct Choice: B**
A careful reading of the poem shows that "Cynthia" provides light on a dark night. The only choice that matches this is B, the moon.

37. **Correct Choice: C**
Boisterous means "noisy and active, unrestrained." Anchored as they are to the ground, trees can only be described this way if they are being blown and tossed about by the wind. *Clownish* also suggests tumbling and movement.

38. **Correct Choice: C**
The context shows that the speaker is talking about the views she can see in the moonlight once she passes through the trees.

39. **Correct Choice: E**
The speaker pays homage to the moon because she is afraid of the dark. The "sable mantle" is a metaphor for the dark sky.

40. **Correct Choice: D**
A river cannot feel surly, trees cannot act clownish, a person's vital organs cannot literally faint, and night is not "an old hag." Only choice D, "the ambient air," is a literal expression; *ambient* means "surrounding."

41. **Correct Choice: A**
Context shows that the speaker feels she is wiser and smarter for having survived the experience of crossing the "surly river."

42. **Correct Choice: A**
The line might be rewritten "I surprise swelling fears." In this sense, *surprise* means "discover." The speaker is saying that she discovers a fear of the darkness rising inside her.

43. **Correct Choice: E**
All five choices are true statements, but only choice E accounts for the connection in Amory's imagination between the upperclassmen and ghosts. Like ghosts, the boys are dimly seen white figures at night.

44. **Correct Choice: B**
A *phalanx* is a closely massed group of soldiers; a *platoon* is a subdivision of a military company or troop.

45. **Correct Choice: B**
Amory is captivated by Princeton. He responds strongly to sensory impressions. He feels a sense of mystery, unreality, enchantment, and exultation, very much like falling in love. *Romance* is the choice that best describes this mood.

46. **Correct Choice: A**
Something *infinite* lasts forever; something *transient* has only a momentary existence or presence.

47. **Correct Choice: D**
The numerous references to ghosts, shadows, and illusions show that Amory feels almost as if he is caught up in a magic spell. The idea of college buildings as living creatures with human personalities suggests that they too are enchanted by magic.

48. **Correct Choice: B**
Because Allenby must "dodge through the heavy blue and crimson lines" to achieve victory, the lines must be those of a rival team or teams. (Many readers would know that blue and crimson represent Yale and Harvard, Princeton's two main rivals.)

49. **Correct Choice: A**
Amory wants to explore the "shadowy scented lanes" so that he will better understand the mysteries of a place that is new and strange to him.

50. **Correct Choice: A**
The author's main purpose in the passage appears to be to evoke the sounds and sights of a Princeton freshman's first night on campus. Part of this experience is Amory's knowledge of Princeton's traditions—old buildings that have been part of the campus for many years, students singing at night, and football games against other universities.

51. **Correct Choice: D**
This phrase is intended literally; Tarkington was literally out alone at night, singing to the stars in the sky. The other four choices make imaginative, direct comparisons between two things—for example, songs cannot literally "weave."

52. **Correct Choice: E**
A heroic couplet is two rhymed lines of iambic pentameter. "Strange Meeting" is composed entirely of such couplets, although they differ from standard heroic couplets because the rhymes are not exact (i.e., *mystery/mastery, killed/cold*).

53. **Correct Choice: B**
The lines "no blood reached there from the upper ground, / And no guns thumped or down the flues made moan," show that Option II is correct. Finding oneself in Hell is certainly "cause to mourn," and many of the soldiers are groaning, so Options I and III are wrong.

54. **Correct Choice: D**
"The steady running of the hour" refers to the page of time, measured out at a steady rate by a clock. Beauty is so confident that it does not yet fear the future, in which it will grow old and may fade.

55. **Correct Choice: C**
The pity of war—in which young men who have no personal quarrel kill one another, and the dead are prevented from growing to adulthood and fulfilling their potential for good—is the main theme of the poem.

56. **Correct Choice: A**
The stranger looks toward the future and predicts that men will either accept the world, which has been spoiled by war, or they will go to war again.

57. **Correct Choice: B**
To *loathe* is to hate. To be *loath* to do something is to hate having to do it, or to be unwilling to do it.

58. **Correct Choice: A**
Progress implies motion toward something, not away from it. Citadels, by definition, are walled. If foreheads bleed, they must be wounded. A man cannot be both an enemy and a friend.

59. **Correct Choice: D**
The stranger suggests that he would have made men laugh and weep (lines 22–23) and also that he wants to share the truth. This accurately describes the aim of any creative artist. Therefore, *writer* is the best of the five choices.

60. **Correct Choice: E**
To *taint* means to infect something with poison or disease. When something is *tainted*, it is contaminated or corrupted.

![] HOW TO CALCULATE YOUR SCORE

Count the number of correct answers and enter the total below.
Count the number of wrong answers. Do NOT include any questions you did not answer.
Multiply the number of wrong answers by 0.25 and enter the total below.
Do the subtraction. The answer is your raw score. Use the scoring scale to find your scaled score.

$$\underset{\text{(number of correct answers)}}{\underline{\text{[short WOL]}}} - \underset{\text{(number of wrong answers} \times 0.25)}{\underline{\text{[short WOL]}}} = \underset{\text{(raw score)}}{\underline{\text{[short WOL]}}}$$

Raw Score	Scaled Score	Raw Score	Scaled Score	Raw Score	Scaled Score	Raw Score	Scaled Score	Raw Score	Scaled Score
60	800	44	710	28	560	12	420	−4	260
59	800	43	700	27	550	11	410	−5	250
58	800	42	690	26	540	10	400	−6	240
57	800	41	690	25	530	9	390	−7	230
56	800	40	680	24	520	8	380	−8	220
55	800	39	670	23	510	7	370	−9	210
54	790	38	660	22	500	6	360	−10	200
53	790	37	650	21	500	5	350	−11	200
52	780	36	640	20	490	4	340	−12	200
51	770	35	630	19	490	3	330	−13	200
50	760	34	620	18	480	2	320	−14	200
49	750	33	610	17	470	1	310	−15	200
48	740	32	600	16	460	0	300		
47	740	31	590	15	450	−1	290		
46	730	30	580	14	440	−2	280		
45	720	29	570	13	430	−3	270		

Note: This is only a sample scoring scale. Scoring scales differ from exam to exam.

LITERARY RESOURCES

Authors and Texts Used in *McGraw-Hill's SAT Subject Test: Literature*

PRACTICE TEST 5

PRACTICE TEST 6